PERGAMON INTERNATIONAL LIBRARY
of Science, Technology, Engineering and Social Studies
The 1000-volume original paperback library in aid of education,
industrial training and the enjoyment of leisure
Publisher: Robert Maxwell, M.C.

Environmental Oceanography

An Introduction to the
Behaviour of Coastal Waters

THE PERGAMON TEXTBOOK
INSPECTION COPY SERVICE

An inspection copy of any book published in the Pergamon International Library will gladly be sent to academic staff without obligation for their consideration for course adoption or recommendation. Copies may be retained for a period of 60 days from receipt and returned if not suitable. When a particular title is adopted or recommended for adoption for class use and the recommendation results in a sale of 12 or more copies, the inspection copy may be retained with our compliments. The Publishers will be pleased to receive suggestions for revised editions and new titles to be published in this important International Library.

Related Pergamon Titles of Interest

Books

BRUCE & CLARK: Introduction to Hydrometeorology

FEDOROV: The Thermohaline Finestructure of the Ocean

*GORSHKOV: World Ocean Atlas
      Volume 1: Pacific Ocean
      Volume 2: Atlantic and Indian Oceans
      Volume 3: Antarctic Ocean

KEEN: An Introduction to Marine Geology

KRAUS: Modelling and Prediction of the Upper Layers of the Ocean

*MARCHUK & KAGAN: Ocean Tides (Mathematical Models and
    Numerical Experiments)

*MELCHIOR: The Tides of the Planet Earth, 2nd edition

PICKARD & EMERY: Descriptive Physical Oceanography,
    4th edition

POND & PICKARD: Introductory Dynamic Oceanography,
    2nd edition

TCHERNIA: Descriptive Regional Oceanography

UN: Coastal Area Management and Development

WHO: Waste Discharge into the Marine Environment (Principles and
    Guidelines for the Mediterranean Action Plan)

Journals

Continental Shelf Research

Deep-Sea Research

Environment International

Marine Pollution Bulletin

Progress in Oceanography

*Full details of all Pergamon publications/free specimen copy of any Pergamon
Journal available on request from your nearest Pergamon office.*

*Not available under the Pergamon textbook inspection copy service.

Environmental Oceanography

An Introduction to the Behaviour of Coastal Waters

by

TOM BEER

Natural Systems Research Pty. Ltd.,
(Environmental Consultants), Hawthorn, Victoria, Australia

PERGAMON PRESS

OXFORD · NEW YORK · TORONTO · SYDNEY · PARIS · FRANKFURT

U.K.	Pergamon Press Ltd., Headington Hill Hall, Oxford OX3 0BW, England
U.S.A.	Pergamon Press Inc., Maxwell House, Fairview Park, Elmsford, New York 10523, U.S.A.
CANADA	Pergamon Press Canada Ltd., Suite 104, 150 Consumers Rd., Willowdale, Ontario M2J 1P9, Canada
AUSTRALIA	Pergamon Press (Aust.) Pty. Ltd., P.O. Box 544, Potts Point, N.S.W. 2011, Australia
FRANCE	Pergamon Press SARL, 24 rue des Ecoles, 75240 Paris, Cedex 05, France
FEDERAL REPUBLIC OF GERMANY	Pergamon Press GmbH, Hammerweg 6, D-6242 Kronberg-Taunus, Federal Republic of Germany

First edition 1983

Library of Congress Cataloging in Publication Data
Beer, Tom.
Environmental oceanography.
(Pergamon international library of science, technology, engineering, and social studies)
A project of the Australian Centre for Maritime Studies.
Includes bibliographies and index.
1. Oceanography. 2. Coasts. I. Australian Centre for Maritime Studies. II. Title. III. Series.
GC28.B44 1983   551.3'6   82-18099

British Library Cataloguing in Publication Data
Beer, Tom
Environmental oceanography.
1. Oceanography
I. Title
551.46   GC11.2
ISBN 0-08-026291-0 Hardcover
ISBN 0-08-026290-2 Flexicover

This book was a project of the Australian Centre for Maritime Studies, PO Box 20, Canberra ACT 2600.

Printed in Great Britain by A. Wheaton & Co. Ltd., Exeter.

Dedicated to
Jane, Dugald, Tansy and Kenn

Preface

The past decade has been characterised by sustained interest in, and concern for, the environment. In response to this public demand many governments established environmental regulatory agencies, and tertiary institutions were not far behind in initiating courses to train the staff for these agencies. I have been involved with two of these: the Graduate Diploma in Natural Resources at the Western Australian Institute of Technology and the Master of Resource and Environmental Studies at the Australian National University. Whilst lecturing to the students in these programmes it became apparent that there was a lack of suitable textbooks about the marine environment. There were two reasons for this. In the first place, oceanography texts fall into two distinct groups – the highly technical intended for those pursuing a career as a research oceanographer and the profusely illustrated general level texts aimed at introductory courses. There is poor catering for the intelligent, interested graduate from a non-scientific background. In the second place, environmental concern is primarily directed at coastal waters, whereas most scientific interest, as reflected in the textbooks, is in the deep sea.

This book, then, is intended for environmental managers, environmental administrators and for students destined for these roles. These people need to be able to understand the technical reports submitted by their oceanographic consultants and, if necessary, be able to mount their own environmental investigation. It is intended as an introduction to the physical environment of coastal waters, and thus may prove useful to students in engineering, physics and mathematics before they commence more rigorous courses that provide the analytical background to the phenomena described herein. To this extent I see this volume as a companion to Professor Pickard's excellent text *Descriptive Physical Oceanography*.

The ordering of chapters is determined by the fact that the text is graded in both mathematical and conceptual difficulty. The first few chapters have little mathematics, but more is steadily introduced as one progresses. It is for this reason that the chapter on coasts contains a simplified account of relevant wave properties and precedes the detailed chapter on waves. Another consequence is that some of the formulae in earlier chapters will look strange to the practising physical oceanographer. I made a conscious decision to express variables in terms of observables; wavelength (λ) instead of wavenumber (k), inertial period (T_i)

instead of Coriolis parameter (f). Later, when the concepts are familiar, the formulae revert to standard forms.

There is a list of further reading at the end of each chapter. These lists are not exhaustive bibliographies but reflect a personal choice of works that I found useful or interesting. Any student wishing to pursue a topic further should also check the original source of any diagrams on that topic. These sources are given in the acknowledgement section which comes after this preface.

Natural Systems Research Pty Ltd   TOM BEER
(Environmental Consultants)
Melbourne, Victoria 3122

Acknowledgements

I would like to record my gratitude to Bob Houghton, John Penrose and Bob Humphries who were responsible for initiating and sustaining my interest in coastal water. Their companionship was invaluable. I am also obliged to the many friends and colleagues who read parts of the manuscript and gave me encouragement. Especial thanks must go to Phil Wilkinson, Bruce Hamon, George Pickard, Mike Collins and Tony Bayes who made incisive comments on the work as a whole. In addition I would, of course, like to thank the students of my various classes who gave the contents of the book the acid test.

I wish to thank the following journals, publishers, organisations and individuals for their permission to reproduce or adapt previously published material or for providing illustrations.

1.1   From D. L. Inman & B. M. Brush, *Science*, **181**, 20–31, 1973.

1.2   Based on R. W. Galloway & M. E. Bahr, *Australian Geographer*, **14**, 244–247, 1979, and B. B. Mandlebrot, *Fractals*, W. H. Freeman, 1977.

1.3   From A. S. Monin, V. M. Kamenkovich & V. G. Kort, *Variability of the Oceans*, John Wiley, 1977.

1.4   Courtesy of Dr R. Legeckis, ESSA, NOAA.

1.5   From G. A. Riley, H. Stommel & D. Bumpus, *Bull. Bingham Oceanog. Coll.* **12**, 1–169, 1949.

1.6   Courtesy of Esso Australia Ltd, from *Oil – The Vital Search*.

1.7   From G. W. P. George (ed.), *Australia's Offshore Resources: Implications of the 200-mile Zone*, Australian Academy of Science, 1978 (p. 99).

2.5   From P. D. Komar, *Beach Processes and Sedimentation*, Prentice Hall, 1976, and from C. J. Galvin, *J. Geophys. Res.* **73**, 3651–3659, 1968.

2.6   Based on data of C. J. Galvin in *J. Geophys. Res.* **73**, 3651–3659, 1968, and in R. E. Meyer (ed.), *Waves on Beaches and Resulting Sediment Transport*, Academic Press, 1972 (pp. 413–455).

2.8   Based on F. Hjulstrom, *Uppsala Univ. Geol. Inst. B.* **25**, 221–527, 1935, and updated by H. Postma in G. H. Lauff (ed.), *Estuaries*, American

Assoc. Advancement Science, Washington 1967 (pp. 158–179). See Chapter 7 of A. J. Raudkivi, *Loose Boundary Hydraulics*, Pergamon, 1967, or Chapter 9 of Komar, op. cit., for information about the Shields curve.

2.9   From Komar, op. cit., after P. D. Komar & D. L. Inman, *J. Geophys. Res.* **75**, 5914–5927, 1970.

3.2   From B. Kinsman, *Wind Waves*, Prentice Hall, 1965.

3.5   From M. S. Longuet-Higgins, *Proc. Roy. Soc.* **A352**, 463–480, 1977.

3.6, 3.7, From W. J. Pierson, G. Neumann & R. W. James, *Practical Methods for*
Table *Observing and Forecasting Ocean Waves by Means of Wave Spectra and*
3.2   *Statistics*, U.S. Hydrographic Office Publication 603, 1955.

3.8   From *New Scientist*, 6 January 1977 (Vol. 73, No. 1033).

3.9   From D. L. Cutchin & R. L. Smith, *J. Phys. Oceanog.* **3**, 73–82, 1973.

Table Equilibrium tidal amplitudes are from E. W. Schwiderski, *Rev. Geophys.*
4.2   *Space Phys.* **18**, 243–268, 1980. The Hook of Holland values are taken from J. J. Dronkers, *Advances in Hydroscience*, **10**, 145–230, 1975.

4.4   Based on C. L. Pekeris & Y. Accad, *Phil. Trans. Roy. Soc.* **A265**, 413–436, 1969.

4.6   Courtesy of the French Embassy, Canberra.

4.7   From *Australian National Tide Tables*, courtesy of the Hydrographer, R.A.N.

4.8. From D. G. Provis & R. Radok, *Aust. J. Mar. Freshwater Res.* **30**, 295–301, 1979.

4.9   From C. D. Winant, *Rev. Geophys. Space. Phys.* **17**, 89–98, 1979.

5.1, 5.2 Based on data in Unesco, *National Oceanographic Tables,* National Institute of Oceanography, Great Britain and Unesco, Paris, 1966. Updated by W. Wilson & D. Bradley, *Deep Sea Res.* **15**, 355–363, 1968 and R. G. Perkins & E. R. Walker, *J. Geophys. Res.* **77**, 6618–6621, 1972.

Table Based on seawater data in J. P. Riley and G. Skirrow, *Chemical Oceano-*
5.1,   *graphy*, Academic Press, 1965, and freshwater data in B. A. Whitton
Table (ed.), *River Ecology*, Blackwell, Oxford, 1975.
5.2

5.3   Based on R. W. Houghton, *J. Phys. Oceanog.* **6**, 909–924, 1976.

Table From *Cockburn Sound Environmental Study, 1976–1979*, Report No.
5.3,   2, Dept. Conservation & Environment, Western Australia, 1979.
Table
5.4

5.5   Based on data in H. W. Harvey: *The Chemistry and Fertility of Sea-water*, Cambridge University Press, 1960.

6.5   Based on data of T. Gustafson & B. Kullenberg, *Goteborgs K. Vet. Vitt. – Samih. Handl. Femte Fljoden* (Goteborgs Oceanog. Inst.), 3 (6), 1933.

6.7   Based on G. R. Cresswell, T. J. Golding & F. M. Boland, *J. Phys. Oceanog.* 8, 315–320, 1978.

6.8, 6.9 From C. D. Booth, Tom Beer and J. D. Penrose, *Am. J. Phys.* **46**, 525–527, 1978.

7.1   From E. B. Kraus (ed.), *Modelling and Prediction of the Upper Layers of the Ocean*, Pergamon Press, 1977.

7.3   From T. J. Hart and R. I. Currie, *"Discovery" Reports*, **31**, 123–298, 1960.

7.4   From H. U. Sverdrup, M. W. Johnson & R. H. Fleming, *The Oceans: Their Physics, Chemistry and General Biology*, Prentice Hall, 1942.

7.5   From E. B. Kraus, 1977, op. cit.

7.6   From P. Petrusevics, Major factors in nearshore water movement, M.App.Sci. thesis, Western Australian Institute of Technology, 1981.

8.1   From Tom Beer, *Atmospheric Waves*, Adam Hilger, 1974.

8.3   From B. R. Ruddick & J. S. Turner, *Deep Sea Res.* **26**, 903–914, 1979.

8.6   From A. Okubo, *Deep Sea Res.* **18**, 789, 1971.

8.7   From G. T. Csanady, Circulation in the coastal ocean, *EOS, Transactions of the American Geophysical Union*, **62**, 9–11, 1981.

8.8   From M. Bowman & W. Esaiais (eds.), *Oceanic Fronts in Coastal Processes*, Springer Verlag, 1979.

8.9   From R. A. Kerr, *Science*, 28 October 1977, vol. 198, p. 387 (source: P. L. Richardson).

8.10   From J. C. Andrews, *Deep Sea Res.* **24**, 1133–1148, 1977.

Table 9.1   From N. Bowditch, *American Practical Navigator*, U.S. Defence Mapping Hydrographic Center, 1977.

9.2   Photograph courtesy of A. Scott.

Table 9.2   Mainly based on data in *The State of the Environment in OECD Member Countries*, OECD, Paris, 1979.

9.6   From Natural Systems Research Pty Ltd, Liquids Project Oil Spill Trajectory Study, 1981.

9.7   From *Report by Director of Meteorology on Cyclone Althea*, Aust. Govt. Publishing Service, Canberra, 1972. Reproduced by permission of the Director of Meteorology.

9.9   Based on D. P. Hoult (ed.), *Oil on the Sea*, Plenum Press, New York, 1969 (pp. 53–63).

9.10   From S. D. Gedzelman & W. L. Donn, *Monthly Weather Rev.* **107**, 667–681. For a diagram of a coastal low see *Q. J. Roy. Met. Soc.* **103**, 432–433, 1977.

10.1   From E. P. Hodgkin, P. B. Birch, R. E. Black & R. B. Humphries, *The*
10.2   *Peel–Harvey Estuarine System Study (1976–1980)*, Report No. 9, Department of Conservation & Environment, Western Australia, 1980.

Table All data except for the Fly river are based on J. N. Holeman, *Water*
10.1   *Resources Res.* **4**, 737–741, 1968. His flow estimates tend to be high when compared to more recent determinations of mean flow in major rivers. The Fly river data are from Natural Systems Research Pty. Ltd.

Table From M. R. Gourlay and P. G. Flood, *Proc. Conf. Environmental*
10.2   *Engineering, Townsville*, pp. 159–163, Australian Inst. Engineers, 1981.

10.3   From G. L. Pickard, *Descriptive Physical Oceanography* (2nd edition), Pergamon Press, 1975.

10.4   From D. I. Smith & P. Stopp, *The River Basin*, Cambridge University Press, Cambridge, 1978.

10.7   From E. C. F. Bird, *Coasts* (2nd edition), A.N.U. Press, Canberra, 1976.

10.8   From G. R. Cresswell & M. A. Greig, *Aust. J. Mar. Freshwater Res.* **29**, 345–353, 1978.

11.2, Courtesy of Dr. J. D. Penrose.
11.3

11.5   Based on data from R. J. List (ed.), *Smithsonian Meteorological Tables* (6th edition), Smithsonian Institution, Washington, 1951.

11.6   Based on A. Defant, *Physical Oceanography*, Pergamon, 1961.

11.7   From Sverdrup *et al.*, op. cit., 1942.

11.8   From N. G. Jerlov, *Marine Optics*, Elsevier, Amsterdam, 1976.

11.9   Based on J. H. Steele, *Limnology & Oceanography*, **7**, 137–150, 1962.

11.10 From D. E. Barrick, M. W. Evans & B. L. Weber, *Science*, **198**, 138–144, 1977 (courtesy of D. E. Barrick).

11.11 From T. Beer, *Remote Sensing Env.* **9**, 65–85, 1980.

11.12 Courtesy of NOAA.

12.1, Courtesy of Natural Systems Research Pty Ltd.
12.4

12.2   Based on R. L. Falconer & D. J. Linforth, *Winds and Waves in Bass Strait*, Meteorological Summary, Commonwealth of Australia Bureau of Meteorology, Melbourne, 1972. Reproduced by permission of the Director of Meteorology.

13.2   From C. J. Krebs, *Ecology*, 2nd edition Harper & Row, New York, 1978 (p. 530).

Table   From J. H. Ryther, *Science,* **166**, 72–76, 1969. There is an extensive
13.1   discussion on the reliability of these estimates in Chapter 6 of G. A. Rounsefell, 'Ecology, utilization and management of marine fisheries', C. V. Mosby Co., Saint Louis, 1975.

Contents

LIST OF SYMBOLS   xviii

ACRONYMS   xxi

CHAPTER 1. COASTAL OCEANOGRAPHY   1

1.1 Introduction   1
1.2 Coastal Waters   2
1.3 Fishing and Biology   6
1.4 Economics and Geology   10
1.5 Units and Dimensions   15

CHAPTER 2. SHORE PROCESSES   20

2.1 Introduction   20
2.2 Wave Refraction   21
2.3 Breakers   23
2.4 Beach Processes   26
2.5 Coastal Engineering   31
2.6 Coastal Zone Management   33

CHAPTER 3. WAVES   37

3.1 Surface Waves   38
3.2 Energy Propagation   41
3.3 Wave Set-up   45
3.4 Wave Spectra   48
3.5 Trapped Waves   53
3.6 Long Wavelength Waves   55
3.7 Internal Waves   59
3.8 Seasickness   60

CHAPTER 4. TIDES   63

4.1 Astronomical Tides   64
4.2 Dynamical Theory   67
4.3 Tidal Prediction   69
4.4 Tidal Power   73
4.5 Long Period Tides   77

4.6 Internal Tides   78
4.7 The Littoral Zone   80

CHAPTER 5. WATER COMPOSITION   83

5.1 Introduction   83
5.2 Density   84
5.3 Vertical Temperature   85
5.4 Salinity   86
5.5 Dissolved Gases   90
5.6 Nutrients   94
5.7 Rivers   95
5.8 Water Quality   96

CHAPTER 6. WATER CIRCULATION   100

6.1 Introduction   100
6.2 Pressure Forces   102
6.3 Coriolis Force   106
6.4 Diffusion   111
6.5 Viscosity   114

CHAPTER 7. BOUNDARY LAYERS   117

7.1 Introduction   117
7.2 Ekman Layers   119
7.3 Benthic Boundary Layers   125
7.4 Coastal Boundary Layers   126

CHAPTER 8. MIXING   130

8.1 Turbulence   130
8.2 Convection   132
8.3 Turbulent Entrainment   134
8.4 Dispersion   136
8.5 Oceanic Fronts   139
8.6 Large-scale Mixing   141

CHAPTER 9. COASTAL METEOROLOGY   146

9.1 Introduction   146
9.2 Hydrological Cycle   146
9.3 Winds   153
9.4 Aerosols   160
9.5 Oil Spills   161
9.6 Coastal Lows   165

CHAPTER 10. ESTUARIES AND REEFS   169

10.1 Introduction   169

10.2 Geomorphological Classification of Estuaries 170
10.3 Estuarine Hydrology 172
10.4 Estuarine Pollution 178
10.5 Coral Reefs 185

CHAPTER 11. DIRECT AND REMOTE SENSING 191

11.1 Instruments and Methods 191
11.2 Remote Sensing 195
11.3 Acoustics 196
11.4 Electromagnetic Radiation 202
11.5 Marine Optics 204
11.6 Radar 212
11.7 Satellites 213

CHAPTER 12. DATA ANALYSIS 219

12.1 Data Presentation 219
12.2 Data Analysis and Statistics 220
12.3 Time Series Analysis 223
12.4 Modelling 229
12.5 Ecosystems Analysis 233

CHAPTER 13. COASTAL ASSESSMENT 236

13.1 Introduction 236
13.2 Cost-Benefit Analysis 238
13.3 Aquatic Ecosystems 239
13.4 Pollution 242

APPENDICES 248

Appendix 1 SI Units 248
Appendix 2 Sample Equipment Checklist 249
Appendix 3 Wave Glossary 252
Appendix 4 Oceanographic Glossary 254

INDEX 257

List of Symbols

a	acceleration
a_T	autocorrelation coefficient
A	wave amplitude
A	albedo
b	windrow spacing
B	Bowen's ratio
B_D	bottom drag coefficient
c	wave speed (light, sound or water waves)
c_T	cross correlation coefficient
C_p	specific heat
C_D	drag coefficient
d	relative density (specific gravity)
d	distance
D	diameter
D	distance
D_O	dissolved oxygen concentration
D_E	Ekman depth
e	vapour pressure
E	energy per unit area
E	evaporation
f	Coriolis parameter
F	force
g	acceleration due to gravity
g'	modified (reduced) gravity
h	wave height
h	Planck's constant
H	depth
H_s	Secchi disc depth
I	intensity (energy flux) of a wave
I_0	reference intensity
I_b	energy flux of black body
J	longshore sand transport

k	wavenumber
K	diffusivity
l	eddy length
L	distance
L	latent heat of vaporisation
m	mass
M	momentum
n	number
N	particles per unit volume
p	pressure
P	power per unit crest length
P_T	total power
P_l	onshore flux of longshore directed energy (onshore power per unit length)
q	specific humidity
Q	river flow
Q	rate of transfer of heat energy
r	radius
R	reflection coefficient
r_i	radius of inertial oscillations
s	optical scattering coefficient
S	salinity
S_H	stratification parameter
SL	sound level
t	time
t_f	flushing time
T	wave period
T_i	inertial period
T	temperature
TS	target strength
u, v	horizontal velocity components
$u*$	friction (shear) velocity
U	speed
U_e	entrainment speed
V	volume
V_g	speed of wave energy propagation (group velocity)
w	vertical speed
w'	vertical wind speed fluctuations
W	wind speed
x, y	horizontal distance
x_t, y_t	data sets

X		cross-sectional area
z		vertical distance
Z		acoustic impedance
Z		Z transform (forward shift operator)

	α	wind factor
alpha	α	horizontal angle between wind and current directions
beta	β	volume scattering function
gamma	γ	psychrometric constant
	Γ	extinction distance
delta	δ	Fractal dimension
	Δ	vapour pressure gradient
epsilon	ϵ	emissivity
zeta	ζ	wind factor
eta	η	Austausch coefficient (eddy viscosity)
theta	θ	angle
kappa	κ	extinction or attenuation coefficient
lambda	λ	wavelength
	Λ	dispersion coefficient
mu	μ	coefficient of dynamic viscosity
nu	ν	frequency
rho	ρ	density of water
	ρ_a	density of air
sigma	σ	Knudsen parameter
	σ^2	variance
tau	τ	shear stress
	τ	lag
phi	ϕ	latitude
chi	χ	scattering cross-section
xi	ξ	beach slope
psi	ψ	angle between wave crests and shore
omega	ω	angular frequency (same as angular velocity)
	Ω	angular frequency of Earth's rotation

Acronyms

AOU	Apparent Oxygen Utilisation
ARAND	Computer programs for Analysis of Random noise
AXBT	Airborne expendable bathythermograph
BOD	Biochemical Oxygen Demand
BTG	Bathythermograph
CAPTAIN	Computer Aided Programs for Time series Analysis Including Noise
CTD	Conductivity – Temperature – Depth
CZCS	Coastal Zone Colour Scanner
DDT	Dichloro-diphenyl-trichloro-ethane
DO	Dissolved Oxygen
EEZ	Exclusive Economic Zone
FAS	Fully Arisen Sea
FFT	Fast Fourier Transform
GENSTAT	General Statistical Package
GOSSTCOMP	Global Operational Sea Surface Temperature Computation
IAPSO	International Association for Physical Sciences of the Ocean
IMSL	International Mathematics and Statistical Library
IUGG	International Union of Geodesy and Geophysics
LANDSAT	Land observing Satellite
MBT	Mechanical Bathythermograph
MSY	Maximum Sustainable Yield
NAVSAT	Navigation Satellite
NOAA	National Oceanic and Atmospheric Administration (USA)
OTEC	Ocean Thermal Energy Conversion
PAR	Photosynthetically Active Radiation
RADAR	Radio Detection And Ranging
SAR	Synthetic Aperture Radar
SCUBA	Self Contained Underwater Breathing Apparatus
SI	Système International
SL	Sound Level
SST	Sea Surface Temperature
STD	Salinity – Temperature – Depth
TS	Temperature – Salinity

TS	Target Strength
UK	United Kingdom
UN	United Nations
UNCLOS	United Nations Conference on the Law of the Sea
US, USA	United States of America
VHRR	Very High Resolution infra-red Radiometer
XBT	Expendable Bathythermograph

CHAPTER 1

Coastal Oceanography

1.1 Introduction

Oceanography – or oceanology as the Chinese and Russians prefer to call it – is the scientific study of the deep and coastal waters of our planet. It consists of four branches: physical oceanography, chemical oceanography, biological oceanography and geological oceanography. This book deals mainly with physical oceanography, which describes the oceans in terms of their physical characteristics and attempts to explain their behaviour in terms of physical mechanisms. In particular, it deals with the interrelation and interaction between physical oceanography and oceanography's three other branches.

Physical oceanography is a fascinating and challenging field of science that may be studied for its own sake. And it also provides answers to some of the questions that will be asked during our future exploitation of oceanic resources. For example: ocean surface currents play an important role in maritime transportation; subsurface currents may carry industrial waste into unwanted locations; ocean waves can damage drilling platforms at sea, and harm coastal structures on land.

During the past three decades there has been a vast increase in our knowledge and understanding of physical oceanography. Some of this has come from laboratory work and experiments, but most of it has come from data painstakingly collected in the deep oceans of the world. For a long time, the excitement, adventure and discovery involved in deep water oceanography overshadowed coastal and estuarine oceanography. But when renewed interest in man's nearshore environment surfaced, scientists started to apply their knowledge of physical oceanography to nearshore and estuarine situations. And occasionally the knowledge was found to be lacking. Coastal waters have an inherent variability that greatly complicates attempts to understand them. Furthermore, the knowledge gained in the ocean, where salinity variations are small, needs to be applied carefully to the estuarine situation where the salinity variations can be huge.

Physical oceanography is itself considered to be composed of two parts. Synoptic oceanography refers to the observation, preparation and interpretation of oceanographic data, and is generally the branch of oceanography in which most geographers are interested. Dynamic oceanography applies the already known laws of physics to the ocean, regarding it as a fluid acted upon by forces and solves the resulting mathematical equations. Of course, neither part can stand alone. The predictions of the dynamic oceanographer need to be tested by the synoptic oceanographer; the results of the synoptician explained by the dynamicist.

This division into synoptic and dynamic parts is also true of meteorology — the study of the atmosphere. There is a close symbiosis between meteorology and oceanography. Both study environmental fluids — a liquid in one case, a gas in the other — and the same mathematical tools can pry at both fields. They are also interconnected. Ocean temperatures affect the atmosphere. Hurricanes are a dramatic example of this, since they can form only if the sea surface temperature exceeds 27°C. But the atmosphere also affects the oceans: winds drive upper layer currents and they determine the nature of the waves generated on the ocean surface. The oceans and the atmosphere are an extremely complicated mutually interacting system.

There is, however, one important difference between meteorologists and oceanographers. Oceanographers talk of the direction towards which a current is moving, whereas meteorologists refer to the direction from which a wind has come. The meteorologist's westerly wind will, in the first instance, generate an eastward drift of water.

In this volume we present a physical description of coastal waters and explain in a simplified form some of the dynamic theories believed to control them. The average biologist, chemist, geologist or environmental scientist when tackling a marine problem may well find that he or she can manage adequately at first with no input from the physical oceanographer. But as the investigation continues there will be many vexing physical questions unanswered, and an inadequate knowledge of these can lead to problems. Because of this, most modern coastal oceanographic and estuarine work is carried out by interdisciplinary teams working together, but to obtain the best results from these teams, each specialist must be able to communicate sensibly with the other specialists. The aim of this volume is to provide environmental practitioners with the necessary skills to communicate with physical oceanographers, and to introduce physical oceanographers to the type of problems which interest the wider community.

1.2 Coastal Waters

What is the coast and what are coastal waters? There is no unique definition and the military, political, scientific and economic uses of the terms differ. In order to cover as broad a scan as possible, this book treats the coast as being synonymous with the coastal zone depicted in Fig. 1.1. This extends from the edge of the continental shelf (if there is one) to the limits of geologically recent marine influence. Nevertheless, other definitions and views are important — nations tend to wage war when their coast is invaded — and we shall examine some of them in more detail.

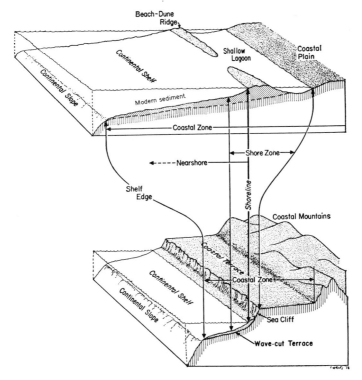

FIG. 1.1. *Typical coastal depth profile showing the names of various geomorphological features. The waters in the depicted region are sometimes called neritic waters.*

The Coastal Zone

Coastal zone managers need a legal definition to set their jurisdiction. The exact wording will vary from state to state, but one definition of the coastal zone that is in common use, and was adopted by Western Australia, is:

> The land and waters extending inland for one kilometre from high water mark on the foreshore and extending seaward to the thirty metre depth contour line, and also including the waters, beds and banks of all rivers, estuaries, inlets, creeks, bays or lakes subject to the ebb and flow of the tide.

The concern here is to define the inward extent of coastal waters as much as their outward extent. The overriding consideration is tidal penetration which has here been defined in terms of movement. It is also possible to examine tidal effects in terms of salt fluctuations. Coastal waters extend inland as far as do tidal effects; so that estuaries and deltaic river mouths can be thought of as comprising coastal waters. Notice, however, that our working definition is broader than the legal one given above. Our seaward limit extends to the continental shelf slope — explained more fully later — which may be deeper than 30 m. Similarly, the landward extent of recent marine influence may be greater than 1 km.

The Continental Shelf

The continental shelf refers to a physical concept and also nowadays to a legal concept. The physical concept is that of the seaward prolongation of the continental land mass. The enormous number of measurements made around the world's continental margins have led to a composite picture of the average continental shelf. This mythical entity consists of a shelf 65 km wide which descends at a gradient of 1 in 500 (or $0°7'$) to a water depth of 128 m at its outer edge. The continental shelf terminates at the shelf break, which is the point at which the gradient increases to 1 in 20, and seaward of the break lies the continental slope.

Unfortunately for the legal concept of the continental shelf the distance over which the continental shelf will stretch from the coast varies considerably. In some places a well-defined continental shelf does not exist. Many Pacific islands are virtually mountains poking out of the deep sea. Elsewhere the shelf may stretch for several hundred kilometres — as it does off the north-west coast of Australia.

This book focuses attention mainly on the waters of the continental shelf, known to biologists as the neritic waters. There are occasions when coastal nations consider their coastal waters to comprise the waters above their continental shelf and their continental slope. This extended boundary is called the continental margin and lawyers involved with the United Nations Conference on the Law of the Sea (UNCLOS) are experimenting with a number of alternative definitions for it. These include:

(i) A line fixed 200 nautical miles (370 km) from the coast.

(ii) The 500-m depth contour, known as the 500-m isobath.

(iii) A line at the foot of the continental slope.

Territorial Waters

The traditional international law of the sea, which has prevailed from the early seventeenth century to the middle of this century, rests upon a clear distinction between the territorial seas and the high seas. Territorial seas consist of the belt of water immediately adjacent to each coastal nation. In these waters the coastal State possesses, subject to one limitation, the same fullness of sovereignty as it has on land, and those absolute rights extend to the bed and subsoil of the territorial sea. The limitation upon the rights of the coastal State is the enjoyment by vessels of all nations of a right of "innocent passage" through a territorial sea on their way to and from foreign ports.

Although there is general agreement on the legal content of the territorial sea concept, there was wide variation in the width of claims made to it. While a majority of nations favoured 3 miles, many spread their claims over belts of 4, 6, 12, 25 and even in recent years, 200 miles.

The idea of territorial seas being synonymous with coastal seas was eroded as coastal States became aware of the existence and exploitability of the mineral and living resources of the continental shelf. The first significant indication of this was the Truman proclamation of 1945 by which the United States asserted the exclusive right to explore and exploit the resources of the continental shelf adjacent to its coasts, regions which had hitherto been seen as part of the high seas. Since that time interest has turned to means of defining the continental shelf and the continental margin, and methods of resolving conflicts arising from competing claims to the same waters.

The Exclusive Economic Zone (EEZ)

The idea of an exclusive economic zone represents a kind of "functional" sovereignty: that is to say, a sovereignty limited to a particular aspect of State activity – control over the economic exploitation of an area. Full sovereignty still ends at the outer limit of the territorial sea (which it is now generally agreed should be 12 nautical miles) but the coastal state is to enjoy beyond that limit, for a further 188 nautical miles, "sovereign rights" for the exploration and exploitation of non-living resources and the conservation and management of living resources.

The exclusive economic zone concept first emerged in 1974, and since that time it has rapidly gained acceptance as a part of customary international law. Over 52 countries have claimed EEZs and another 22 countries have claimed something less in content but not in area, namely 200-mile exclusive fishing zones. Essentially, the coastal nation is under a duty to take measures to conserve the living resources in its EEZ by pursuing the objective of optimum utilisation. Most countries interpret this as, in the first place, determining the maximum sustainable yield. It enjoys the first access to the determined yield. If it is not capable of utilising the whole stock, the right of first access is coupled with the obligation to accord to other nations access to the surplus, under such terms and conditions as the coastal nation may determine.

To many nations, the proclamation of their EEZ has suddenly brought them to the threshold of a number of important issues related to the fishing, mining and drilling of the region. Within Australia there is considerable uncertainty over the extent to which the local fishing industry is capable of catching the sustainable yield and what to do with the surplus. This surplus is already being seen by governments as an important and constructive element of foreign policy and its future importance looms so large in much official thinking that much of the present worldwide interest in and financial support for oceanography, and coastal oceanography, can be traced back to the idea of the exclusive economic zone.

The Shoreline

The simplest view of a coast is that of the boundary between land and sea. A topographic map makes it look well defined, but, as may be seen in Fig. 1.1, this boundary is often discontinuous or poorly defined. The boundary between land and sea constitutes the shoreline which many people equate with the coastline.

The shore is the portion of the land mass close to the sea which has been modified by the action of the sea. It is as well to note in this connection that there is ample evidence to indicate that sea level in the past has varied over a range of about 100 m when glaciers were smaller or larger than they are now. The beach is the seaward limit of the shore and extends roughly from the highest to the lowest tide levels. As we shall see later on, beaches are often in a state of dynamic equilibrium. A sandy beach, for example, may always be sandy, but it will not always be the same sand. This may be continually moving along the shore under the influence of waves and nearshore currents.

Besides defining the coast, agencies of government are also interested in measuring the length of a particular coastline. This is generally done by measuring the coastline on a topographic map of the scale most commonly employed by that agency and adopting the resulting figure which then finds its way into encyclopedias and almanacs. However, if you think about it you will see that a coastline length calculated from a large-scale map, say 1 : 12,000,000 in scale, will be shorter than one calculated from a more detailed map, say 1 : 10,000, because the large-scale map will smooth out all but the largest bays, inlets, capes and estuaries. This problem has recently attracted the attention of mathematicians who are trying to model the roughness and irregularity of real coastlines in terms of a class of shapes known as fractals. Some of their results are shown in Fig. 1.2, which calculates the decreasing total length of the Australian, South African and British west coast if measurements are made with an ever-increasing length scale. To the mathematicians the slope of these lines (on double logarithmic paper) is a measure of $1 - \delta$, where δ is the dimension of the fractal necessary to model that particular stretch of coast.

1.3 Fishing and Biology

The unique resource of the sea is its fish. It is a renewable resource that can provide sustenance and nourishment if it is wisely managed. The exclusive economic zone concept has, as we have seen, put a premium upon accurate scientific knowledge of a nation's coastal fisheries. The contribution of the marine biologist

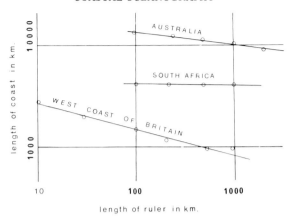

FIG. 1.2. *The apparent length of a coastline depends on the scale of the map (or the length of the ruler) used in making the measurements. The lines are drawn on logarithmic graph paper in which equal lengths correspond to an increase by a factor of ten.*

or biological oceanographer is well accepted, but there are also physical processes involved.

Physical characteristics of the water can be important in determining optimum fish yields. Figure 1.3 depicts the optimum temperature at which the most valuable commercial fish can be found off the coast of Japan. Knowledge of the ocean temperature can improve fishing yields, and modern technology is being applied to determine sea surface temperatures and to disseminate the results. The National Oceanic and Atmospheric Administration (NOAA) of the USA produces weekly maps of the world's sea surface temperature deduced from satellite observations. A typical example of one of these maps is shown in Fig. 1.4. These maps are relayed to those fishermen who wish to receive them, and who can then base their subsequent trawling locations upon the information contained within them.

Fishermen have also been quick to utilise the physics of acoustics in their profession. An echo-sounder is now standard equipment, even on very small boats, because it is very useful as a hydrographic tool in determining water depth. However, shoals of fish also emit characteristic acoustic reflections which an echo-sounder will pick up. The technological fisherman can now pick his general area of interest on the basis of the satellite deduced sea surface temperature maps, and narrow it down by using acoustic techniques with his echo-sounder.

An example in which physical measurement complemented biological information and political action concerns the western rock lobster. In its larval form, this little beastie is carried about by ocean currents. The government of the

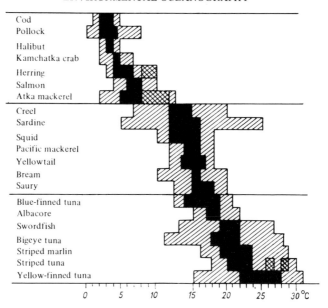

FIG. 1.3. *The temperature range in which various commercial fish species prefer to live.*

state of Western Australia, whose fishery is dominated by the western rock lobster, was concerned that foreign fishing vessels may be seriously depleting their stocks. It wanted to know where the ocean currents took the larvae and whether they spent all their lives within the exclusive economic zone or whether they spent considerable periods outside of it. The answer was quite complex. Physical oceanographers studied the water movement off the Western Australian coast for a number of years and discovered that the Western Australian current did not flow in the way that atlases claimed. The Western Australian current was supposed to flow slowly but steadily equatorward up the Western Australian coast. In fact it seems to do no such thing and may really consist of a succession of closed circular currents known as gyres. The flow in each gyre may be speedy, but the string of gyres only moves slowly along the coast.

The single physical factor that is most important in all biological productivity is light. Plant growth cannot take place in the absence of solar radiation and phytoplankton, small marine plant life, is the basic food for the inhabitants of the sea. This means that the euphotic zone, the topmost 200 m of the sea into which light can penetrate, is also the most productive. Phytoplankton accumulate in the euphotic zone, and will rise at night — and during solar eclipses. Certain regions near coasts have very high rates of phytoplankton and fish productivity. This occurs in regions where the water movement carries phytoplankton and other nutrients upwards from the ocean bottom. This process is called upwelling,

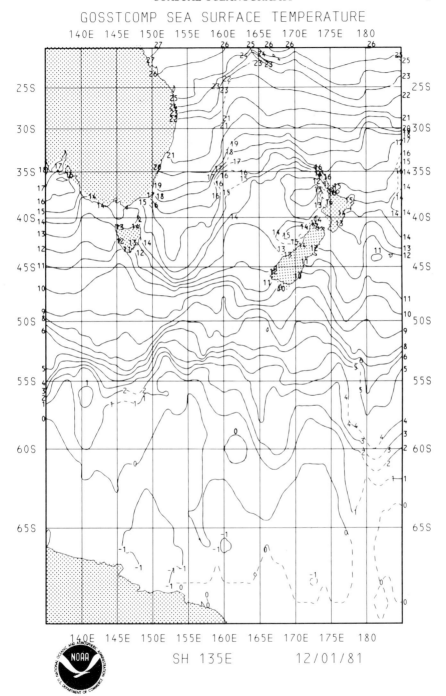

FIG. 1.4. *A GOSSTCOMP map of sea surface temperature. Maps like this are produced weekly from the infra-red observations relayed to Earth by satellites.*

and upwelling regions occur on the eastern boundaries of oceans — Peru, California, Somalia, South Africa are all examples. These upwellings depend on the wind direction. If it changes, upwelling ceases and fishing declines.

Most of the examples that have been given so far can be quantified, that is expressed in terms of mathematical equations. If the biological processes can also be expressed mathematically, then it is possible to develop models to predict the future behaviour of organisms. These ecosystem models are still in their infancy. Phytoplankton models, for example, are generally based upon an equation that describes the change in the total number of phytoplankton — the continuity equation — and it is necessary to find a mathematical form for the flux of phytoplankton, that is the number traversing a given area in a given time, and for their production and loss. One of the earliest attempts to derive phytoplankton models based on physical ideas was that by Riley, Stommel and Bumpus in 1949. They sought a steady-state depth distribution of phytoplankton that did not vary with time, and to do so assumed that the vertical variation of phytoplankton concentration could be described by a second-order differential equation relating three factors: a vertical eddy diffusivity, that moves plankton in the direction of decreasing vertical concentration gradient, a settling velocity, which measures the rate at which they sink, and a term to allow for production and grazing. In the euphotic zone this term is taken as positive, indicating that phytoplankton grow there, but is taken as negative in deeper waters, where fish and other predators graze on the plankton biomass.

Having made these assumptions, development of the model is purely mathematical, but leads to some interesting results. For a steady-state vertical plankton distribution to exist there must first be a limit to the depth of the euphotic zone. Secondly, there are only a fixed set of values of the settling velocity and eddy diffusivity for which the steady state is possible, and thirdly, there is a tendency for the plankton concentration to maximise at the base of the euphotic zone. Figure 1.5 depicts the comparison between this simple theory and the observed vertical distribution of phytoplankton in various parts of the Atlantic.

Modifications of phytoplankton models since 1949 have utilised our improved understanding of the mixing processes in the upper ocean. Though there is little doubt that the euphotic zone is important, the upper parts of it generally constitute a "well-mixed layer" in which wind stirring causes all the physical parameters to stay constant. The coarse vertical sampling of Fig. 1.5 has missed the details of this fine structure, which will be discussed later in the chapter on mixing processes.

1.4 Economics and Geology

Over the past decade, rising petroleum prices have fuelled interest in the non-renewable resources of the ocean. Foremost amongst these are the hydro-

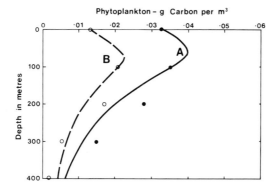

FIG. 1.5. *Relation between the observed vertical distribution of phytoplankton (dots) and the distribution predicted by theory (lines) for A: Florida Straits and B: Gulf Stream off Montauk Point.*

carbons, such as oil and gas, which are found buried within sediments of continental shelves, and possibly also in the deeper parts of the ocean.

Preliminary exploration of the sea bed relies heavily on acoustic techniques. The technology of marine seismic surveys (Fig. 1.6) has progressed remarkably over recent years. The internal structure and stratigraphic relationships of sedimentary layers beneath the ocean floor can be revealed in much greater detail than was previously possible. The general workings of a marine seismic survey can be thought of as a cross between an echo-sounder and a seismograph. Instead of the gentle pinger of an echo-sounder, a towed sleeve exploder generates strong shock waves that penetrate the sea floor and are reflected from underlying layers of rock. The reflected waves of energy are detected by a receiving cable towed behind the exploration vessel and their arrival times are recorded by instruments on the ship. From these data the configuration and depths of strata are calculated, once the unwanted multiple reflections are filtered out of the record by a set of numerical calculations similar to those described in Chapter 12.

The final analysis of offshore oil and gas reserves relies on drilling. The first offshore operations were in water depths of only a few metres, in areas such as Lake Maracaibo in Venezuela, the Gulf of Mexico and the Caspian Sea in the USSR. These initial steps were followed by ventures into deeper water. The technology involved in the manufacture of coastal drilling platforms has advanced apace, but the design criteria used in their planning and manufacture rely heavily on knowledge of the physical oceanic and atmospheric environment. Information on such factors as water depth, tidal range, wave height, the surface currents and bottom currents, wind velocity — both the gust velocity and the sustained wind velocity — water temperature, marine growth and foundation conditions

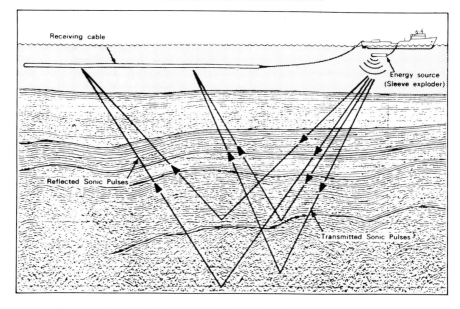

FIG. 1.6. *A marine seismic survey produces a profile such as the one shown. Shock waves generated by the towed sleeve exploder penetrate the sea floor and are reflected from underlying layers of rock. The reflected waves of energy are detected by the receiving cable and their arrival time are recorded by instruments on the ship. From these data the configuration and strata depths are calculated.*

must be obtained and it must be accurate. The gathering of such information is time-consuming, and in many of the less-inhabited areas of the coast the historical information on these physical parameters must be used with the utmost caution.

As nearshore areas become more and more developed, future development will move into more remote regions where the records of past weather and sea states are more limited and less reliable. Moreover, the need for accuracy of such information increases with water depth. Figure 1.7 shows how the overturning moment of a platform in 125 m of water will increase as the height of the wave crests increases. A 1-m shift in the design wave height (i.e. the maximum wave height which the structure is designed to withstand) necessitates a much larger, stronger and more expensive structure. Furthermore, since the moment on a structure is defined as the product of its length and the force which it experiences, structures in deeper waters will be longer and experience even greater overturning moments.

The haphazard way in which painstakingly collected oceanographic and hydrographic baseline data is archived is the best illustration of the scientific infancy of oceanography. It is well accepted that the acquisition of meteorological data is a social function worthy of being subsidised by the taxpayer and co-

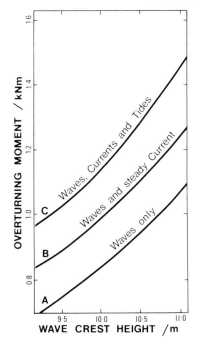

FIG. 1.7. *The overturning moment, or rotational force, on an oil drilling platform increases as the square of the wave height. Accurate information on the wave climate means that cheaper structures can be designed. The three curves are the results of calculations which (a) took only wave forces into account, (b) added the effects of steady current and (c) added the varying effects of oscillatory tidal currents. The axes labels on this graph follow the SI recommendations to use a slash to divide a quantity by its units to produce a dimensionless number as depicted on the axes.*

ordinated at the national level by a weather bureau. Oceanographic data in most parts of the world is fragmented amongst different organisations. In some countries tide gauge records are centrally stored; elsewhere they remain the property of the individual instrumentality that collected them. In general, the monitoring of ocean conditions still seems to be carried out by research organisations rather than service departments, and often exploration companies have to gather their own data, or hire consultants to obtain it for them. Though research organisations generally tend to deposit their data with a national oceanographic data centre, exploration companies – for obvious reasons – tend to remain particularly secretive about their own data.

Alternative Technology

In addition to exploitable non-renewable energy resources, the ocean is a store for renewable energy resources that can, potentially, be tapped. Some of these – such as the production and use of hydrogen gas by electrolytic dissociation of sea water – lie outside the scope of this book. Those alternative technologies based upon physical principles fall into three categories: (i) ocean thermal energy conversion devices, (ii) wave energy extraction devices and (iii) tidal power stations.

The idea of harnessing the tidal energy of the ocean has a special fascination for many scientists. Various ideas and schemes have been devised whereby the rise and fall of the tides could be used to drive electrical turbines or other devices. But the development of many of these ideas has been hampered by the vast capital expenditure necessary to implement them. The world's first major tidal power system, built on the Rance River in France, cost about 100 million dollars, and supplies 65 MW of electricity into the national grid system. Plans to build tidal power stations near the Severn estuary in Britain, and close to the Bay of Fundy in Canada, have existed for years. Various reasons, usually political, have hindered the development of these potential sources of new power.

Actually, tidal power is only one form, and a small one at that, of energy that could be harvested from the sea. The force of waves is known to anyone who lives near the sea or has seen the effects of a severe storm. There are a large number of different patented wave energy extraction devices, some of which are floating converters whereas other types are fixed to the seabed. The world's first full-scale wave-powered turbine generators went into test operation aboard a floating power plant off the Sea of Japan in August 1978. It utilises Masuda buoys in which air inside the buoy is compressed by the motion of the waves, driving a turbine to produce power. There are three turbines in the Japanese plant, built at a cost of more than 1 billion yen, that are each rated at 125 kW. The possibility of linking large numbers of such vessels in tandem for large-scale power generation is currently under study.

The oceans also contain vast amounts of thermal energy that could be used to warm large areas of the world – the main question is, How? The concept of ocean thermal energy conversion (OTEC) was first proposed in 1881 by Arsène d'Arsonval. OTEC aims at harnessing temperature differences between surface ocean waters heated by the sun and cold water drawn from lower layers in order to drive a turbo-generator. As with wave energy extraction devices, a wide variety of different mechanisms of doing this have been proposed. One innovative way is to drive the generating turbine by propane that is alternately cooled and heated, respectively, by the deep and surface waters. The plant would be floating with propane containers below the surface.

Whatever technology is proposed, each generator is expected to supply from 10 to 400 MW of power, in the form of electricity, which can then be transported by underwater cable to coastal and island sites in the OTEC belt (the tropics) or by shipping its associated products – ammonia, or hydrogen – worldwide. The French have a plan to get a 10 MW working system into the water by 1985 at a cost of about 50 million dollars.

There is little doubt that with petroleum prices jumping steeply, and projected costs for coal and nuclear energy costs rising, nations will have to give serious consideration to alternative energy sources that exploit oceanic properties. Successful implementation of these schemes will require accurate information on the coastal physical environment combined with technological and engineering skill.

1.5 Units and Dimensions

In dealing with oceanographic quantities it is necessary to differentiate between the quantity, its symbol, its value, its units and its dimensions. For example, the acceleration due to gravity is generally denoted by the symbol g, and has a numerical value of about 9.8 when its units are metres per second per second. Some of you may find 32 feet per second squared more familiar, which illustrates the fact that the system of units is arbitrary. I have written most of this volume in the International System of Units (abbreviated SI) which is coming into general use. This system recognises the following base units:

Base unit	Abbreviation	Dimension
metre	m	Length, or [L]
kilogram	kg	Mass, or [M]
second	s	Time, or [T]
Kelvin*	K	Temperature, or [K]
ampere	A	Electric current, or [A]

so that we may now write

$$g = 9.8 \text{ m s}^{-2} \text{ or } 9.8 \text{ m/s}^2 \text{ (not m/s/s)}.$$

However, in many cases these base units are either too big or too small. The SI system recognises this by using prefixes to indicate multiples of the base units. A centimetre is one-hundredth, or 10^{-2}, of a metre. The SI prefixes are:

Factor	Prefix	Symbol	Factor	Prefix	Symbol
10^{18}	exa	E	10^{-1}	deci	d
10^{15}	peta	P	10^{-2}	centi	c
10^{12}	tera	T	10^{-3}	milli	m
10^{9}	giga	G	10^{-6}	micro	μ
10^{6}	mega	M	10^{-9}	nano	n
10^{3}	kilo	k	10^{-12}	pico	p
10^{2}	hecto	h	10^{-15}	femto	f
10^{1}	deca	da	10^{-18}	atto	a

We could then write $g = 980 \text{ cm s}^{-2}$, which would be correct, but where possible it is preferable to use base units. On the other hand, certain commonly occurring quantities have been given their own unit. Force is measured in newtons, abbreviated N (note the absence of a full stop), energy is in joules (J), power in watts (W) and pressure in pascals (Pa). A more complete list is given in Appendix 1. Unfortunately oceanography, like many other fields, uses a mixed system of

*The degree Celsius ($^\circ$C) is the Kelvin temperature minus 273.16 degrees. It has dimensions [K].

units and in order that the reader be able to recognise some of the more common ones they are occasionally used in the text.

There are three reasons why non-SI units are used. Firstly, familiarity. Many people still talk and think in the imperial unit the knot (0.514 m s^{-1}). The highly unofficial SI knot is one half of a metre per second. Secondly, convenience. The decibar (10 kPa), the litre (1 dm^3), the dynamic metre (10 m^2 s^{-2}) and the Sverdrup (10^6 m^3 s^{-1}) are examples of these. Thirdly, ignorance. Many people are unfamiliar with some of the details of the SI recommendations. For example, the official abbreviation for a year is a (from the latin *annum*) so that "per year" becomes a^{-1}. The IAPSO working group on symbols, units and nomenclature in physical oceanography has also made a number of, as yet, little known recommendations that include the abandonment of the symbol "^{o}/oo" and its replacement by 10^{-3} as well as the abandonment of % ($=10^{-2}$), ppm ($=10^{-6}$) and so on. They also abandoned the term specific gravity in favour of relative density. The definition, nomenclature and symbol for the Knudsen parameter, σ (sigma), to be defined in Chapter 5, is under a cloud and is to be discussed again at a future date.

Dimensional Analysis

All the derived units can be expressed as multiples and powers of the base units. A newton, for example, is the force required to give 1 kg mass an acceleration of 1 m s^{-2}. A newton is then equivalent to a kg m s^{-2} and it has dimensions [MLT^{-2}]. A pascal is a newton per square metre and has dimensions [ML^{-1}T^{-2}]. And so it goes.

If you become proficient at dimensional analysis, then you have a very powerful tool for checking and deriving physical formulae. Here is how it works: the dimensions on both sides of an equation must be identical, and if they are not then there is something wrong. The hydrostatic pressure, p, exerted by a body of water of density ρ (rho) at a depth H is given by the hydrostatic formula $p = \rho g H$ which links the quantities through g the acceleration. The left-hand side of this equation, being a pressure, has dimensions [ML^{-1}T^{-2}]. Density is measured in kg m^{-3} and thus has dimensions [ML^{-3}], g we already know has dimensions [LT^{-2}], whereas depth is measured in metres and has dimensions [L]. We can then see that

$$[ML^{-3}] \times [LT^{-2}] \times [L] = [ML^{-3+1+1}T^{-2}] = [ML^{-1}T^{-2}]$$

so that the formula is dimensionally correct. This does not guarantee that the formula is absolutely correct because there are dimensionless quantities that could be involved. Angles, pure numbers, and mathematical functions are all dimensionless quantities. However, dimensional checking will immediately detect hopelessly incorrect formulae. An environmental consultant using an unfamiliar formula should first of all check its dimensional consistency.

Dimensional analysis also has a more powerful use. If one has a good idea of the quantities involved then it can be used to deduce the correct form for an equation. The speed (dimensions $[LT^{-1}]$) of long waves in water depends on the acceleration due to gravity, g, with dimensions $[LT^{-2}]$ and the depth of water H, of dimensions $[L]$. If we assume that the speed, c, varies as some power of g and H,

$$c \sim g^i H^j$$

then the only dimensionally consistent choice is $i = j = 1/2$, or

$$c \sim \sqrt{gH}.$$

In this particular case, a full mathematical analysis based on the equations that describe wave motion confirms this and in fact tells us that

$$c = \sqrt{gH},$$

which may also be written as

$$c = (gH)^{1/2} \text{ or } c = (gH)^{0.5}.$$

Further Reading

1. General Oceanography

There is a veritable plethora of elementary general oceanography texts. Two that appeal to me are:

K. K. TUREKIAN: *Oceans*, Prentice Hall, Englewood Cliffs, N.J. (2nd edition, 1976), is cheap and concise and slanted towards geology.

D. A. ROSS: *Introduction to Oceanography*, Prentice-Hall (2nd edition, 1977), is both clear and comprehensive.

More biologically oriented introductions are given by

F. S. RUSSELL & C. M. YONGE: *The Seas*, Frederick Warne & Co., London (4th edition, 1975).

R. V. TAIT: *Elements of Marine Ecology*, Butterworths, London (2nd edition, 1972).

At a more advanced level, the standard treatise – still in print – on biological and physical oceanography is still

H. U. SVERDRUP, M. W. JOHNSON & R. H. FLEMING: *The Oceans:* Their Physics, Chemistry and General Biology, Prentice-Hall (1942).

2. Physical Oceanography

In recent years a number of intermediate level books on physical oceanography have appeared. These include:

G. L. PICKARD & W. J. EMERY: *Descriptive Physical Oceanography*, Pergamon (4th edition, 1982).

J. A. KNAUSS: *Introduction to Physical Oceanography*, Prentice-Hall, 1978.

S. POND & G. L. PICKARD: *Introductory Dynamic Oceanography*, Pergamon, 1978.

The last two of these assume fairly sophisticated mathematical abilities. The classical textbook on physical oceanography is

G. NEUMANN & W. J. PIERSON: *Principles of Physical Oceanography*, Prentice-Hall, 1966.

However, any serious student of the subject is well advised to also consult

B. A. WARREN & C. WUNSCH (editors): *The Evolution of Physical Oceanography*, M.I.T. Press, Cambridge, Mass., 1980.

Of greater interest to neritic oceanographers requiring a more advanced treatment will be

C. B. OFFICER: *Physical Oceanography of Estuaries and Associated Coastal Waters*, John Wiley & Sons, New York, 1976.

3. Specialised Topics

(a) *Fractals*

B. B. MANDELBROT: *Fractals – Form, Chance and Dimension*, W. H. Freeman & Co., 1977.

(b) *Law of the Sea*

There is an extensive literature on the law of the sea and the 200 mile zone, but most of it treats only the concerns of the home country of the author. In order to stay within that tradition I could recommend

G. W. P. GEORGE (ed.): *Australia's Offshore Resources: Implications of the 200-mile Zone*, Australian Academy of Science, 1978.

Or for the British:

Sea floor development: moving into deep water, *Phil. Trans. Roy. Soc.* 290, 1–189, 1978.

(c) *Energy*

Energy problems are well dealt with by

M. KENWARD: *Potential Energy*, Cambridge University Press, 1976,

who covers both traditional and alternative energy resources and

J. A. CONSTANS: *Marine Sources of Energy*, Pergamon Press, 1979,

who considers seven sources of marine energy – tides, waves, offshore winds, marine bioconversion, thermal gradients, salinity gradients, and marine currents.

4. Units and Dimensions

Most elementary physics textbooks contain discussions on units and dimensions. Most countries (with the notable exception of the USA) have accepted the SI system as their national standard with details in documents available from either the Standards Association or the National Institute of Physics. Oceanographers should also consult the SUN report (see Further Reading section of Chapter 5).

5. Biological Modelling

There are six reviews covering the present status of biological modelling in

E. D. GOLDBERG, I. N. McCAVE, J. J. O'BRIEN & J. H. STEELE (eds.): *The Sea*, Vol. 6 (Marine Modelling), John Wiley & Sons, New York, 1977.

CHAPTER 2

Shore Processes

2.1 Introduction

The shoreline is the sedimentary and solid surface associated directly with the interaction of waves and wave-induced currents on the land and on the runoff products from the land. The shore zone includes the beach, the surf zone, and the nearshore waters where wave action moves bottom sediments. The shore zone extends landward to the sea cliffs or dunes that border the backshore of a beach, and, where wave-deposited structures such as barrier islands and spits are narrow, across these features to the cliff or coastal plains bordering shallow lagoons. All bodies of water have shore zones, the extent and configuration of which depend upon the frequency and height of the waves, the range of the tide, the degree of exposure to winds, size of the wave-deposited structures, and parent geology. The names of common shore features are indicated in Fig. 2.1.

The coastal environment means one thing to most people — beaches; and their sun, surf and sand. For many, the coastline is a static environment that does not change from day to day. Nothing could be further from the truth. The coastline as a whole, and in particular the beaches, are dynamic systems of

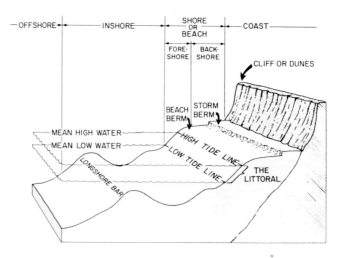

FIG. 2.1. *Beach profile illustrating terminology.*

continual change. The beaches themselves are composed of whatever material is locally in greatest abundance now, or was abundant in past geological times. The principal sources of beach and nearshore sediments are as follows: rivers which bring large quantities of sand and mud directly to the coast; the unconsolidated material of sea cliffs, which are eroded by waves; and material of biological origin, such as shells, coral fragments, and skeletons of small marine organisms. Many beaches, such as those along the east coast of the United States, are supplied by sand that has been reworked by waves and currents from ancient river and glacial material deposited during former times when the sea level was in a different position.

The energy carried by waves provides the predominant natural tool by which the shore's continual sculpture is wrought. Waves can transport large amounts of energy, and the continual dissipation of this energy can, with time, wear away the toughest of stone. This is erosion. Yet at different locations, waves can transport sand and build up beaches. This is accretion. In recent years urbanisation has produced a far greater threat via crowding coastlines than natural wave action. In many parts of the world beaches have been lost through lax building standards allowing real estate development on fragile sand dunes.

Natural processes continue to occur, even if man's activities have disrupted them. Development must work in with and understand the forces shaping the coastline. Most important of all is the behaviour of waves, and their interaction with the shallow bottom and the shore in the nearshore wave zone. We shall defer until the next chapter a detailed discussion of the nature of the waves themselves.

2.2 Wave Refraction

Waves in deep water and waves in shallow water basically behave differently. Upon entering shallow water the forward speed, c, of a wave is given by

$$c = \sqrt{gH}, \tag{2.1}$$

where g is the acceleration due to gravity (9.8 m s^{-2}) and H is the depth. As the wave moves closer to the shore, the depth will decrease and so the forward speed of the wave will also decrease. If the waves are aimed directly at the shoreline in such a way that their crests are parallel to it, then this slowing of the waves will bunch them closer together and decrease the wavelength between successive crests. Waves arriving with the lines of their crests at an angle to the shoreline will be subject to refraction, a phenomenon in which the direction of wave travel changes with decreasing depth of water in such a way that the crests tend to parallel the depth contours. For straight deepening coasts the wave crests bend parallel to the shoreline (Fig. 2.2). The refraction of water waves is analogous to the bending of light rays and the change in direction is related to the change in the wave speed through Snell's law:

ENVIRONMENTAL OCEANOGRAPHY

$$\frac{c}{\sin \psi} = \text{constant},\qquad(2.2)$$

where ψ is the angle between the line of wave crests and the shoreline.

Figure 2.2 illustrates the way in which this occurs. As a wave approaches a beach at an oblique angle, the portions of it that are in shallow water will move more slowly than the portions of it that are in slightly deeper water, since we can use $c = \sqrt{gH}$ for the wave velocity. This velocity differential turns the wave fronts (the line of crests) around so that it lies nearly parallel to the beach. It is for this reason that, no matter what the direction of incoming swell in the deep sea, breakers will break in lines parallel to the beach.

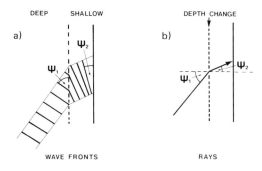

FIG. 2.2. *Wave refraction. As a line of waves approaches a beach it bends parallel to the shore; in this case we assume a sudden depth change at the dotted line to show the effect. A gradually sloping beach will continuously bend waves.*

Wave refraction can cause either a spreading out or a convergence of the wave energy. This effect can best be examined by concentrating on the wave rays (Fig. 2.2b), the lines drawn perpendicular to the wave crests and in the direction of wave advance and energy propagation.

Irregular bottom topography refracts waves in a complex way and produces variations in the wave height and energy along the coast. Waves refract and diverge over the deeper water of a submarine canyon or other depression so that the waves on the beach shoreward of the canyon are reduced in height while those to either side, where the rays converge, are somewhat higher (Fig. 2.3). Waves also refract and bend towards headlands because of the offshore shoal area associated with the headland (Fig. 2.3). The wave energy is therefore concentrated on the headland and the wave heights there may be several times as large as in adjacent embayments.

Wave convergence or divergence is important in deciding where to construct a pier or other structure along a particular stretch of coast. An oil-loading wharf was built in El Segundo, California, before wave refraction techniques came into

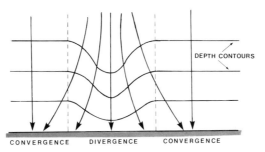

DEPTH CONTOURS

CONVERGENCE   DIVERGENCE   CONVERGENCE

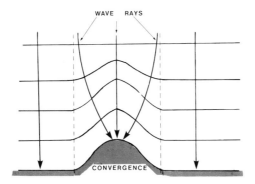

WAVE   RAYS

CONVERGENCE

FIG. 2.3. *An undersea canyon refracts waves away, and a headland refracts waves towards itself. Zones of convergence have substantial wave activity. Divergence zones are calm.*

general practice. As a result, it was unwittingly located in an area of strong wave convergence. Under certain wave conditions, huge breaking waves were produced at the oil wharf site, closing it for extended periods of time.

If we look again at Fig. 2.3 we can see the effect that waves have in shaping the coastline. It is one tending to uniformity. A headland often forms because it is composed of harder rock than the surrounding countryside, so that the aeons of wave action wear it down more slowly. The protrusion that then forms, and its associated offshore terrain, act to converge wave action upon itself, decreasing the wear of adjacent areas and increasing the slow, but subtle, degradation of the headland.

2.3 Breakers

As a wave moves into shallow water its speed will become $\sqrt{gH}$, where H is the depth of the water. But as it runs up to the shoreline the value of H will differ for the wave crests and troughs (Fig. 2.4). At the crests H will be greater than at

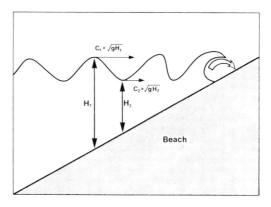

FIG. 2.4. *Breakers occur when the height of the wave is significantly affected by the bottom so that the wave speed,* $\sqrt{gH}$, *differs from crest to trough. The faster moving crest eventually overtakes the trough and topples to form a breaker.*

the troughs and the wave will then move faster at the crests than at the troughs. Each crest will steadily overtake the trough in front of it until there is an unsupported overhanging wall of water (the crest). At this point the crest topples to produce a breaker.

Types of Breakers

Certain beaches in the world are famed for their surf. When surfboard riding was in its infancy and long boards were in vogue the ideal beach was one in which the bottom was nearly horizontal for a long distance out. The incoming waves gently broke at their tops and continued breaking as they came into shore. It was even better if the waves arrived at an angle, so that the breaking region moved in the longshore direction. A well-defined long-lived break point guaranteed a long ride. In scientific parlance these waves are known as spilling breakers (Fig. 2.5).

In those days surfers dreaded plunging breakers — commonly known as dumpers — because the unwary swimmer would be caught up by the fast water flow, carried into the overhanging top and "dumped" down as the wall of water collapsed. The trick to avoid this rather painful process was to dive under the incoming dumper and let it pass overhead. Modern surfers love, and actively seek, plunging breakers in which the whole wave does not break as one. Euphoria for a surfer is to be "tubed" in the cylinder of water that moves along the wave as it breaks. The bottom topography is important in determining the speed of "peel off" and the steepness and therefore hollowness of the wave. There are

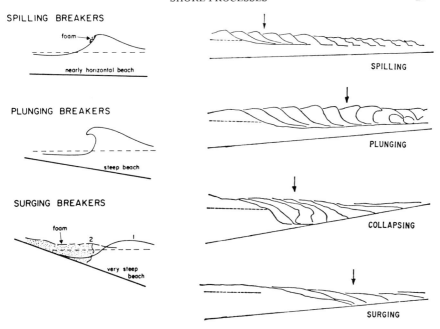

FIG. 2.5. *Types of breaking waves. Vertical arrows mark the break point.*

point, reef and beach breaks, with the former two producing the most predictable and best shaped waves. In Sydney, a wave produced by a shallow reef is known as a bombora.

Finally there are two types of breaking waves that don't quite make it as far as the surfing world is concerned. Collapsing breakers occur on steep beaches when the wave delays its break until what is virtually its last moment so that it foams at the same time as it produces its final surge. On very steep beaches the collapsing breakers don't even foam and are known as surging breakers. They are really only the rise in water level as the wave reaches its end point.

So far we have implied that the wave type — and its suitability for surfing — is determined solely by the steepness of the bottom slope in the run-up to the beach. This is certainly important, but the nature of the incoming swell (good surf breakers always form from swell-induced waves) is also important. The wave steepness — the ratio between wave height and wavelength — is the crucial factor in determining the type of wave formed (Fig. 2.6). Ideal surfing conditions consist of predictable spilling or plunging breakers (depending on your skill and courage). The most orderly swell arises from waves produced by storms thousands of miles from the coastline upon which they eventually break. Hawaii, California and Australia all have exposed coastlines which can produce the ideal wave, though perfectly shaped waves are rare. Surfers congregate where they occur.

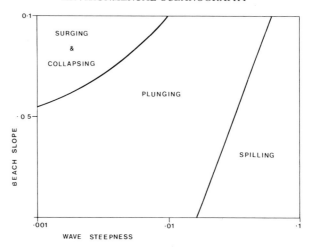

FIG. 2.6. *The type of breaker is determined by
the beach slope and the wave steepness (the ratio
of deep water wave height to wave length).*

2.4 Beach Processes

The shape and nature of a beach depends on the tide height and wave action.
A long sandy exposed beach at low tide can completely disappear underwater
at high tide. This is normal enough and does not cause any concern since the
reappearance of the beach is fairly certain. However, after a heavy winter storm
a beach can completely disappear and fail to reappear. This process, called
erosion, warrants careful study, since it can be greatly aggravated by poor
building codes.

Erosion (Degradation)

The energy in an incoming wave varies as the square of its amplitude, so that
the larger the waves the more energy is pounding the beach. Storms produce
large waves, so that beach erosion is most liable to occur during heavy storms.
The mechanism is as follows (Fig. 2.7). Large waves pound the beach, quickly
removing the flat sandy part until they reach the first line of sand dunes behind
the beach (the foredunes). Sand from these foredunes is carried out to sea by the
backwash near the sea bottom and collects offshore. Eventually the collected
sand forms a bar (a ridge of high ground) or a series of bars and the incoming
large waves then break over the bar, dissipate their energy whilst they are still
at sea and cease to erode any further sand from the beach.

Beach protection is then a case of zealous conservation of the foredune
system. If there is sufficient sand in the foredunes to build an offshore bar,

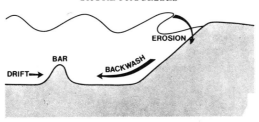

FIG. 2.7. *During storm activity large waves erode the sand dunes until a bar forms out at sea which protects the beach from further erosion. During calm periods the sand in the bar is slowly redeposited on the beach.*

then erosion will be temporary and the beach will be rebuilt over summer. If the foredunes do not exist, then erosion will continue unchecked and threaten structures a considerable distance inland from the original beach. The three most common reasons for the disappearance of the foredunes are:

(i) beach mining of sand;
(ii) levelling of the dunes to build beachfront houses; and
(iii) destruction of the dune vegetation by cattle or humans. Dune buggies indiscriminately ridden over foredunes are especially destructive.

Vegetation holds the dune together and once it disappears the wind will, with time, blow the dune away.

Beaches that are protected by permanent bars, such as coral atolls of the Pacific, do not suffer from this type of problem. Nevertheless, these permanent reefs are a major problem for navigators. Boats venturing in the Pacific need to keep a sharp lookout for areas of breaking waves which may mark shallow coral reefs that can damage their boat. *The Admiralty Pilot* (a book) for the Pacific used to warn mariners to beware of vigias, that is "shoals, the locality and even existence of which is doubtful".

Accretion (Progradation)

Beaches gradually restore during calm periods. There is a build-up of the sand that was lost in storms. The gentle wave action has a bottom drift shorewards and this drift carries with it the sand from the offshore bar and redeposits it on the beach. During this quiescent period, the beach profile is characterised by a wide berm, the flat shoreward portion of the profile (Fig. 2.1) and by a smooth offshore profile with no bars except perhaps in relatively deep water. This contrasts with the storm profile which has almost no berm, the sand having shifted offshore to form a bar parallel to the shoreline.

In fact, accretion is taking place all the time, during both storm and quiescent periods. Erosion is so much greater during storms that it nullifies the positive effects of accretion. To accrete, waves must have sufficient energy to raise sediments from the sea floor, carry them to the beach and deposit them in their swash. This process tends to favour small, fine particles since they are light enough to be lifted and propelled forward, and it is for this reason that most beaches are composed of fine-grained material. Of course, the beach composition can only reflect whatever is available to build it up. Local pocket beaches with a limited source area may have exotic sediments, even on continents where quartz-feldspar sand beaches otherwise predominate. The beautiful pocket beach at Tintagel, Cornwall, England, below the castle of the legendary King Arthur is made up of flat pebbles and shingle composed of very-fine-grained mica schist from the surrounding metamorphic terrain.

Before undertaking any beach restoration work it is advisable to analyse the composition and grain size distribution of the beach. It is common practice to add a foreign sand supply in order to replenish sand that has been lost. If the environmental officer improperly chooses the sand to be ministered to the beach, he may find that all or part of it is quickly shifted to deep water by the waves and his purpose defeated.

The exact grain size found on a beach berm depends on the nature of the incoming waves and the steepness of the beach slope. We can get a rough idea of what is liable to happen from studies on sedimentation and erosion of rivers. In these experiments the speed of water flow was progressively increased over different sized beds. The relationship between the velocity needed to move a particle – the erosion velocity – and its size is illustrated in the curve of Fig. 2.8, known as the Hjulstrom curve, after a pioneer worker on sediments. Erosion velocity is represented by a large band, because other factors such as the shape of the channel bed also influence whether particles are picked up or not. A non-dimensional variation of the Hjulstrom curve, used extensively by coastal engineers, is the Shield's curve.

Large velocities are needed to pick up large particles because of their weight. What is more surprising is that large velocities are needed to pick up small particles as well. The reason is that small grains form a colloid in which they are bound together by electrical forces. However, once the erosion velocity has been reached small particles tend to move as suspended load, and will continue to remain as suspended sediment even if the flow velocity drops below the erosion velocity. They will remain as suspended sediment until the flow velocity drops below the fall velocity, the lower line of Fig. 2.8, when they settle out.

The bottom of the graph denotes grain diameter in millimetres. On the top we have given the appropriate ϕ (phi) units, a common geomorphological measure defined as the negative logarithm to base 2 of the diameter in millimetres. The lowest erosion velocities are needed to move sand of diameter approximately 0.25 mm to 0.5 mm (2ϕ to 1ϕ) and the median grain size of most beaches does indeed fall into this size range.

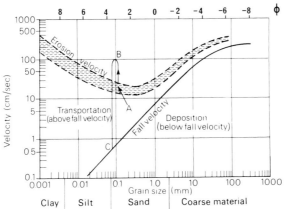

FIG. 2.8. *Hjulstrom curve of erosion and deposition for uniform material. The fate of a 0.1-mm sand particle is shown. It starts to move if the water velocity exceeds that at A and continues to move even if the velocity drops from its peak value (B) until the water velocity drops below the fall velocity at C.*

Nearshore Currents

There are two wave-induced current systems in the nearshore zone which dominate water movement, in addition to the to-and-fro motions produced by the waves directly which will be discussed in Chapter 3.1. These are longshore currents produced by an oblique wave approach to the shoreline; and a cell circulation system of rip currents and associated longshore currents. Rip currents are strong jets of seaward-flowing water which flush the nearshore waters and replace them with cleaner offshore waters.

The cell circulation is shown schematically in Fig. 2.9a. Rip currents are the most obvious feature of this circulation, but they are relatively narrow, so that any bather caught in one should swim parallel to the shore for a time to escape the current before attempting to swim back to shore. Surfers sometimes use rip currents for a free ride seaward of the breakers. The rips are fed by a system of longshore currents which increase in velocity from zero about midway between two adjacent rips. To make up for the water moving seaward out of rip currents, there must also be a slow mass transport of water moving shoreward through the breaker zone in the area between the rips. All these components together make up the nearshore cell circulation system.

A longshore current is established when waves approach a straight coastline at an oblique angle. It flows parallel to the coastline in the nearshore zone. The velocity of the current decreases quickly to zero outside the breaker zone, so it is clearly wave-induced and cannot be attributed to ocean currents or tides.

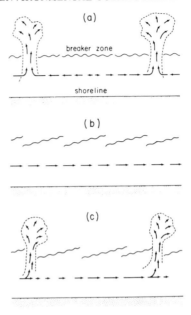

FIG. 2.9. *The summation of a cell circulation (a), with a longshore current from an oblique wave approach (b), resulting in the observed nearshore current pattern (c).*

This current, depicted in Fig. 2.9b, is particularly significant in that it is responsible for the nett transport of sand or other beach material along the shore. The immersed weight of sand-transported longshore, J, expressed in units of Newtons per second, is

$$J = 0.77\, P \sin \psi \cos \psi,$$

where P is the power per unit crest length of the breaking wave and ψ is the angle that the breaking wave crests make with the shoreline. Ways of evaluating P are discussed in the next chapter, but it is worth mentioning that the product $(P \sin \psi \cos \psi)$ is usually denoted by P_l and given a wide variety of different names. One of the most common geomorphological features of this transport is the occurrence of sand bars across river mouths (virtually every river in the southern part of Western Australia is closed by a sand bar that is periodically breached) or the formation of a spit, a beach that is tied to the coast at one end and free at the other.

When breaking waves approach a beach there is a rise in mean water level.

This is called wave set-up and will be more fully explained in the next chapter. Variations in wave set-up provide a longshore head of water. This head of water drives feeder longshore currents and produces rip currents. Wave set-up variations are, in turn, due to longshore variations in the incoming wave height — the higher the waves the greater the wave set-up. Therefore, the currents flow from positions of highest breaker height and turn seaward as rip currents at positions of lowest wave height.

2.5 Coastal Engineering

There is considerable controversy as to whether a beach, left free of human influences, undergoes permanent changes, cyclic changes, or whether it reaches a state of equilibrium between sediment sources and wave action. The existence of the controversy indicates that whatever happens, it will take a long time to do it — years and decades. When jetties, breakwaters, or other structures are constructed in the coastal zone, then the natural readjustment processes may be upset, sometimes with disastrous consequences. Many of the most severe cases of coastal erosion can be attributed to this disturbance of natural readjustment processes.

Structures are constructed in nearshore waters for two main purposes: to improve navigation and to diminish coastal erosion. Jetties and breakwaters are built for the protection of boats and to aid navigation, whereas groins (or groynes) and various types of seawalls are constructed to prevent erosion of the coast. If there are deleterious effects after these structures are built, they may not be noticeable for some years. This is because the wave climate can fluctuate from year to year and because the beach zone has reserves which cover immediate contingencies.

Unlike erosion, accretion against a man-made obstacle is very swift, since much of the action takes place within the surf zone. This speedy reaction has tended to give engineers the impression of swift success with erosion abatement structures, though the more experienced of their profession have always been aware of the difficulty of maintaining long-term shore stability through artificial means.

Jetties (or training walls) are built at the mouth of a river or tidal inlet to help deepen and stabilise a channel, to prevent shoaling by littoral drift and to protect the channel entrance from storm waves. Jetties direct or confine the stream and tidal flow to aid the channel's self-scouring ability. In order to prevent littoral drift from entering the channel, jetties generally extend through the entire nearshore to beyond the breaker zone. However, in doing so, they also act as a dam to the longshore drift of sand in the nearshore. As the sand moves alongshore under the natural processes of waves breaking obliquely to the shoreline, the drift must stop when it reaches an obstacle placed across the littoral zone. As a result the sand accumulates on the updrift side of the jetty and the same processes scour the sand away from the downdrift side.

Breakwaters are structures which protect a portion of the shoreline area, thus providing a harbour or anchorage shielded from waves — provided the harbour entrance has not been inadvertently chosen at a point of wave convergence. Breakwaters are constructed in a variety of shapes, but are generally attached to the coast at one or both ends, with a gap for a boat entrance. One variety, the offshore or detached breakwater which is illustrated in Fig. 2.10, is built parallel to the shoreline. The jetty and breakwater combination of Fig. 2.10 has been used at a couple of marinas in California. Initially it was thought that such a

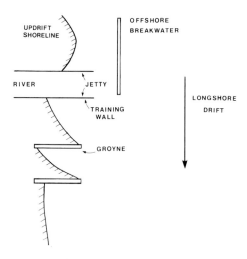

FIG 2.10. *A sketch of the effects of a jetty, breakwater, groin combination.*

construction would provide a protected passage for boats whilst offering no impediment to the natural drift of longshore sand. However, breakwaters diminish the wave energy at the shoreline and thus reduce the capacity for waves to transport the sand alongshore. The result is a deposition of littoral sands within the protected lee of the detached breakwater which acts as a sand trap. After sufficient time a spit of sand would form to connect the breakwater with the land, and thus negate the supposed advantages of having originally constructed an offshore breakwater.

Virtually all jetty, or jetty and breakwater combinations, built in areas of strong alongshore sediment drift have to be periodically dredged and in extreme cases, have to have the sand bypassed from the updrift side to the downdrift side. This bypassing is either done by fixed or floating mechanical pumps, or by trucking the sand around from one location to the next. The best documented examples are the harbours of Santa Barbara, California and Madras, India, though many dozens of other examples abound.

Seawalls are built along the shoreline to prevent property erosion and other damage due to wave action. They are placed parallel, or nearly parallel, to the shoreline separating the land from the water. Older seawalls were constructed as vertical walls, but it was found that the reflected wave energy interacted with the incoming waves to produce standing waves known as clapotis, which promote erosion at the toe of the wall. Nowadays seawalls are built so as to slope upwards toward the land and gradually diminish the incoming wave energy as it dissipates in its run up the sea wall.

A groin (or groyne) is a shore protection structure usually built perpendicular to the shoreline in order to trap sand that is drifting along the coast. This helps prevent further erosion of the beach updrift of the groin. Groins rarely exist in isolation, and the segment of beach between two adjacent groins acts as a small pocket beach which aligns itself with the crests of incoming waves. Unfortunately groins cannot prevent continued erosion on their downdrift side, and indeed, by trapping the sand that would have replaced the eroded material they actively aggravate the erosion until the groin is filled with sand and the drift can then continue by passing its seaward end. To prevent excess downdrift damage groins can be artificially filled with sand, or used in conjunction with sand pumping (Fig. 2.11).

We have so far concentrated on the standard type of shore protection features commonly used. New types are being investigated, but their practical application is fraught with legal and environmental dangers. Even when standard techniques are used it is considered prudent to seek legal counsel at the earliest stages. Municipalities downdrift of groins and suffering accelerated erosion are usually quick to instigate a court action. Legal considerations may even arise over a beach artificially created by sand-bypassing, despite the obvious advantages to most property owners. In one case a pier that had been used for fishing was left stranded after beach nourishment work was started. The owner then brought suit, seeking payment for the loss of value of his pier.

2.6 Coastal Zone Management

The example of coastal engineering outlined in the previous section is one example of the wider problem of coastal zone management. How does one obtain the maximum benefit from the coast; from its estuaries, rivers, beaches, headlands, aquatic resources and underwater facilities? Total protection is unrealistic. People cannot be kept away from all beaches; offshore drilling has become vital in our oil-short era. Equally, total destruction is unthinkable in our environmentally conscious age. People will no longer tolerate the indiscriminate usage of waterfront areas for those industries that could well be established elsewhere. Each coastal community has to work out its own priorities and its own needs, and they need to sort these out before their coastline has reached the stage where it is so despoiled that there is nothing left to manage.

FIG. 2.11. *Groins near Perth, Western Australia. Note that seawalls have been built where the dune system was flattened to provide car-parks.*

In many cases coastal zone management has become equated with land use practices and zoning regulation. Though these are certainly very important considerations it is dangerous to neglect marine considerations in coastal zone planning. The most visible cases involve beach erosion or accretion as a result of harbour or other foreshore construction. More insidious problems can arise from waterfront factories whose waste discharge contains noxious chemicals. Similarly, care must be exercised when deciding on the location of sewage discharge pipes in order to ensure that the resulting effluent will not migrate shoreward and pollute recreational beaches.

Thorough planning and design require that the full ecological and aesthetic impact of any modification be considered and understood. Many States have legislated to this effect by requiring an environmental impact statement to be approved by an environmental protection board before construction — or sometimes even demolition — can begin. If there is potential for significant adverse effect to any environmental feature, then the design analysis of the project should include alternatives for avoiding or mitigating that adverse effect. Therefore, design analysis should include a multidisciplinary appraisal of the total impact of the project, to include environmental quality as well as economic benefits. Accurate assessment of the pre-project environment, in general through base-line studies, is essential. This helps initial planning and design, and provides the data to evaluate later design modification or alternatives.

From an environmental standpoint there are three fundamental steps necessary for the good design of coastal structures: (i) identification of the important processes operative in an environment, (ii) understanding of their relative importance and their mutual interactions, and (iii) the correct analysis of their interaction with the contemplated design. There is no substitute for direct measurements in identifying and determining the relative importance of the various environmental parameters. It is also necessary that measurements be continued over a sufficient length of time so that predictions based on an earlier series of measurements can be tested for agreement with subsequent series.

Marine Parks

Particularly scenic pieces of coastline can best be managed by their being declared a marine park. In Australia, the Great Barrier Reef has been given this status and is administered by a national authority known as the Great Barrier Reef Marine Park Authority. One of the first acts of this body was to divide the reef into management sections and develop zoning plans for those nearest to heavily populated centres.

The Authority chose a zoning plan based on five classifications:

   (i) general use A zones in which trawling and commercial fishing was permitted;

(ii) general use B zones in which only recreational fishing was permitted;
(iii) a Marine National Park in which all fishing was prohibited and access limited to designated tourist boats;
(iv) a scientific research zone which allows for the conduct of a research station;
(v) a preservation zone of prohibited access;

and in addition specified areas in which there would be intermittent and seasonal restrictions on fishing.

It may be noted that the Authority basically saw a marine park as an entity in which licensed and regulated fishing could take place, as opposed to a Marine National Park in which it could not.

Further Reading

A simple textbook with some good diagrams is

W. BASCOM: *Waves and Beaches*, Anchor Books, Doubleday & Co. Inc., New York, 1964.

The best textbook on shore processes is

P. D. KOMAR: *Beach Processes and Sedimentation*, Prentice-Hall, Englewood Cliffs, N.J. 1976 (429pp).

The "bible" of the coastal engineer is the three-volume set entitled

Shore Protection Manual, published by the US Army Coastal Engineering Research Center (3rd edn, 1977). It is sold through the US Government Printing Office.

Other textbooks related to coastal engineering are

R. L. WIEGEL: *Oceanographical Engineering*, Prentice-Hall, Englewood Cliffs, N.J. 1964 (532pp).
R. SILVESTER: *Coastal Engineering* (2 volumes), Elsevier Scientific Publishing, Amsterdam, 1974.

There are few textbooks devoted to coastal zone management, though there is a recent journal entitled *Coastal Zone Management Journal* published by Crane, Russak & Co., to which the reader can turn. Otherwise

B. H. KETCHUM (ed.): *The Water's Edge, Critical Problems of the Coastal Zone*, MIT Press, Mass., 1972 (393pp)
and
J. R. CLARK: *Coastal Ecosystems Management (A Technical Manual for the Conservation of Coastal Zone Resources)*, John Wiley & Son, New York, 1977 (928pp)

provide good starting points.

CHAPTER 3

Waves

We are all familiar with the concept of a water wave. A sugar cube dropped into a cup of tea will generate waves that travel radially outwards; a breeze blowing over a river will produce waves that will move in the direction of the wind on the surface of the river, even though the current may be flowing in some other direction. These examples of wave motions in a liquid have two properties in common with all other types of waves: firstly, energy is being propagated from one point to another; secondly, the disturbance travels through the medium without giving the medium as a whole any permanent displacement.

Follow the motion of a cork floating on the water surface as waves pass; the cork rises and falls and at the same time moves back and forth, describing a circular motion whose diameter is the wave height. The cork makes very little nett advance in the direction of wave motion, illustrating that the water itself does not move along with the wave form.

The period of a wave is the time for successive crests to arrive at the cork and it is an easily measured quantity, provided that you are equipped with a watch. Waves on the surface of the sea can be conveniently grouped in terms of their period as shown in Table 3.1.

TABLE 3.1. *Surface Wave Types*

Period (T)	Wave type	Commonly seen as
< 1 s	capillary waves	ripples
~ 1 s	wind waves (chop)	"cat's paws"
~ 10 s	swell	breakers
minutes	seiches	harbour oscillations
hours	tides	tides

The wind is responsible for generating both wind waves and swell. Wind waves, or chop, are the short, bumpy, sharp crested waves that appear in windy conditions. Swell is the slow, gently rolling waves that impinge on an exposed shoreline even on calm days. Swell is produced by storms a long way away from the point of observation. Typically, the swell on the Californian coast is a product of storms near New Zealand. On the other hand, choppy seas due to strong wind conditions are the result of local wind generation. Capillary waves form on the back of large waves even when there is no wind, and exist in profusion when there is a wind. They are easy enough to generate in a kitchen sink by rapidly moving your finger through the water — capillary waves are the ones that appear in front of your moving finger. These waves, also known as surface tension waves, were just a curious oddity until recently. They are now treated with renewed respect since it appears that they are responsible for much of the depolarisation of microwave signals being used to infer sea surface wind speeds, as described in Chapter 11. Thus a better understanding of surface tension ripples could lead to better satellite-determined oceanic wind speeds.

3.1 Surface Waves

Wave motion is periodic; that is, it is repetitive through fixed periods of time. At some stationary position — say the post in Fig. 3.1 — a succession of wave crests (or troughs) pass at fixed intervals of time, T, the period. The horizontal

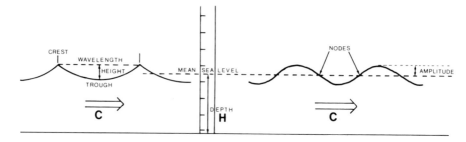

FIG 3.1. *Nomenclature for wave parameters. The wave on the left represents a realistic surface wave. The one on the right a more idealised sinusoidal wave.* c *denotes the celerity or phase speed.*

distance between successive crests (or troughs) is called the wavelength, λ (lambda), and it is related to the velocity of propagation of the crests and troughs, c, by

$$c = \lambda/T. \tag{3.1}$$

This relationship (3.1) is true for all periodic waves, though, as we shall see later, there are also other expressions that can be used to find the velocity of water waves. The speed, c, is sometimes called the celerity of the wave.

The simple theory for water waves was first presented by G.B. Airy (1801–1892) who developed a theory for waves travelling over a horizontal bottom in any depth of water. He pointed out that the restoring force for these waves is the gravitational force and that there are two limiting cases: deep water waves and shallow water waves.

(i) *Deep water waves*

The restoring force for water waves is gravitational, and one would expect g, the acceleration due to gravity, to appear in any expression linking the wave speed and the other wave parameters. Since c can be expressed completely in terms of either period or wavelength, let us choose the wavelength and use dimensional analysis to show that

$$c = (\text{constant}) \times \sqrt{g\lambda} = \sqrt{\frac{g\lambda}{2\pi}},$$ (3.2)

where the value of the constant ($\sqrt{1/2\pi}$) must be supplied by the complete mathematical argument, based on the equations of fluid motions. The reason for this, as explained in section 1.5, is that $\sqrt{1/2\pi}$ is a pure dimensionless number which cannot be found by dimensional analysis. The symbol π (pi), which represents the number 3.142, crops up frequently in wave theory because wave motion can be related to circular motion. π is the ratio of the area of any circle to its circumference.

(ii) *Shallow water waves*

In shallow water, the mean depth of water, H, becomes the dominant length scale and we find that the wave speed

$$c = \sqrt{gH}.$$ (3.3)

The transition between deep and shallow water waves depends on the ratio of the mean water depth to the wavelength. Water in a pan may be "deep" if the surface waves are very short, and the ocean over the Tongan trench will be "shallow" for waves as long as those of tsunamis (Chapter 3.6). If you can make your wave measurements to within 5% accuracy, then

$$H/\lambda > 1/4 \text{ implies deep water}$$
$$H/\lambda < 1/20 \text{ implies shallow water}$$

and values in between these two represent intermediate water in which the full mathematical expression for c would need to be used namely:

$$c^2 = (g\lambda/2\pi) \tanh (2\pi H/\lambda),$$ (3.4)

where the hyperbolic tangent is the following function:

$$\tanh (x) = \frac{e^x - e^{-x}}{e^x + e^{-x}},$$

and e is mathematical shorthand for the number 2.718.

Wavenumber and Angular Velocity

The terms $2\pi/\lambda$ and $2\pi/T$ appear so frequently in wave analyses that special names have been assigned to them. $2\pi/\lambda$ is known as the wavenumber and it is generally denoted by the symbol k and has unit m^{-1} — that is dimensions $[L^{-1}]$.

The term $2\pi/T$ is denoted by the Greek omega, ω, and is called either the angular velocity or the angular frequency. The reason for the latter term is that the frequency of a wave, ν, is defined as $1/T$.

Unless you have a particular interest in wave theory you should now proceed to the next section on particle motion, for in the remainder of the text we shall continue to use λ and T because they are directly measurable quantities. However, anyone reading the literature about water waves will be confronted by strange formulae which often turn out to be 3.1, 3.2, 3.3 or 3.4 in a different form. These different forms arise because

$$k = 2\pi/\lambda$$
$$\omega = 2\pi\nu = 2\pi/T,$$

so that 2.1 can be changed by multiplying top and bottom by 2π

$$c = \lambda/T = \frac{\lambda}{2\pi} \cdot \frac{2\pi}{T} = \frac{1}{k}. \; \omega = \omega/k.$$

Similarly deep water waves, expressed in terms of ω and k, are

$$c = \omega/k = \sqrt{\frac{g\lambda}{2\pi}} = \sqrt{g/k}$$

which is often written as $\omega^2 = gk$.

As waves move from deep water into shallow water, the wavelength and hence the wavenumber alters, but the wave period, and hence ω, stays the same. If one knows the deep water values for these quantities, then it is possible to calculate their subsequent shallow water values.

Particle Motion

As a wave travels through the water, the particles of water comprising the wave move up and down in simple harmonic motion, and they also move forward and backward in simple harmonic motion. There are two quite distinct ways of considering and depicting this and all other fluid motions – the Lagrangian presentation and the Eulerian presentation.

The Lagrangian approach is based on the idea of following the particle displacements so as to map out their trajectories. We considered a cork earlier on. It traces out a circle at the surface of deep water, and so the trajectories at the surface in this case are circles. Any particle rolling on the bottom must have a straight line trajectory because water cannot bore through the bottom. At intermediate positions the trajectories, as depicted in Fig. 3.2, are either ellipses – if the waves "feel" the bottom – or circles – if the waves do not "feel" the bottom. Remember; waves feel bottom if the depth-to-wavelength (H/λ) ratio is small.

The Eulerian representation emphasises particle velocities and produces a set

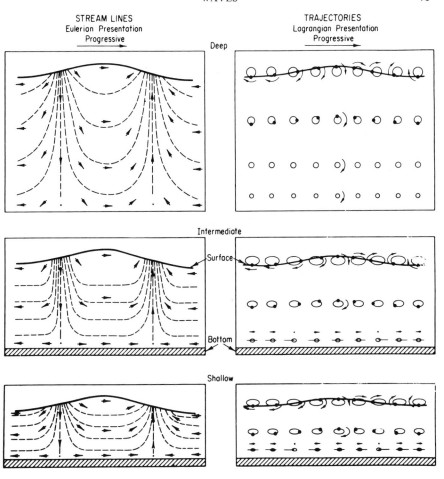

FIG. 3.2. *Eulerian (streamline) and Lagrangian (trajectories) representation of deep, shallow and intermediate waves moving towards the right.*

of stream lines that denote the direction of the velocity at each point of the water. The water flows towards the node of the wave just ahead of the crest, because in a few instants of time that is where the new crest will be, and sufficient water must have moved there to make up the new crest. At the crest itself, the water is moving neither up nor down but horizontally (Fig. 3.2).

3.2 Energy Propagation

A wave on the surface of water consists of an initial transient heap of water that is pulled down by gravity, overshoots its mean level and so forces an adjacent patch of water upwards. The energy in the wave is equally divided between potential energy, which is energy arising from the displacement of water above its equilibrium position, and kinetic energy, which is the energy associated with particle movement.

Energy is conserved. This means that the wave carries its energy along until it is dissipated through friction – in which case the wave dies away and the water heats up ever so slightly – or through wave breaking. A breaking wave redistributes some of its energy into stirring up the bottom sediment, some into heat and some into sound.

The energy of a water wave is independent of wave period or wavelength. The only wave parameter which determines a wave's energy content is the wave height. The energy increases as the square of the wave height. A wave twice as high as its neighbour carries four times the energy. This means that the destructive power of large storm waves is substantial.

The speed at which wave energy travels is not, in general, the same speed at which wave peaks and wave troughs move. This is illustrated in Fig. 3.3. Energy moves in parcels called wavepackets with a velocity called the group velocity.

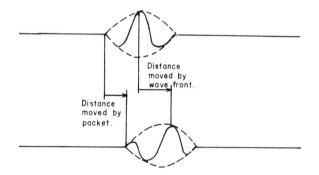

FIG. 3.3. *The velocity of the peaks and troughs
(the phase velocity) does not always equal the
velocity of the wavepackets (the group velocity).
Energy travels with the wavepackets.*

Wave peaks and troughs move at the phase velocity. The fact that they can be unequal may be demonstrated by dropping a stone into a still lake. This generates a wavepacket composed of two or three crests. As the wavepacket moves along the surface of the water, away from the spot where the stone was dropped in, the leading trough is gradually overtaken by the crest behind it. Thus the trough moves out of the packet which now has a crest leading it. This crest also moves faster than the packet and soon disappears to be replaced by a trough, and so on.

The wave speed, c, that was discussed in section 3.1 dealt with crests and troughs (not wavepackets) and it is identical to the phase velocity. The group velocity, which we shall call V_g, is in the same direction as c but will be some proportion of it. For deep water waves (the ones formed when you throw a stone into a still lake) $V_g = (1/2)c$, but in shallow water $V_g = c$. Waves for which $V_g \neq c$ are called dispersive. Deep water waves are dispersive, shallow water waves are non-dispersive.

The power per unit crest length, P, of a wave is the rate at which it transports its energy. Mathematically, it is the product of the energy per unit area, E, carried by the waves and the group velocity V_g, which is the speed at which the energy moves.

$$P = EV_g. \tag{3.5}$$

On a worldwide basis, the total energy in the waves of all the seas is about 5×10^{17} Joules spread over some 3.6×10^{14} m^2. If we take a wave period $T = 10$ s as a reasonable average period, then V_g can be calculated from 3.1 and 3.2. To do this notice that

$$c^2 = \lambda^2 / T^2 = g\lambda/2\pi$$

for deep water waves, so that for these waves λ and T are related by

$$\lambda = gT^2/2\pi,$$

which, when substituted back into 3.2 tells us that

$$c = gT/2\pi.$$

But for deep water waves $V_g = (1/2)c$ so that V_g, for 10-s period waves is about 9 m s^{-1}. Thus, very approximately, 10^4 Watts power is being dissipated, on average, along each metre of the world's shoreline. The shoreline of the entire earth is about 500,000 km so that there is a continuous power dissipation of about 5×10^{12} W along world shorelines.

Because of this continuous transfer of energy to the shoreline, alternative energy sources based on wave action have been proposed, and a number are under serious consideration. Wave energy advocates are not new and there are over a hundred British patents covering proposals of varying feasibility for extracting wave energy. There was a spate of these proposals after the First World War. Flaps, floats, ramps, converging channels and liquid pistons have all been advocated, but most of these earlier proposals showed poor efficiency on model tests. In recent years Japan and Britain have been in the forefront of wave energy work because they are both island nations with long coastlines regularly subject to swell waves whose heights — especially in winter — can be appreciable. Based on historical records of waves impinging on the coast of the United Kingdom, it is estimated that 7 GW of power could be available even at a 30% efficiency of conversion.

Despite the continuing succession of new and ingenious wave energy extraction devices, most interest is centred on three devices: the Masuda buoy, the

Cockerell raft, and the Salter cam. The most developed of these is the Masuda buoy, in which air is compressed by the motion of the waves, driving a turbine to produce power. This principle has, in fact, been used at low power levels (50 to 60 kW) to light navigational aids in Japanese waters for some 15 years, but in August 1978 the Japanese launched their full-scale wave turbine proto- type power plant with three 125-kW generators.

Cockerell rafts consist of a chain of floats, hinged together and aligned so that waves travel down the chain. Pumps on the hinges absorb power from the relative rotation of adjacent floats. The length of individual floats should be less than a quarter of the dominant wavelength, and about the minimum wave width. Typical sizes are 10 m long and 30 m wide. In laboratory tests Cockerell rafts and Salter cams (or Salter ducks) have comparable efficiencies of around 50% or higher. The Salter duck abandons the idea of using an object bobbing up and down, and utilises the to-and-fro motion of the water. It consists of a vane designed somewhat in the shape of the number 6, which turns out to be the optimum shape for garnering waves' to-and-fro motions. The energy in the rotation of the vanes is stored by its connection to a unidirectional pump.

Despite the experimental nature of wave energy generation devices, questions are already being asked as to whether this apparently benign source of electrical power presents side effects that are in any way comparable with those of the more familiar fossil fuel generating stations or nuclear power. If wave energy grows to that dominant a role, then the answer must be yes, though the scale and scope of the effects are different. Wave power devices would primarily be navigation hazards, but they have a significant potential for changing the sea state climatology.

As the very purpose of wave power devices is to extract energy from the sea, they will act as floating or fixed breakwaters. By preferentially absorbing the large winter swell waves it would seem likely that beaches in the lee of the generators would suffer increased sediment deposition. Depending on the marine flora and fauna of the area, this could be ecologically disruptive, though in other regions it could be a positive boon. These types of questions will need to be answered in detail if specific plans to site wave power stations proceed.

Wave Momentum

Equation (3.5) represents the energy flux of waves: the energy passing a unit distance in a unit of time. In addition to their energy flux, surface waves also transmit momentum. The average horizontal momentum per unit area, M, is

$$M = E/c, \tag{3.6}$$

where E is the energy per unit area and c is the wave phase speed. Hence we expect a horizontal flux of momentum MV_g, where V_g is the group velocity — the speed at which energy travels. In deep water $V_g = (1/2)c$, so that we expect a momentum flux

$$MV_g = EV_g/c = (1/2)E \qquad (3.7)$$

per unit distance across the wave.

Suppose we have a wave power device or other offshore structure being acted on by waves. If it absorbs all the wave energy, then it must also absorb the momentum. Now the momentum flux represents the flow of momentum per unit time per unit distance across the wave, and Newton's laws of motion inform us that a time rate of change of momentum produces a force, so the wave power device will experience a mean horizontal force per unit distance across the waves. If all the wave energy is reflected, then the momentum is all reversed, and the resulting force is just doubled. In general a wave power device will reflect some of the wave momentum M_{ref}, and allow some of it to pass through, M_{trans}. In general, we expect that any such body will be subject to a force per unit distance

$$F = (M_{in} + M_{ref} - M_{trans})V_g,$$

where M_{in} is the incident momentum. The anchoring system of any wave power device needs to be built to withstand these types of forces.

In the next section we shall look at some of the nearshore consequences of this momentum flux in breaking waves. Before we do this, it is interesting to consider that it is possible to use the momentum flux force to propel a small craft. A laboratory prototype attached a Salter cam to the stern of a small balsa-wood raft and oscillated the cam with a small electric motor. At wave maker frequencies of 3 s^{-1} the boat was propelled along at speeds of 10 to 15 cm s^{-1}. The ratio of thrust to power expended is given by

$$F/P = MV_g/EV_g = 1/c,$$

which is larger than for some conventional propellors.

3.3 Wave Set-up

Field observations indicate that part of the variation in mean water level near shore is a function of the incoming wave field. Both laboratory studies and theoretical investigations indicate that for waves breaking on a slope there is a decrease in the mean water level relative to the stillwater level just prior to breaking, with a maximum depression, or *set-down*, at about the breaking point. These studies also indicated that from the breaking point the mean water surface slopes upwards to the point of intersection with the shore and this has been termed wave set-up. Wave set-up is defined as that super-elevation of the mean water level caused by wave action alone. The process of wave set-down and set-up for breaking waves on a beach is illustrated in Fig. 3.4 in which the dashed line represents the normal stillwater level, that is the water level that would exist if no wave action were present. The solid line represents the mean water level when wave shoaling and breaking do occur.

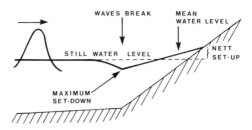

FIG. 3.4. *A wave approaching a beach initiates wave set-down of the mean sea level until it breaks. A breaking wave produces set-up of the mean sea level and the overall effect at the shore is one of set-up. The bottom topography is shaded.*

Wave set-up calculations must be done when designing coastal industry or housing to ensure it is not flooded in a severe storm. For major engineering structures, such as nuclear power plants, it is quite important to consider all possible causes of water level rise. This is especially so in hurricane-prone areas for the effect of wave set-up during a hurricane will exacerbate the coastal flooding.

Calculations of the expected wave set-down and set-up can be made by invoking the momentum flux, or radiation stress as it is called in this context. On entering shallow water the wave amplitude, after an initial decrease, begins to increase sharply. This produces an increase in the radiation stress which has to be offset by a *decrease* in the hydrostatic pressure of the weight of the water. Alternatively, in energy terms, the waves as they grow are gaining in energy and the source upon which they draw is the potential energy of the water surface. The mean sea level therefore falls, and there is wave set-down. The set-down increases almost till the breaking point, when the waves begin to lose height and the radiation stress diminishes. The static pressure must now increase, and there is a dramatic rise in sea level, producing the much larger wave set-up. In energetic terms, the original incoming wave energy is now transferred into oceanic potential energy. Shoreward of the breaking point, the surface tilt is about 20% of the bottom slope.

Stokes Drift

Surface wave theory, as presented up until now, is based on a mathematical procedure that omits terms involving the wave height, h, to the second (h^2) and higher orders. It is thus limited to waves of infinitesimally small amplitude which are sometimes called Airy waves. One consequence of this is that the particle orbits for surface waves turn out to be closed loops (Fig. 3.2) so that a floating object will not have changed its location after one complete wave period. In practice waves do not behave quite like this, and an object floating in the water will move in the direction of the waves. You can float a soap dish from one end of a bath to the other by continually beating the water in order to produce waves.

G. G. Stokes (1819–1903) considered waves of small but finite height progressing over still water. The Stokes wave profile has steeper crests separated by flatter troughs than does the sinusoidal Airy wave so that the general shape of the Stokes wave more closely conforms with the profile of swell waves as they enter shallow water. An interesting departure of the Stokes wave from the Airy wave is that the particle orbits are not closed. This leads to a nonperiodic drift, or mass transport, in the direction of wave advance with an associated Stokes drift near the bottom. This nett shoreward velocity near the bottom may be important in producing a slow transport of sediment toward the beach. Such a sediment drift is known to occur and it is possible that this is the cause.

The forces acting on offshore bars must produce effects more complicated than just a Stokes drift. Though the gradual return of the bar to the beach during storm-free periods may, in part, be a result of a Stokes drift; the reversal of its mass transport during storms suggests that other mechanisms are at work. Experiments with model bars mimic the behaviour of off-shore sand bars in that long low waves propel the bar towards the shore, whereas steep breaking waves propel it seaward. It is possible to explain this behaviour in terms of the forces on the bar induced by wave set-down and set-up effects, by considering a cylindrical bar as two beaches, back to back (Fig. 3.5).

Suppose first that there is no breaking (Fig. 3.5a). Then there will be a small wave set-down, but no set-up, which induces a small vertical force directed upwards. The effects of finite amplitude, and fluid friction make the mean level unsymmetrical and there will be a small horizontal force as well as a mean vertical force. Now let us suppose the waves are breaking (Fig. 3.5b, c). The points where waves begin and end their breaking are shown by B and B' respectively. Outside these limits, approximately, there is a wave set-down. But inside, there is a much larger wave set-up to balance the loss of horizontal momentum flux. If the wavelength of the incoming waves is long compared to the diameter of the submerged bar, there will be a nett horizontal force to the right (Fig. 3.5b). The waves are forced to break, from their point of view, without much warning, but the breaker height adjusts to the local depth of water above the bar. To the right of mid-point, when depth begins to increase, breaking soon ceases because the waves will no longer be forced to try to become steeper.

When the wavelength is small compared to the dimensions of the bar, the waves do not interact with the bottom until it is much shallower and there is a delay in the onset of breaking until near the point of minimum depth. Moreover, breaking continues until some time after the depth begins to increase again. Hence the wave set-up is unsymmetrical occurring on the right. This produces a nett force to the left as shown.

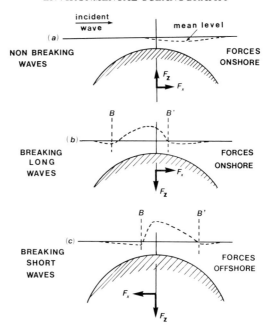

FIG. 3.5. *Schematic sketch — based on laboratory experiments — of the changes in mean sea level of waves in the presence of an offshore bar. The waves, which come from the left, break at B and cease breaking at B'. (a) Non-breaking waves produce a shoreward force on the bar. (b) Long wavelength breakers produce a shoreward force. (c) Short wavelength breakers produce an offshore force on the bar.*

Thus long low waves exert a shoreward force and drift sand shoreward. Short waves exert an offshore force and remove sand from the shore.

3.4 Wave Spectra

Real waves in the ocean are seldom as simple as we have pretended in the preceding sections on wave theories. Any storm will generate a whole spectrum of waves and not a simple train of one fixed period and height. In addition, more than one major storm may be present, so that waves may be arriving simultaneously at a beach from different directions with different heights and periods.

One solution to this dilemma (Fig. 3.6) is to divide the real sea into a set of sinusoidal waves of different periods and directions (remember that if you know

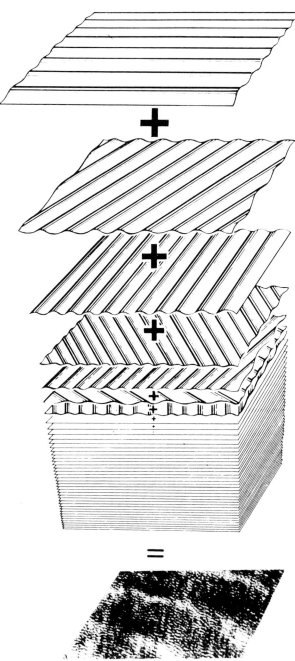

FIG. 3.6. *The sea surface can be represented by the sum of many simple sinusoidal wave trains of different periods and amplitudes moving in different directions.*

the period and water depth then you can work out the wavelength). This is done by a mathematical technique known as harmonic or spectral analysis, based on the mathematics of J.B. Fourier (1768–1830) who pointed out that any curve — provided it has only one value at every point — can be obtained by adding together an infinite number of perfect sinusoidal curves.

As might be expected, wave spectra vary depending upon the strength of the wind and how long (the duration) and over what distance (the fetch) it has been blowing. For any given wind speed there is an equilibrium point at which the energy imparted to the waves by the wind equals the energy lost by the waves through breaking. This is called the fully arisen sea (FAS) or the fully developed sea. The fetch and duration needed to generate it are given in Table 3.2, along with some statistics of the waves generated.

TABLE 3.2. *Characteristics of a Fully Developed Sea*

Wind speed ($m\ s^{-1}$)	Minimum fetch (km)	Minimum duration (hr)	Peak wave period (s)	Average wave period (s)	Total wave energy ($J\ m^{-2}$)	Significant wave height (m)	Average wave height (m)
5	10	2	4.0	2.8	55	0.43	0.27
10	100	10	8.1	5.7	17.6×10^2	2.44	1.52
15	250	22	12.1	8.5	13.4×10^3	6.58	4.11
20	750	45	16.1	11.4	56.3×10^3	13.8	8.50
25	1400	70	20.2	14.2	17.2×10^4	23.8	14.9

A fully developed sea will generate wave spectra as depicted in Fig. 3.7. This diagram indicates, for example, that a fully arisen sea generated by wind speeds of 40 knots will have most energy contained in 16-s waves (i.e. their frequency is $0.06\ s^{-1}$). In other words, if the fully arisen sea were decomposed into its constituent sinusoids — as done in Fig. 3.6 — then waves of 16-s period would be largest, and waves of both higher and lower period would exist in profusion but with smaller amplitudes. If you have obtained a series of wave spectra from some appropriate instruments (pressure recorders, wave staffs, etc.) and they have a strong peak at say 20 s — then you would normally consult Table 3.2 and assume that they were generated by a 25-m s^{-1} wind somewhere along the great circle route along which the wave has travelled.

Oceanographers often refer to both the significant wave height and the average wave height. For a given wave record the average wave height is found by measuring the distance from crest to trough of each record and then doing the appropriate averaging. Significant wave height is defined as the average of the highest one-third of the waves in the record, and is often used because there is good evidence that when a careful observer at sea visually estimates the average sea height he is approximating the significant wave height, because he commonly eliminates the smaller perturbations of the sea surface from his visual average.

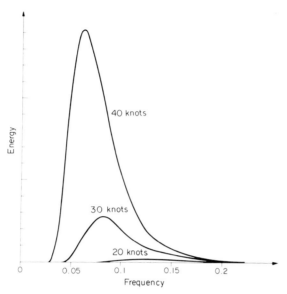

FIG. 3.7. *Idealised wave spectra for a fully developed sea for various wind speeds. The displacement of the peak of the curves from higher to lower frequencies with increasing wind speeds means that the waves of largest amplitude will be of longer period the stronger the wind.*

Giant Waves

If waves are regarded as having heights that are more or less randomly distributed then there will always be some small finite possibility that a giant wave will occur. For example, three large waves travelling in different directions could meet at some point and have their crests pile up into a massive wave. Recently, however, there has been a lot of concern that certain areas of the world — notably the eastern coast of South Africa — have more frequent occurrences of giant waves than one would statistically expect, and that there may be an interaction between the shelf break, the Agulhas current, and certain weather conditions that combine to produce these waves (Fig. 3.8).

The hazard to shipping of the unusual waves on the Agulhas current is due to the combination of large steepness and large wave height. If the waves were less steep, then a vessel could ride over them, and if the wave height were less then there would not be such a tremendous weight of water crashing onto the bow of the vessel. The mariner's reports seem to suggest that the most destructive waves have the added feature of being steepest on the forward face. This reduces the time available for the ship's forepart to rise to meet the oncoming wave crest.

FIG. 3.8. *Giant waves.*

With large tankers there is a considerable premium on speed and an understandable tendency to disregard the wave conditions. Thus, having successfully risen over one large wave the ship ends up steaming (possibly at full speed) downhill and buries its bow in the next wave with disastrous effects.

3.5 Trapped Waves

Trapped wave is a term used for waves that owe their existence to the presence of physical or dynamical boundaries. The shoreline is a physical boundary that can trap waves. The equator is a dynamical boundary that can trap waves. In this section we shall discuss a few of the short period trapped waves that play a role in coastal dynamics. We shall defer long period trapped waves to the next section.

Edge Waves

Edge waves are a type of ocean surface wave that move parallel to the shore with crests normal to the shoreline. Their height diminishes rapidly seaward and is negligible at a distance of one wavelength offshore. The edge waves that are going to be discussed in this section are ones that are of importance in nearshore dynamics, whose propagation is controlled by the beach slope. There is also a similar type of long period wave which will be discussed in section 3.6, which differs mainly in scale, so that Fig. 3.9 provides a visual representation of both these types of trapped waves.

One can understand how an edge wave maintains itself in terms of wave refraction, as described by Snell's law (equation 2.2), and in terms of the changing wave speed (equation 3.4). As the speed of surface waves increases with water depth, rays travelling towards deep water are refracted back on shore

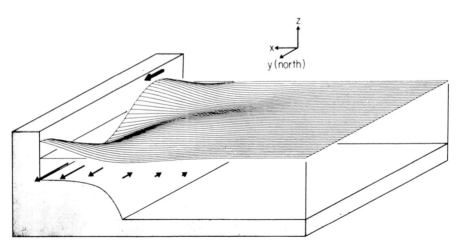

FIG. 3.9. *Representation of a trapped wave in the Northern Hemisphere. The heavy arrow indicates the direction of phase propagation and the lighter arrows indicate the water velocity under the crest. The vertical displacement of the sea surface is greatly exaggerated.*

where they are reflected back offshore to be refracted anew. As a quantitative example, if a ray (or wave orthogonal) is directed seawards at $45°$ to the coast when $H/\lambda = 0.01$, then on a uniform slope the ray will run parallel to the beach when $H/\lambda = 0.01885$ and thence run back towards the beach.

For a long time edge waves (like capillary waves) were considered a mere curiosity. Nowadays their importance in nearshore dynamics has been recognised. In particular, when the edge wave period equals the period of incoming swell, then the interaction of this swell with edge waves travelling along the shore produces alternate zones of high and low waves that determine the position of rip currents, and the spacing between the rip currents will be the edge wave length. In addition, the puzzling rhythmic pointed indentations in beach sands known as beach cusps can be explained in terms of the action of edge waves excited by surf.

Edge waves, or similar trapped waves, can occur at ridges and around islands. One recent patent for a wave energy extraction device consists of an artificial atoll in which the shape has been mathematically refined to make waves spiral into the core of the unit to produce a whirlpool action, which then drives a turbine.

Seiching

Sometimes one can stand on the shore of a lake and see the water slowly rising as if the tide were coming in. But the rise goes on only for a minute or two (it can be several minutes if the lake is large) and then it reverses. The rise and fall will probably be only a few centimetres. The water level goes on rising and falling in this way for as long as you care to watch. The motion is larger on some days than on others.

As you watch the water level slowly rising at your side of the lake, someone on the opposite shore would see it falling. The water in the lake is slowly sloshing from side to side. There is a standing wave in the lake water which is called a seiche. It is easy to generate a small seiche in a rectangular cake tin.

The dominant period of seiching can be calculated for a lake whose width is a distance L. If we treat the maximum water rise as the crest of a seiche wave, then the wave must travel a distance $2L$ before the next crest is seen. As most lakes are much longer than they are deep, the seiche wave will be a shallow water wave with a speed $\sqrt{gH}$. Hence the period is

$$T = 2L/\sqrt{gH,}$$

which is known as Merian's formula. Seiching can also occur in nearshore areas of the sea. For example, in Western Australia, the coastline near Perth has a conspicuous reef system running parallel to the shoreline and situated a few kilometres out. This reef comes almost to the water surface, and the water trapped between the reef and the shoreline (known as the reef lagoon) will start seiching during strong winds.

Harbour Resonance

Though it is easiest to picture seiching taking place in a closed basin such as a lake, it can occur in semi-closed basins and also in open embayments. In an open harbour, such as the one depicted in Fig. 3.10, strong seiching occurs if there is a node in the velocity fluctuations at the shoreline, combined with an antinode — a region of maximum velocity amplitude — at the harbour entrance. The

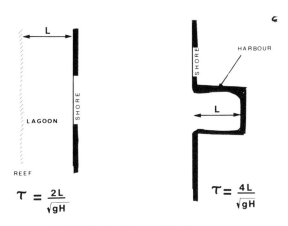

FIG. 3.10. *Seiching and harbour resonance. The formulae relate the seiching or resonant period to the distance L, as shown, and to the depth of water H.*

effective wavelength of this strong seiching wave is then $4L$. There can thus be seiching with a period

$$T = 4L/\sqrt{gH}.$$

This is known as harbour resonance. Engineers try to design harbours so that harbour resonance does not occur.

Harbour resonances can be excited by a number of different causes. The wind is one of them. Strong longshore currents can generate harbour resonances in exactly the same way that blowing across the top of an empty bottle will resonate the air inside. There are also long period waves which travel along shorelines that can excite harbour resonances. Let us now study these long waves.

3.6 Long Wavelength Waves

So far we have almost always been talking about waves that are easily visible to the naked eye. Yet people who live near the sea shore know that the daily variation of the sea level due to the tides is far greater than any variation normally produced by wind waves or by swell. We shall see in the next chapter that tides can also be treated as if they are waves, albeit waves of very long period and wavelength. In addition to tides there are a number of other long period waves that can exist, for all of which

$$c = \sqrt{gH},$$

since long period waves have wavelengths that approximate, or exceed, the mean depth of the water and hence act like shallow water waves.

There are also waves of even longer period and wavelength that are affected by the rotation of the Earth. Effects of the Earth's rotation will be discussed in Chapter 6, but be aware that at any latitude, ϕ, on the Earth's surface there is a period, T_i known as the inertial period and defined by

$$T_i = 12/\sin \phi \text{ (hours)}.$$

Waves whose period exceed the inertial period are long waves that are known under a variety of names: "second-class waves", "planetary waves", or "Rossby waves", and in each case their motion, and that of the particles comprising the wave, is influenced by the Earth's rotation. For these waves c does not necessarily depend on H, and more complicated expressions involving the inertial period describe their phase speed.

Tsunamis

A tsunami is popularly (but erroneously) called a "tidal wave". It is a long, low wave travelling at the maximum speed for open ocean depths from the site of some cataclysmic disturbance such as a slipping fault, submarine landslide, or volcanic explosion. These waves spread outward over the ocean at the shallow water rate

$$c = \sqrt{gH} = \sqrt{10 \times 4000} \text{ m s}^{-1} = 200 \text{ m s}^{-1},$$

with an energy density that decreases as the inverse first power of the distance travelled. Some consist of a single crest; others develop a broad trough in advance of the main wave and a succession of smaller waves behind. It is the preceding trough, together with man's curiosity, that has been the cause of much loss of life. People attracted by the very low stand of sea level as the tsunami approaches have gone out to walk on the newly exposed sea floor and have been drowned as the rising crest suddenly flooded shorewards.

At sea, the tsunami has a very small amplitude and long wavelength, with wavelengths typically being within the range 100 km to 200 km. As the tsunami approaches the shore it will build up in height, in the same way that swell coming into the shore builds up into breakers. At sea a tsunami can have an amplitude of 2 m yet build up into a 15-m crest (a huge wave!) as it comes in to the shore. In the open ocean a 2-m wave with such a long wavelength would take about 15 min to pass and hence go unnoticed.

Long Period Trapped Waves

A variety of non-tidal long period waves can be discovered if you carefully examine sea level records, from harbour or coastal tide gauges. The periods of these waves range from a few hours up to many days. Figure 3.11 shows the results of this examination for the Ghanaian port of Tema. The figure is called

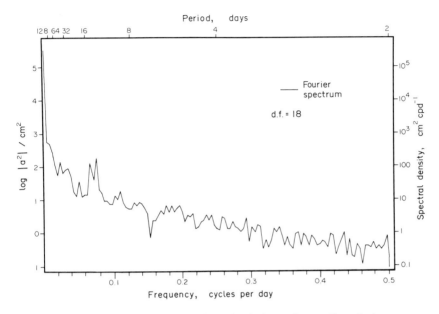

FIG. 3.11. *Power spectrum of daily sea level observations at Tema harbour in West Africa. The peaks indicate that a long period wave exists with a period of about 14 days.*

a power spectrum, and it plots some measure of wave energy on the ordinate (the y axis) and some measure of the period on the abscissa (the x axis). Subsequent chapters will talk more about power spectra. All you need to notice at the moment is that there is a peak at around a 14-days period. This alerts us to look for interesting phenomena at this periodicity, and when we do, we find that there is a wavelike fluctuation of 14-day period which travels along the coast.

These long period oscillations are trapped waves to the extent that their existence requires either a boundary such as a coastline, or a sudden depth change. Figure 3.9 illustrates, with greatly exaggerated sea surface displacements, the nature of a trapped wave in the Northern Hemisphere. These waves move parallel to the coast and propagate in only one direction. In the Northern Hemisphere they travel with the coast to the right, whereas in the Southern Hemisphere they travel with the coast to the left, down the west coast and up the east coast of Australia.

The best known trapped wave is the Kelvin wave. It propagates at the shallow water wave speed $(gH)^{1/2}$, with the depth H being that appropriate to the deep ocean off the continental shelf. It spans the whole frequency range and can exist with periodicities measured in hours as well as periodicities measured in days. Its amplitude decays exponentially away from the coastline with a length scale (i.e. the distance in which the amplitude drops to $1/e = 0.368$ of its maximum value) given by $[T_i\,(gH)^{1/2}]/2\pi$. Kelvin waves are the dominant coastal response of the coastal waters to any major disturbances.

Two distinct classes of trapped waves exist in addition to the Kelvin wave:

(i) Edge waves whose periods lie below the inertial period and whose periodicities are generally measured in hours. They behave like surface waves and are trapped by refraction.

(ii) Shelf waves whose periods lie above the inertial period and are generally measured in days. They are strongly affected by the Earth's rotation and are trapped by its effects. Figure 3.12 sketches the division between these two classes of trapped waves.

The exact means by which these waves are excited is not known. Long period shelf waves that travel northward up the east coast of Australia appear to be generated by wind changes during the eastward passage of storms across south-

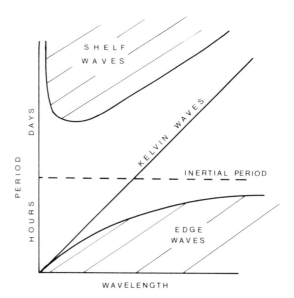

FIG. 3.12. *Trapped wave nomenclature in terms of wave period and wavelength. A diagram relating these two quantities (or frequency and wavenumber) is called a dispersion diagram.*

eastern Australia. Tropical cyclones generate shelf waves that travel southward down the Western Australian coast. Theory suggests that poleward travelling shelf waves on the western coasts of North and South America are generated by large-scale changes in the trade wind field over the whole tropical Pacific Ocean.

3.7 Internal Waves

In days of yore, when sailing vessels plied the Seven Seas, captains reported that their vessels occasionally appeared to "stick" in the water. This occurred during a light breeze when the vessel would behave sluggishly and make little headway. The experience was particularly common in Arctic waters when there was a thin top layer of fresh water from melting ice. Slowly moving steamers have had similar experiences, but when their speed was increased the "dead-water" effect disappeared.

This dead water is due to the fact that a slowly moving vessel creates internal waves at the fresh–salt water boundary if this boundary lies close to the surface (Fig. 3.13). Energy, which would normally be used to propel the vessel, is now used to generate and maintain internal waves. This is the reason the vessel appears to stick in the water.

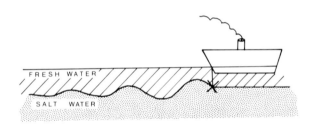

FIG. 3.13. *Internal waves can exist at a boundary between different layers of fluid. In this case the ship's propeller is generating internal waves rather than moving the ship forward.*

The speed of internal waves depends on the density difference, as well as on gravity and on the depth of the fluid. For a thin layer of density ρ_1 and depth H overlying a larger layer of density ρ_2 the speed is given by

$$c^2 = \frac{(\rho_2 - \rho_1)}{\rho_2} gH. \tag{3.8}$$

A more complete explanation of this formula will be given in section 6.2. Notice, however, that (3.8) can be made to look like equation (3.3), the speed of propagation of shallow water waves either by defining a reduced gravity

$$g' = \frac{(\rho_2 - \rho_1)}{\rho_2} g$$

or by defining an equivalent depth

$$H_e = \frac{(\rho_2 - \rho_1)}{\rho_2} H$$

and both of these concepts are frequently used when internal wave effects are important.

The amplitude of internal waves is a maximum at the boundary between fluids of different densities, and the amplitude of these internal oscillations can far exceed the oscillations of the water surface. You can find the denser water slowly rising and falling by as much as 30 m whilst the air—sea boundary hardly moves at all. The motion is slow because the pressure forces that cause the motion arise from very small density differences between the two types of sea water. Such slow motion, with periods of 30 min or thereabouts, means that there is little energy associated with them. (Unlike surface waves, whose energy is independent of period, internal wave energy decreases as the period increases.) Despite their low energy, breaking internal waves can mix oceanic waters and produce turbulence.

Internal waves can exist whenever there are density variations in the water column. The water is said to be stratified when these vertical density variations are gradual, and said to be layered when they are abrupt. Internal waves can exist in both situations with their greatest amplitude occurring where the density variations are greatest. Their period ranges from tens of minutes to a few hours and it can never exceed the inertial period.

Barotropic and Baroclinic Motions

The terms barotropic and baroclinic are often used in describing fluid motions. They have a strict definition based on the behaviour of surfaces of constant density and surfaces of constant pressure. In practice, the important point is to realise that baroclinic motions are associated with density stratification — and they can arise from either temperature or salinity changes. Internal waves are baroclinic motions. Surface waves are barotropic because they will exist even if the fluid density is constant throughout the water column.

3.8 Seasickness

One of the least pleasant aspects of waves is their propensity to induce seasickness in those unaccustomed to working in boats and ships. Any serious student of coastal waters will soon have to learn to face the effects of seasickness.

Its signs and symptoms include malaise, pallor, cold sweating, nausea and vomiting.

Seasickness is caused by the motion of the sea surface, and in this respect is similar to motion sickness experienced in turbulent aircraft and occasionally even in spacecraft. More specifically it appears to be changes in acceleration that trigger it, and these upset the body's balance mechanism. The exact means by which wave action upsets the body's equilibrium is still unknown, but it is certainly related to the vestibular system of the ear. Deaf mutes never feel seasick. Acclimatisation is important, and it would appear that individuals least subject to seasickness have had a childhood acquaintanceship with boats.

However, every normal person will succumb to motion sickness if the motion is appropriate and lasts for a long enough time. A flight simulator can always be "tuned" until those in it experience motion sickness. This parallels the well-known phenomenon that a person habituated to the motion of one kind of ship will frequently suffer from seasickness on a different kind until habituation occurs in the new environment.

Various seasickness remedies are available. They are valuable in prevention but once the sickness develops they are of no value. The only drug that is of value in treating seasickness once it has developed is Valium. Preventative drugs include hyoscine hydrobromide — which works even better combined with amphetamine — taken well before motion is expected. Hyoscine is useful only for motion of short duration and most people suffer from drowsiness and dry mouths after taking it. For motions of long duration the recommended drugs are meclozine (Ancolan, Bonamine, Postafene) or cyclizine (Marzine). Prochlorperazine maleate (Stemetil) is particularly successful, but can have serious side effects in those allergic to it. Each individual needs to experiment to find the best drug, dosage and repetition rate for a particular sea state.

Further Reading

The books by Komar, Wiegel and Silvester mentioned in Chapter 2 all have several chapters on water waves at an intermediate level of mathematical sophistication.

N. F. BARBER: *Water Waves*, Wykeham, London, 1969,

keeps the mathematics low key but emphasises physical reasoning and intuition. The more mathematical approach to surface waves is given by

B. KINSMAN: *Wind Waves*, Prentice-Hall, Englewood Cliffs, N.J., 1965,

whereas

P. H. LE BLOND & L. A. MYSAK: *Waves in the Ocean*, Elsevier, Amsterdam, 1978,

is encyclopaedic in its coverage. They have updated their coverage with two reviews

P. H. LE BLOND & L. A. MYSAK: Ocean waves: a survey of some recent results, *SIAM Review* 21, 289–328, 1978.
L. A. MYSAK: Recent advances in shelf wave dynamics, *Rev. Geophys. Space Phys.* 18, 211–241, 1980.

Any reader requiring an elementary monograph on the physics of waves in general should turn to

F. B. CRAWFORD: *Waves,* McGraw-Hill, N.Y., 1968, or
H. J. PAIN: *Physics of Wave Motion*, John Wiley, N.Y. (2nd edition, 1976).

The most recent comprehensive review of motion sickness is

K. E. MONEY: Motion sickness, *Physiological Rev.* 50, 1–39, 1970.

CHAPTER 4

Tides

People who live near the seashore soon become accustomed to the periodic rise and fall of the water level twice daily. At certain times rock pools and large stretches of sand will be exposed, yet 6 hr later they will be submerged. However, the traveller who examines the tides at many different locations will find a much more complex behaviour than the stay-at-home who studies it at only one location. The tide height varies considerably. On the Mediterranean coast the tides are almost unnoticeable. In the Bay of Fundy in Canada the shape of the bay augments the tidal range to over 15 m, one of the largest tidal ranges in the world. Even the periodicity changes — most of the world has semidiurnal tides with a period of 12.42 hr, but certain locations, one of which is the southern coast of Western Australia, have diurnal tides with a period close to 24 hr.

The harbour master and harbour engineer are concerned with tidal prediction. They need to know the times of high and low water and, as accurately as possible, its exact height. The navigator and captain of a vessel also need to know the strengths and directions of tidal currents — the water movements associated with tidal changes. For such purposes very good predictions can be obtained by using the methods of harmonic analysis which, in fact, are used to produce tide tables. Discrepancies between such tables and observed phenomena arise from unpredictable weather-induced effects on the sea surface rather than from errors in the formulation of the astronomically induced tides. (See Chapter 9 for more about this.)

Nevertheless, ocean tides continue to be studied by a large corps of scientists. The reason is that tides are unique among natural physical processes in that one can predict their motions well into the future with acceptable accuracy without learning anything about their physical mechanism. Scientific interest centres around the spatial behaviour of tides. The great majority of tidal records in the past have been taken at coastal ports and river estuaries, mostly in shallow seas where the tides are dissipated. These give the least possible information about tides in the ocean and on the continental shelf. Sophisticated present-day oceanographic instruments have started to generate offshore tide data and the scientific challenge is to produce tide charts for the open oceans that match these data.

4.1 Astronomical Tides

Sir Isaac Newton (1642–1727) was the first to suggest that heavenly bodies, through their mutual gravitation, produced ocean tides. The force of attraction between the earth and the moon is the vector sum of a great many pairs of forces between the elements of mass that make up the two bodies. For spherical bodies like these, the overall nett attraction is the same as if the entire mass of each of the two bodies is concentrated at their respective centres. However, we know that the earth–moon system does not fly apart and in order to present a highly simplified explanation of tides it is convenient to think as if (i) the earth were revolving around the moon – the viewpoint of the man in the moon – and (ii) there is a centrifugal force balancing the gravitational force and thus maintaining a circular orbit (Fig. 4.1).

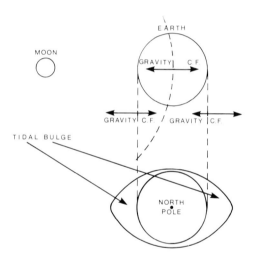

FIG. 4.1. *Schematic representation of the balance between the gravitational and rotational forces (marked C.F. for centrifugal force) at the Earth's centre and their imbalance at the surface, leading to tidal bulges towards and away from the moon.*

The important point to note is that at the centre of the earth – or more precisely at the centre of mass of the earth–moon system – there must be an exact balance between the gravitational force of attraction – which varies as the inverse square of the distance from the moon – and the centrifugal force which varies linearly with distance from the moon. However, at the surface of the earth this delicate balance no longer holds. At the side of the earth furthest from the moon, L, the distance from the moon, is larger so that the centrifugal force which varies as L, exceeds the gravitational force which varies as L^{-2}. There is thus an excess force directed away from the moon. Similarly, at the surface of the earth nearest to the moon, L is smaller and the gravitational force exceeds the centrifugal force, and there is an excess force directed towards the moon.

The nett result of these excess forces according to the equilibrium theory of tides is to produce a tidal bulge (Fig. 4.1) at those locations where the moon is directly overhead, and at the directly opposite point.

As the earth rotates on its diurnal cycle, there will be two high tides at the two bulges, and two low tides between them. The time it takes an observer on earth to traverse the two bulges is longer than 12 hr. Over a 12-hr period the earth will have moved slightly further around the moon and it will take a little longer for the observer to reach the tidal bulge. In fact, astronomical theory predicts a dominant lunar semidiurnal tidal period of 12.42 hr. The agreement between this value and the observed dominant semidiurnal tide around Europe was primarily responsible for the acceptance of the astronomically based equilibrium theory.

Mathematical development of equilibrium tidal theory indicates that the effect described so far is actually outweighed by the equatorward push of fluid that lies out of the moon's rotational plane. The predicted equatorial tidal amplitude is 0.356 m from the effects of the moon. A similar calculation yields an amplitude of 0.162 m from the effects of the sun. These are the only two heavenly bodies to exert any significant tidal forces upon the earth.

When the earth, moon and sun are all approximately in a line then the tidal bulges of the moon and sun are additive, so that extreme high tides are produced. These are called spring tides, not because they have anything to do with the season, but because the term derives from the Old English word *springan* meaning a rising or welling of the water. Conditions favour their occurrence every full moon and every new moon. At the moon's first and third quarters, the sun and moon produce tide-generating forces 90° out of phase and operating at right angles to each other. This produces the minimum tidal ranges — the neap tides.

The variations in distance between the earth and the moon over its 27.55-day cycle, and between the sun and the earth on its 365.25-day cycle, will also generate tidal periodicities, as will the changes in the plane of their orbits. A number of the most important tidal constituents are summarised in Table 4.1. on page 69. Symbols which represent the various forces are also given. The complex tides observed at any location consist of sums of sinusoidal waves with these periodicities but different amplitudes. The sum of these sine waves gives a predicted tidal variation in water level. The nature of the tide at a given location is governed by which of these constituents is dominant — i.e. has the largest amplitude.

Figures 4.2 and 4.3 depict an idealised Western Australian tidal record and the tidal constituents of which the record is composed. The tidal record is

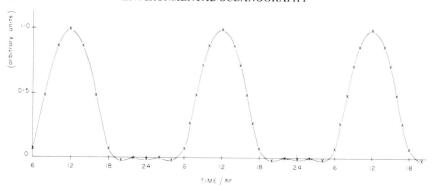

FIG. 4.2. *Idealised representation of tide height readings exhibiting a phenomenon known as double low water.*

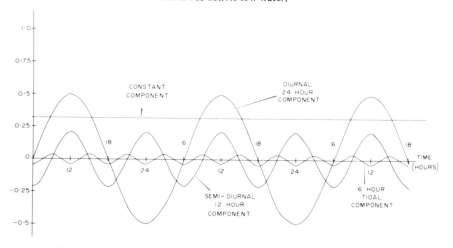

FIG. 4.3. *The tidal components whose sum gives the tide heights of Fig. 4.2.*

shown in Fig. 4.2 and the tidal components that sum together to produce it are shown in Fig. 4.3. The mean water level is labelled the "constant" component. In practice it would vary due to the presence of long period tides. A much longer record is needed to determine mean sea level (19 years of record are generally used). The reason that Figs. 4.2 and 4.3 are idealised is that only one diurnal component and only one semidiurnal component have been considered. This simplifies the diagram, but makes it slightly unrealistic. It is very rare (although it does occasionally happen) for the phases of the dominant diurnal components — K_1 and O_1 — to be such as to allow the amplitude to sum together to produce the nice smooth curve of Fig. 4.3. Another unusual feature is the size of the diurnal component. The diurnal tidal amplitude exceeds the semidiurnal tidal amplitude on the south coast of Western Australia. On most other world coastlines the semidiurnal tidal amplitudes are larger.

The greatest tide-generating forces occur in combination to produce the largest tides when, at the same time, the sun is at its closest, the moon and earth are at their spring tide position, and the moon and earth are in the same plane as the sun. This combination of circumstances occurs every 1800 years, the last occurrence having been in about AD 1400. The tides are now progressively decreasing and will reach a minimum in the year 2300.

4.2 Dynamical Theory

The equilibrium theory demonstrates that tides can exist. The period of these tides is related to dominant astronomical periodicities − those arising from the earth's rotation about its own axis, the moon's rotation about the earth and the earth's rotation about the sun. The fundamental aspect of tides is that the earth is of finite size. If the earth were considerably smaller, then the force imbalance between gravity and rotation would tend to vanish, and so would the tides.

The most obvious criticism of the equilibrium theory of tides is that a tidal crest cannot move over the surface of the earth unless water masses actually change position, but this has been completely disregarded. Though the astronomical theory can explain the presence of tides and their periods, it is unable to explain the actual times of high tide (which, in general, do not occur when the moon is exactly overhead and then 12.42 hr later) and the reasons why certain locations − such as the Western Australian coast − have no appreciable semi-diurnal tides.

The first step towards a dynamical tidal theory is to think of the tide as comprising a long period wave whose crest travels around the earth's surface, and whose wavelength is such that there are two crests around the earth's circumference in the case of the semidiurnal tide, and one crest in the case of the diurnal tide. This wave would be a forced wave, with the astronomical gravitational and rotational forces providing the forcing. If the natural, free motion of this wave were to match the forced motion, then a resonance would occur and the amplitude of the particular tide that is resonant would be greatly augmented.

Though resonances occur in certain locations of the earth's surface, the tides are not resonant with their forcing. Waves of such long wavelengths as the tides would, if free waves, act as shallow water waves and move at a speed given by $\sqrt{gH}$ where H is the mean depth of the ocean. Thus their natural wave speed would be approximately 200 m s^{-1}. However, the rotational speed of the earth does not match this speed at all. Since the earth's circumference moves a distance of $2\pi r_E \cos \phi$ in 24 hr, where ϕ is the latitude, the speed of the forcing is 458 $\cos \phi$ m s^{-1}. This can equal 200 m s^{-1} only at high values of ϕ and in these high latitudes the water is covered by the Arctic ice and blocked by the Antarctic continent.

In fact, examination of a world map reveals that the earth's oceans are mainly large basins with the continents acting as boundaries. Even if the tide was in resonance with the forcing, it would hardly get started on its journey before its growth would be rudely interrupted by a continental margin. In addition, the frictional effects at the continental shelves, as well as the frictional drag of the ocean bottom (remember: tides behave as shallow water waves and can "feel" the bottom) would need to be taken into account.

The mathematical expression of these ideas was undertaken by P. S. Laplace (1749–1827) who developed a complicated system of partial differential equations to describe the dynamics of tidal interactions. Modern attempts to solve these equations have relied on large computers and produce results such as those of Fig. 4.4 in which a particular tidal component – the M_2 tides in this case, is treated as an amphidromic system.

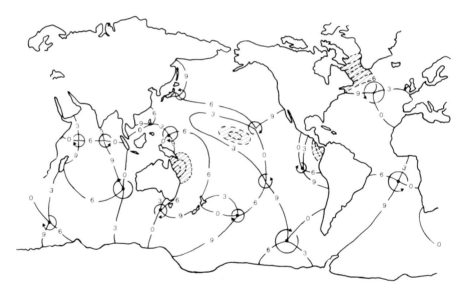

FIG. 4.4. *Theoretical representation of the lunar semidiurnal (M_2) tide. Full curves are loci of equal phase with lunar time marked on them. Regions of tide height greater than 1 m are shaded.*

An amphidromic representation treats the tide as if it were a basin of water rotated in one direction. If you fill a basin with water and rotate it you will find that a wave crest forms and travels around the basin edge in the direction of rotation, whilst the centre of the basin stays relatively calm. The point of no motion is the amphidromic point, and the amphidromic points in the ocean are represented by the dots of Fig. 4.4 from which cotidal lines radiate outwards. These cotidal lines represent points along which the phase of the tide will theoretically be the same. The numbers denote the lunar time. When the moon is directly overhead, and 12.42 hr later, the lunar semidiurnal tide will be at its high tide along the curves labelled zero, and at its low tide on the curves marked 6. In addition, co-range lines join places of equal tide height. The theoretical results on which the results of Fig. 4.4 are based yielded tidal heights in excess of 1 m in only the four shaded locations.

Figure 4.4 represents the results of a world tidal model published in 1969. There are many places where the results do not agree with reality. The clockwise progression southward of tides on the Californian coast is contrary to observation, as is the result on the Brazilian coast. There are also many realistic features. The amphidromic point near South-Western Australia, for example, correctly predicts the low semidiurnal tides to be found there. More recent models have corrected many of these faults and the present-day challenge is to prepare definitive global cotidal maps that are as accurate in deep ocean areas, where measurements are difficult, expensive and scarce, as they are in coastal areas where measurements can be made easily.

4.3 Tidal Prediction

We have mentioned that even though our scientific understanding of tides is incomplete, we are able to predict tide heights to such a degree of accuracy that most discrepancies can be accounted for through weather effects.

In order to produce tidal predictions it is desirable to have at least two years of record from an installed tide gauge. This record is then "decomposed into its harmonics". What this means is that we take the tide to be a sum of each of its tidal constituents (the major tidal constituents are given in Table 4.1) with each

TABLE 4.1. *Dominant Tidal Harmonics*

Name	Symbol	Period (hr)
Semidiurnal components (two tides per day):		
Main lunar	M_2	12.42
Main solar	S_2	12.00
Lunar elliptic	N_2	12.66
Lunisolar	K_2	11.97
Diurnal components (one tide per day):		
Lunisolar	K_1	23.93
Main lunar	O_1	25.82
Solar	P_1	24.07
Longer Period Tides:		
Lunar fortnightly	M_f	327.86 (13.661 days)
Luni-solar fortnightly	M_{sf}	354.36 (14.765 days)
Lunar monthly	M_m	661.30 (27.555 days)
Solar semiannual	S_{Sa}	4384.90 (182.621 days)
Solar annual	S_a	365.242 days

constituent varying as a cosine curve so that at a time t (hours) the tide height due to a particular constituent is

$$y = A \cos \frac{(360°t)}{T},$$

where T is the period (in hours) of the constituent (e.g. $T = 25.82$ for the O_1 tide) and A is its amplitude. For each tidal constituent A and T will be different and, in general, one needs to incorporate a phase angle to allow for the fact that some constituents may be at their highest range whilst others are at mid range or at their lowest. Thus we represent the total tide by a sum of these constituents:

$$y = \sum_{n=1}^{N} A_n \cos \frac{360°t}{T} - \theta_n \qquad (4.1)$$

The more constituents one uses (i.e. the greater N), the more accurate the prediction, but the more time-consuming it is to make the calculations. Modern tidal workers differ in the number of terms that they use, but for most purposes the nine constituents of Table 4.1 would provide adequate results, though at least sixteen are recommended for accurate work.

To illustrate simplified tidal prediction in action we obtained the tide gauge record from Geraldton, on the coast of Western Australia. Approximately one month of the record (from December 1, 1972) is depicted in Fig. 4.5a, and the dominant diurnal nature of the tide at that location is evident. A harmonic decomposition gave the constituent amplitudes, A_n, listed in Table 4.2 and once again, the dominance of the two diurnal tides, O_1 with its 11-cm amplitude and K_1 with its 16-cm amplitude, shows up.

This then raises the question: how good a tidal representation would just these two constituents give? The answer can be seen in Fig. 4.5b, where the curve

$$y = 77.3 + 16 \cos \left(\frac{360°t}{25.82} + 70° \right) + 20 \cos \left(\frac{360°t}{23.93} - 80° \right) \qquad (4.2)$$

is plotted. The representation is good, but far from perfect. Though the times of high and low tide are well reproduced, there are longer-term effects, including the barometric tides, that make the height predictions subject to error.

One may notice that equation (4.2) has used different amplitudes for the tidal constituents than we have given for them in Table 4.2. The reason for this is that Table 4.2 gives the value of each harmonic, assuming the value of all the other harmonics are known as well. However, if one is trying to use two terms to model a short tide record, then the contribution from all tidal constituents close to the O_1 tide and close to the K_1 tide should be considered (for example, the P_1 tide with period 24.07 hr has an amplitude of 5.7 cm at Geraldton). In this case the effect of these other components was to increase the effective amplitudes. The opposite was true of the mean value. Over a one-year period

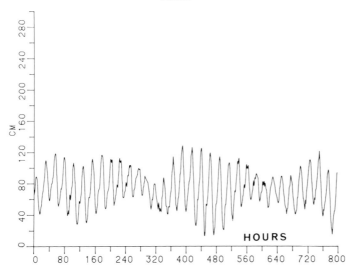

FIG. 4.5a. *The observed tide at Geraldton, Western Australia, during December 1975. The tide is diurnal with small semi-diurnal blips in the record.*

TABLE 4.2. *Equilibrium and Actual Tides at Selected Locations*

Tidal constituent	Equilibrium tide amplitude (cm) at latitude ϕ	Geraldton tide amplitude (cm) ($\phi = 29°$)		Hook of Holland (The Netherlands) tide amplitude (cm) ($\phi = 52°$)	
		Equilibrium	Actual	Equilibrium	Actual
M_2	$24.2 \cos^2 \phi$	18.7	8.8	9.2	80.7
S_2	$11.3 \cos^2 \phi$	8.5	4.4	4.2	20.1
N_2	$4.6 \cos^2 \phi$	3.7	1.2	1.8	11.8
K_2	$3.1 \cos^2 \phi$	2.4	1.6	1.2	6.0
K_1	$14.2 \sin 2 \phi$	12.1	15.6	13.9	7.25
O_1	$10.1 \sin 2 \phi$	8.6	11.1	9.8	10.5
M_f	$4.2 (1{-}3 \sin^2 \phi)$	1.2	2.8	1.8	<6 cm
M_m	$2.2 (1{-}3 \sin^2 \phi)$	0.7	2.8	0.9	<6 cm
S_{Sa}	$1.9 (1{-}3 \sin^2 \phi)$	0.6	0.1	0.8	<6 cm

the mean height of the Geraldton tide gauge was 86 cm, but over the month depicted in Fig. 4.5 the mean value was only 77 cm — the longer period tides had depressed it. Thus the further ahead you want to predict, the more long period constituents you will need to include.

Beats

Take another look at Fig. 4.5 (b). It consists of the sum of two sinusoids; one

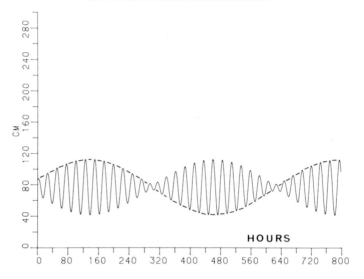

FIG. 4.5b. *A reconstruction of the Geraldton tide record assuming a mean sea level of 77.3 cm, an O_1 tide of amplitude 16 cm and a K_1 tide of amplitude 20 cm. Both the original and reconstructed records show strong beating between the two diurnal tides.*

of period 23.93 hr and one of period 25.82 hr. Yet the resulting curve has a periodicity of about 24 hr, and one of about 327 hr. This demonstrates the phenomenon of beats.

Beats arise when two sinusoids of period T_1 and T_2 are added together.

$$\cos\left(\frac{360°t}{T_1}\right) + \cos\left(\frac{360°t}{T_2}\right) = 2\cos\left(\frac{360°t}{T_3}\right)\cos\left(\frac{360°t}{T_4}\right)$$

where

$$\frac{1}{T_3} = \frac{1}{2}\left(\frac{1}{T_1} + \frac{1}{T_2}\right)$$

and

$$\frac{1}{T_4} = \frac{1}{2}\left(\frac{1}{T_1} - \frac{1}{T_2}\right)$$

so that the final result seems to be a single sinusoid of period $2T_1T_2/(T_1 + T_2)$ whose amplitude is modulated by a sinusoid of period $2T_1T_2/(T_2 - T_1)$. If we substitute $T_2 = 25.82$ and $T_1 = 23.93$ we find a wave produced of period $T_3 = 24.84$ hr that is modulated by a period of 653.83 hr. This modulation wave is shown as a dotted line around the boundary of the curve in Fig. 4.5b and it is clear that the beat period (the time between amplitude maxima) is half of this modulation period.

The name for this phenomenon, beats, comes from acoustics. If you have two identical tuning forks and place a piece of plasticine on the end of one of them, so as to just slightly change the frequency of it, then when the two tuning forks are simultaneously beaten, the result is a sound at the ordinary tuning fork frequency whose intensity waxes and wanes. These are beats.

The beat structure of tidal records is very complicated. This arises because there are many tidal periods, all very close to each other, all of which combine to form beat periods. The semidiurnal M_2 and S_2 tides have a beat period of 355 hr which explains the appearance and disappearance of the little semidiurnal spikes on the tide chart record of Fig. 4.5a. The presence of beats makes it impossible to analyse a tidal record by eye, and sophisticated mathematical tools need to be used.

Local Features

Curious local tidal phenomena can occur through a fortuitous combination of tidal amplitudes and phases. Figure 4.2 depicts a phenomenon known as double low water. Between each of the diurnal tidal peaks, separated by 24 hr, there are two extreme low tides. An actual example of this occurred between hours 300 and 350 of the Geraldton tide record of Fig. 4.5a. Also, in Portland Harbour (UK) the double low water peaks of the semidiurnal tide are so notable that they are locally known as the Gulder.

In the South Australian gulfs people talk of dodge tides. These are fortnightly events when the dominant semidiurnal periodicity is replaced by a diurnal one. They occur because the two dominant semidiurnal constituent amplitudes are almost equal in that part of the world and they beat. Once a fortnight the semidiurnal tides cancel leaving only the dominant diurnal components.

The list of such local events could be extended indefinitely. Bores are probably the most spectacular. These are the tidal equivalent of breaking waves. When the tide propagates into certain rivers or estuaries the rise becomes so rapid that an almost vertical wall of water races up the river with great force. The Severn bore, near Bristol (UK), is the best known bore in the English-speaking world. The bore of the Amazon is an awesome sight, being a kilometre wide at places and up to 5 m high, sweeping upstream at 6 m s^{-1}. The most striking of them all, however, is the bore of the Chinese Yangtze River which has risen as high as 8 m. The Chinese skilfully use the bore to float their junks upstream, ignoring the danger and the helter-skelter ride.

4.4 Tidal Power

Tidal ranges in excess of 4 m, known as macrotidal ranges, are found locally in gulfs, embayments and certain sections along the coast. Macrotides are found in certain sections of all oceans. In the Atlantic they occur in areas along the British, French, Brazilian and Argentinian coasts as well as in the Bay of Fundy, Canada with its 15.6-m spring tide. In the Indian Ocean they occur in areas along the Tanzanian and Burmese coasts, as well as in the Kimberley region of North Western Australia, where peak tides of 12 m occur. In the Pacific they are found in Alaska, the Gulf of California, in the Gulf of Siam and off the North Island of New Zealand. They are also found in certain areas of the Queensland coast where they may be a resonant seiche between the shore and the Great Barrier Reef.

The development of exceptionally high tidal ranges in certain embayments is due to combinations of convergence and resonance effects. As the tide moves into an ever narrower channel, the water movement is constricted and the resulting wedging augments the tide height. The idea of tidal power generation in its simplest form is to dam the embayment, let it fill with water, then close the sluice gates at the tidal maximum when there is sufficient head of water to drive the station's turbines.

The only tidal power projects in the world are one in Russia and one at La Rance in the north-west of France. La Rance averages 65 MW throughout the year since its completion in 1967 (Fig. 4.6). The French experience has shown that tidal power can save some of the fuel that would be burnt in conventional power stations, but it cannot act as a conventional generating station. The reason for this is that tidal power rarely coincides with the peak demand for electricity, so that spare generating capacity has to be available when the tides are mismatched. Electricité de France maximises energy output from the La Rance scheme by using excess electricity elsewhere in the system to pump water at La Rance to even greater heights.

The only other tidal schemes which may yet eventuate are in the Bay of Fundy and in the Severn Estuary of the Bristol Channel. Studies show that a slightly more complex scheme than the French one could supply 12% of the United Kingdom's present electricity demand. Other macrotidal locations are generally too isolated for the tidal power station to be economical and effective. Unless the tidal power generation can be linked into an existing electricity grid, the intermittent and inconvenient times at which it occurs make it less than attractive.

An alternative approach to tidal power generation is to harness the kinetic energy of the water motion, as well as the potential energy associated with the tidal height variations. Locations that experience macrotidal ranges usually also experience strong tidal currents. It is possible to use reversible bladed turbines that are rotated by the movement of the incoming and outgoing water.

Tidal currents (known as tidal streams in nautical parlance) can be a hazard to the unwary mariner and hydrographic charts and tide tables give a summary of their behaviour in macrotidal ports. Figure 4.7 shows the currents at the Port of Broome, Western Australia, during a tidal cycle.

FIG. 4.6. *La Rance Tidal Power Station, France. It has a 15.7-m spillway supplying up to 1360 m³ s⁻¹ to four turbines.*

AUSTRALIA—NORTH WEST COAST—BROOME.

Lat. 18°00′ S. Long. 122°13′ E.

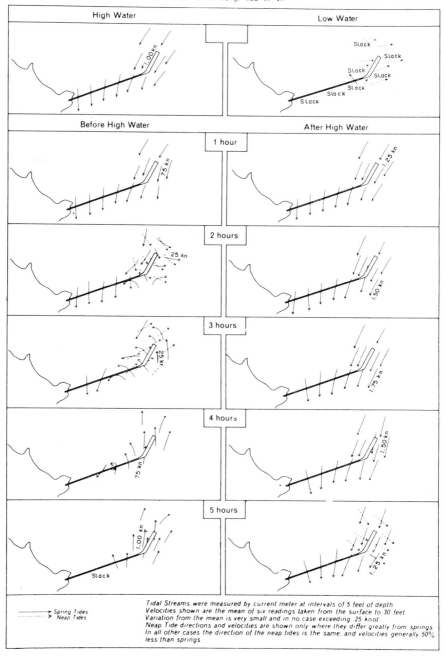

FIG. 4.7. *Tidal currents (also known as tidal streams) during spring tide and neap tide (dotted lines) at the Port of Broome, Western Australia.*

An adequate model of the tidal system must be constructed during the feasibility study for a tidal power station. The philosophy and practice of modelling is detailed in Chapter 12. The tidal model may be a physical small-scale model built with concrete, or it may be a mathematical model stored inside a computer. The importance of modelling is this: Macrotides depend on the shape of the bays and estuaries which channel the wavelike progression of the tide and increase its amplitude. However, by building a dam or barrage, the shape of the bay will be altered and it is vital to ensure that the change will not severely affect the enhancement of the tidal range. Once this vital point has been established then standard economic and environmental assessment of the project can proceed, as described in Chapter 13.

4.5 Long Period Tides

A number of long period tidal constituents are given in Table 4.1. In addition to these one can add an 18.61 nodal cycle due to the revolution of the moon's nodes and the 1600–1800-year cycle when the astronomical alignments are such as to maximise tidal amplitudes.

In practice, however, attempts to determine these long period tides from sea level observations do not produce smooth periodic records. The annual changes in sea level shown in Fig. 4.8 are not smooth sinusoidal curves as they would be if the solar annual tide, S_a, was dominant, but are irregular and peaky. In addition, the equilibrium amplitude of S_a is 0.48 $(1/3 - \sin^2\phi)$ cm at a latitude ϕ, yet annual sea level changes of 20-cm amplitude are reported along many coasts.

Patterns of annual sea level changes are similar in any given region, but vary from one region to another. In general, such annual changes can be attributed to seasonal variations in climate and ocean water properties. One example of this occurs off California where there is a seasonal upwelling of cold deeper water to the surface. This upwelling is initiated by the seasonal wind pattern; during spring and summer winds push surface waters away from the shore and induce upwelling. At these times the sea level is low. Throughout summer upwelling wanes and sea level rises, helped along by the rise in water temperature during summer which expands the water volume (i.e. lowers the density) and lifts the sea level. Other seasonal effects that can affect sea level include changes in barometric pressure and changes in water salinity due, for example, to river discharges. Each of these causes will play different roles in different locations.

Tidal variations are probably the smallest part of longer-term variations in sea level. Over geological time scales there have been a number of large-scale fluctuations in sea level induced by changes in climate. During much of the last ice age, a substantial portion of the earth's total supply of water was locked up within ice sheets covering large areas of the continents. The loss of this water resulted in a lowered sea level, exposing what is now the continental shelf.

It is of interest to note that tides are caused by astronomic forces, and

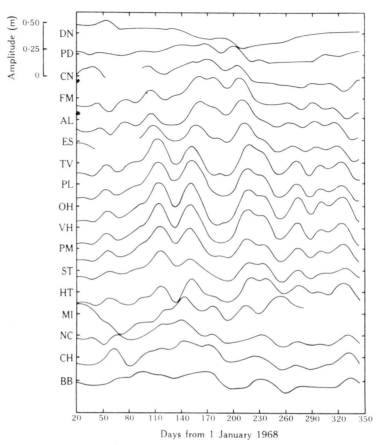

FIG. 4.8. *Annual variation in sea level along the Australian coast.*
Representative stations include Darwin (DN), Fremantle (FM),
Thevenard (TV), Victor Harbour (VH), Hobart (HT), Coffs
Harbour (CH).

nowadays there is a renewed interest in the idea that climatic changes may also be caused by very long-term astronomical changes. These ideas are generally known as the Milankovitch theory and have been used to explain various past ice ages.

4.6 Internal Tides

Oceanic internal tides are internal waves (see section 3.7) with tidal periodicity. They are generated by surface tides in at least two different ways (Fig. 4.9). When coastal waters are layered, or strongly stratified, then surface tides generate internal tides directly on the interface. In water that is not so strongly stratified,

(a)

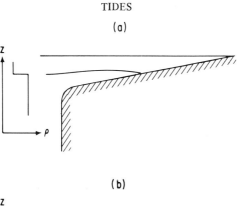

(b)

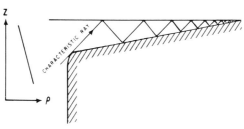

FIG. 4.9. *Schematic picture of internal tides being generated and propagated inshore under (a) strong layering and gentle topography and (b) weaker stratification and bumpy topography.*

internal tides are generated by the passage of a surface tide over sharp changes in the bottom topography – such as the continental shelf break or a protruding sea mount – and thence propagate inshore.

In principle all of the tidal periods in the surface tide should generate internal tides, but in practice only a very few of the dominant terms have ever been definitely identified as internal tides. Specifically, among the semidiurnals the principal lunar and solar tides M_2 and S_2 and among the diurnals O_1, M_1 and K_1 have been seen. Internal semidiurnal tides contain between 10 to 50% of the energy of the surface tide.

Though internal waves of tidal period can sometimes be seen at the surface as "slicks", for the most part they must be measured with subsurface instruments some of which are described in Chapter 11. In shallow water, the extensive use of bathythermographs has given much data, though in recent years measurements of internal tides have mainly come from current meters, thermistors and other devices on moored instrument arrays. Measurements of a tidal periodicity in a temperature record are unambiguous, since the surface tide does not produce any significant vertical displacement of an isotherm (a surface of constant temperature) at depth, and this is the best way to go about searching for them. In velocity records there is no way to distinguish the internal and surface tide contributions.

Even with good temperature records, extraction of the internal tidal component requires sophisticated signal analysis techniques (see Chapter 12 for an introduction to signal analysis) because the signal is often embedded in a lot of background noise. When these powerful signal processing methods are applied to oceanographic records it turns out that internal tides tend to come and go. They appear to be intermittent, and this intermittency is one of the salient features of internal tides.

Exceptionally strong currents occur when internal tides, or internal waves, impinge on a submarine canyon. Submarine canyons are deep gashes in the continental shelf that sometimes extend as far as the shore. Their depth contours and the way they reflect surface waves away from themselves were depicted in Fig. 2.3. However, an internal wave, or internal tide, is less affected by the bottom topography and will penetrate into the submarine canyon if the water is stratified. What then occurs is that the portion of the internal tide that is outside of the canyon generates a force that amplifies the internal tides in the canyon. This generates strong currents where stratification is strongest, and such strong currents can be hazardous to underwater pipelines.

4.7 The Littoral Zone

The littoral zone refers to the area between high watermark and low watermark (the intertidal zone) together with the wave-splashed region above high tide level. The term comes from the latin *litus*, a shore, and carries biological connotations. It is occasionally used to describe all biological activity on the sea bottom out to the continental edge, but this outer area is nowadays called the sublittoral zone.

The littoral zone is a region with unique biological aspects that supports a specialised flora and fauna perfectly adapted to its environment. Though shingle and cobble beaches seem virtually sterile, sand beaches and rocky shorelines are better inhabited. So great are the numbers on some shores that every available surface is colonised, and there is severe competition for living space. A numerous population indicates an abundant supply of food, and this is derived from various sources which include nutrients and plankton from the sea as well as seaweed on the shore.

Spawning is a matter of supreme importance and the special problems of shore life, especially of exposure both to violent water movements and to the air, have to be solved if the species is to be continued. Temperature is the major factor affecting the time of spawning and in the majority of (though not all) shore animals this takes place in spring or early summer when the water teems with microscopic plant life (phytoplankton) which forms ideal food for the newly hatched young. The grunion (*Leurethes tenius*) is a shore dweller that has adjusted its spawning behaviour to the tides. It spawns from March to August and during these months the female ripens a batch of eggs at 2-week intervals. Thus spawning occurs only every 2 weeks and the time required to mature a batch of eggs is so mysteriously adjusted that the fish are ready to spawn only on those three or four nights when exceptionally high spring tides occur.

The spawning runs take place only at night and only on those nights when each succeeding tide is lower than on the preceding night. The run occurs just after the turn of the tide and lasts for about an hour. The grunion are washed up onto the beach with the larger waves, the female quickly digs, tail first into the sand for about half the depth of her body, then extrudes her eggs which are fertilised by the male as he lies arched around her. The whole process of laying takes only about half a minute. The eggs lying buried close to the high water level are buried deeper in the sand as the beach is built up by later but lower tides, and lie in the warm moist sand.

A fortnight later the spring tides erode the beach and free the eggs, which immediately hatch the baby grunion and release them into the water. Thus an extremely delicate adjustment between fish and tidal phenomena assures the perpetuation of a fish unique in its spawning behaviour. If the eggs did not ripen at intervals corresponding to the occurrence of the highest tides, the grunion might spawn on a series of tides which increase in magnitude each tide. This would result in the eggs being dug out and washed back into the sea before hatching time had arrived. For the same reason, if the grunion spawned on any given night before the turn of the tide, the eggs might be washed out to sea. This is avoided because the fish do not run up on the beach until the tide is on the ebb.

Specialised infrequent behaviour like this must be considered in any environmental assessment of the littoral zone. Grunion behaviour is well documented because the fish are kind enough to perform on the doorstep of the Scripps Institution of Oceanography. Equally unusual undocumented behaviour may exist in more remote parts of the world and to guard against this possibility an environmental planner must utilise the local knowledge and folklore of the inhabitants, in combination with past scientific work and his own baseline studies.

Further Reading

A single monograph covering the subject of this chapter is:

E. LISITZIN: *Sea Level Changes*, Elsevier, Amsterdam, 1974.

Komar's book mentioned in Chapter 2 has lucid chapters on tides and the longer-term changes in sea level. Monograph accounts are given by:

Cdr. D. H. MacMILLAN: *Tides*, C.R. Books Ltd., 1966,
G. H. DARWIN: *The Tides*, Freeman, San Francisco, 1962,

the latter of which is a reprint of lectures given in 1897 which still make excellent reading.
Komar gives a simplified account of the mathematical development of equilibrium theory.
The full quantitative treatment may be found in

H. LAMB: *Hydrodynamics*, 6th edition, Dover, New York, 1945.

Tidal analyses are covered by:

G. GODIN: *The Analysis of Tides*, University of Toronto Press, 1972,
J. J. DRONKERS: Tidal theory and computations, *Advances in Hydroscience*, 10, 145–230,
1975,

which are updated by

E. W. SCHWIDERSKI: On charting global ocean tides, *Rev. Geophys. Space Phys.* 18,
243–268, 1980.

Long-term variations in sea level are dealt with in either geological or geomorphological
texts, or more briefly by

J. R. ROSSITER: Long term variations in sea-level, *The Sea*, 1, 590–610, 1962,

whereas internal tides are reviewed by

C. WUNSCH: Internal tides in the ocean, *Rev. Geophys. & Space Phys.* 13, 167–182, 1975.

Milankovitch theory is reviewed by

B. J. MASON: Towards the understanding and prediction of climatic variations, *Q. J. Roy.
Met. Soc.* 102, 473–498, 1976.

The biology of the littoral zone is covered by most basic marine biology texts. The books by
Tait and by Russell & Yonge listed in Chapter 1 both have good elementary chapters on the
biology of the shore environment.

CHAPTER 5

Water Composition

5.1 Introduction

Seawater is a complex solution of dissolved minerals, elements and salts. Virtually all of the known stable elements are found in seawater, although sometimes in only very minute concentrations. Because water is a compound of hydrogen and oxygen, H_2O, these two are the most abundant elements. Sodium chloride (common salt), NaCl, makes up the vast majority of all the dissolved salts, with magnesium, calcium and potassium chlorides and carbonates making up most of the rest. In most of the oceans the ratio between these various salts is remarkably constant and it is sometimes forgotten that this may not be true in some coastal areas. River water has a different saline composition to ocean water, so that coastal areas near major river mouths may have a different ratio of salts.

The hydrostatic parameters of importance are density (ρ) and pressure (p) of water — two variables that are related through the hydrostatic equation

$$p = \rho g z, \tag{5.1}$$

where g is the acceleration due to gravity (9.8 m s^{-2}) and z is the depth. Typical seawater densities are around $1.025 \times 10^3 \text{ kg m}^{-3}$ so that a depth increase of 1 m is very close to a pressure increase of 10^4 Pa, where the pascal, or newton per square metre, is the official SI unit of pressure. In everyday conversation the oceanographer uses the decibar (1 bar = 10^5 Pa) almost synonymously with the metre, and as there is no convenient SI term to cover 10^4 Pa the oceanographic community has strongly resisted the complete introduction of SI metrication. Of course many old sailors still yearn for the fathom (1 fathom = 6 ft = 1.829 m) because it was the length of their outstretched arm when laying out a lead line to measure depth.

Density is influenced principally by the temperature and dissolved salt content of water. Since it is relatively easy to accurately measure water temperature and salinity, but rather difficult to measure density with the precision required in oceanographic work, salinity and temperature are the two prime physical quantities that must always be determined in any oceanic or estuarine investigation. They provide useful information in their own right, as we shall see, but if they are taken together to compute the water density then dynamicists can calculate the stability and flow characteristics of the water. These can then be checked by direct measurement of water movement.

5.2 Density

Pure water

The density of pure water at $4°C$ is exactly 1.0000 g cm^{-3}, or 1000 kg m^{-3}. This is the maximum density which pure water can have. If it is heated, its density will decrease – hot water convects to the surface in a heated saucepan. If it is cooled below $4°C$ its density will decrease – ice floats.

Oceanographers are primarily interested in small variations in density, and have established a convention whereby

$$\sigma = \rho - 1000, \qquad (5.2)$$

where ρ is the numerical value of the density in kg m^{-3}. Thus for a density $\rho = 1025.03$ kg m^{-3}, $\sigma = 25.03$.

The quantity σ (sigma) is called the density excess, or the Knudsen parameter. Its exact definition, symbol and nomenclature are presently under active debate in the oceanographic community, so that in highly accurate density calibrations one needs to explicitly state the definition used. For most work, equation (5.2) is more than adequate, and in coastal oceanography σ is identical to a quantity σ_t (sigma-tee) that often crops up in deep sea oceanography.

The specific volume is the reciprocal of the density, $1/\rho$, and in many theoretical calculations it is of greater convenience. Just as the variations in oceanic density are small, the variations in specific volume are small. For example, when $\sigma = 25.03$ then the specific volume is 0.97558 cm^3 g^{-1} or 9.7558×10^{-4} m^3 kg^{-1}.

Saline Water

The addition of salt increases the density of water if the temperature remains constant. The oceanographic literature has many formulae for calculating the density excess or the steric anomaly (i.e. the departure of the specific volume from a conveniently chosen reference value). There is no single simple formula that gives either of these parameters exactly for all values of salinity, temperature and depth, so that one resorts to tables based on laboratory determinations.

Mathematical formulae for the density excess or the specific volume are usually based on quadratic or higher order curves fitted about the particular salinity and temperature of interest. Formulae for oceanic work will be grossly inaccurate if applied to the density of water in rivers or estuaries. Indeed, for many situations one's interest lies in small density variations about a particular density and a straight line fit is an adequate approximation.

The addition of salt to water markedly affects the water properties. The maximum density of a salt solution occurs below 4°C. The presence of salt lowers the freezing point. This is why Canadians sprinkle salt on their winter roads. Figure 5.1 shows the relation between the freezing point and the temperature of maximum density for water as the salinity increases. There is a cross-over point at a salinity of 24.695°/oo and – 1.33°C, which has important consequences in the freezing patterns of low and high saline waters.

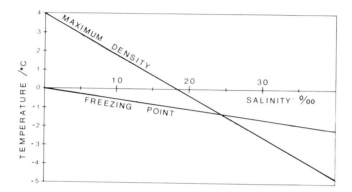

FIG. 5.1. *Salinity dependence of the freezing point of water and the temperature of maximum density. The intersection of the curves, at a salinity of 0.025, represents a change in the freezing properties of saline water.*

(i) *Low salinity waters (lakes, the Baltic Sea)*

At low temperatures, these waters circulate with the colder water, near 4°C, dropping to the bottom until the whole water body is at the temperature of maximum density. Further cooling then *lightens* the topmost water which does not sink. The topmost water then cools rapidly and ice forms at the top surface.

(ii) *High salinity waters (S > 25°/oo)*

In this case convection continues until the whole water column is at the freezing temperature, and the whole water column then freezes. Because of the vast heat extraction required to cool a 4-km depth of ocean water to its freezing temperature, this type of freezing will only occur in the shallower parts of the Arctic and Antarctic waters.

5.3 Vertical Temperature

The density of water decreases with increasing temperature, hence one would expect to find colder water below the sea surface than at the surface. This is indeed the case, but the transition is not the smooth gradual one that one would intuitively expect. Basically, the wind acting on the surface of the water produces a mixed layer which is almost isothermal in the vertical. This mixed layer extends from the surface to a depth that can vary from 50 m to 200 m. There is then a zone below this, which can extend for another 500 m to 1000 m over which the temperature decreases rapidly, and then below this there is a deep region of cold water in which the temperature decreases very slowly.

The depth interval in which the relatively rapid transition between the warm waters of the upper mixed layer and the cold bottom water occurs is called the thermocline. Detailed surroundings of the upper waters reveal that, in fact, the temperature distribution consists of a large number of mini-thermoclines. In low and middle latitudes there is a distinct thermocline present at all times at depths between 200 m and 2000 m. This is referred to as the "main" or "permanent" thermocline. It is rarely found in coastal waters, and then only during upwellings when constant temperature surfaces − isotherms − tilt upwards as cold water rises from the depths. More about upwellings in Chapter 7.

5.4 Salinity

Salinity of water is an important term in the equation of state (i.e. the formula linking density, temperature and salinity). If the sea were composed of only one type of salt (e.g. NaCl), then there would be little problem in defining salinity in terms of the weight of dissolved salt per unit weight of pure water. In fact, seawater is a mixture of many different types of salts, with a most remarkable property: the ionic composition of seawater is virtually the same, with the composition shown in Table 5.1, wherever and whenever readings are taken; provided only that they are not taken close to the discharge of a large river. The

TABLE 5.1. *Ionic Composition*
(by weight) in Seawater

Ion	Symbol	Seawater %
Chloride	Cl^-	55.04
Sodium	Na^+	30.62
Sulphate	SO_4^{--}	7.68
Magnesium	Mg^{++}	3.69
Calcium	Ca^{++}	1.15
Potassium	K^+	1.10
Bicarbonate	HCO_3^-	0.41

remarkable constancy in the ionic composition of seawater is evidence of a continual, and highly effective, mixing taking place in the world's oceans.

On the basis of the chloride ion concentration the definition of salinity was originally based on its determination by chemical titration with silver nitrate so that salinity was defined historically as 1.80655 times chlorinity. In late 1979 this definition was officially abandoned and a new definition for salinity was introduced based on the relationships between electrical conductivity, chlorinity, salinity and density of seawater. This is now termed the practical salinity, in order to distinguish it from the absolute salinity which is the ratio of mass of dissolved material in a seawater sample to the mass of the sample.

Practical salinity is plotted on a practical salinity scale, an example of which is given in Fig. 5.2. The scale is based on a standard seawater having, at 15°C and

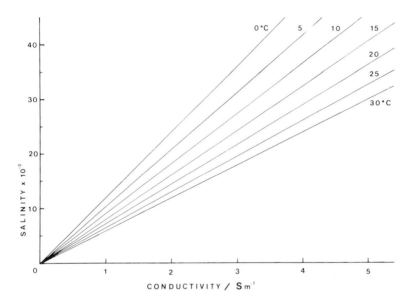

FIG. 5.2. *Practical salinity scale relating salinity to conductivity, as a function of temperature.*

under normal atmosphere pressure, an electrical conductivity equal to that of a standard potassium chloride solution containing 32.4357 g of KCl per kilogram of solution. This particular standard seawater comes from the North Atlantic and used to be known as Copenhagen water. Its chlorinity equals 19.374×10^{-3}, and it has received a practical salinity value equal by definition to 35×10^{-3}, or $35^o/oo$, exactly.

In electrical conductivity units, pure water with a salinity of zero has zero conductivity, but at a practical salinity of 35×10^{-3} its conductivity is 4.29 Siemens per metre at 15°C or 2.904 S m^{-1} at 0°C.

Salinity Distribution

The salinity distribution at the surface of the world's oceans is almost completely controlled by the world's rainfall pattern. Regions of high rainfall and low evaporation, such as areas of the tropics, have low surface salinity due to rainfall dilution of the waters. Regions of low rainfall, namely those situated in the vicinity of the subtropical high-pressure zone between $20°$ and $40°$ latitude, have high surface salinity due to marked evaporation of the surface waters.

The salinity distribution in the vertical direction can be quite variable. It is the *density* that controls the vertical distribution of water, with the less dense water overlying more dense water.

As a rough-and-ready rule of thumb, a salinity increase of $1°/oo$ produces much the same density change as a $4°C$ decrease in temperature. In offshore waters the salinity range is normally small, and it is predominantly temperature that controls the density. In estuaries there can be a relatively sharp transition between salt and fresh water. This is known as a halocline, in the same way that a sharp change in temperature is a thermocline. Generally, haloclines and thermoclines are identified with pycnoclines as well — a region in which the density changes sharply.

A pycnocline will then be either a thermocline, a halocline, or both and it is only worth using the term in this latter situation. Conversely, in special circumstances one may have a region in which there is both a thermocline and a halocline but no pycnocline. This can occur when two bodies of water with identical densities but different temperature and salt compositions come together. Because heat and salt mix at different rates the boundary will undergo a complicated mixing process, which will be examined in more detail in Chapter 8.2.

Temperature–Salinity Diagrams

Water which originates in a particular region possesses a distinctive salinity and temperature and it tends to retain them as it moves. Polar waters have low temperature and salinity; mid-latitude waters have high salinities. Salt and heat diffuse very slowly, so that these properties can be used as tracers of subsurface waters.

Water mass identification is usually done by plotting a diagram of temperature and salinity known as a TS diagram. This gives the temperature and salinity of the whole water mass from top to bottom. In Fig. 5.3 there are at least three water types present. Warm low salinity water (tropical surface water) at about $28°C$, $35°/oo$; cooler high salinity water (Atlantic central water) at about $18°$, $35.6°/oo$; and cold low saline water (subarctic water) near the bottom, $6°C$, $34.7°/oo$. If there was no diffusion and no mixing between these water masses, the TS diagram would consist of three isolated dots. In fact, mixing and diffusion spread the results into the typical curve of Fig. 5.3.

In addition, the TS diagram has at least two further uses. Firstly, a TS diagram provides a graphical method for determining σ at a particular temperature and

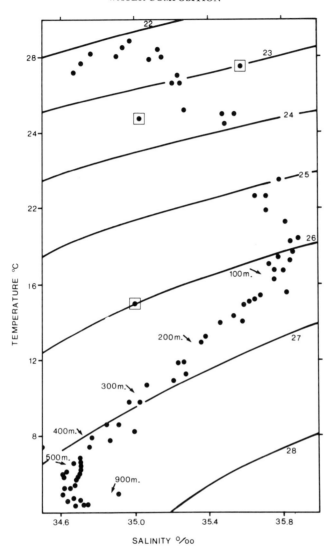

FIG. 5.3. *TS diagram for waters near the coast of Ghana, West Africa. Suspect data points are boxed. The solid lines are isopycnals joining constant values of density. The value of σ is indicated on the line.*

salinity. As shown in Fig. 5.3, the shape of the σ isopycnals (lines of constant density) is a curved line, convex towards the T axis. Secondly, the TS diagram is extremely useful for data verification, and any data point that lies well off the historically determined TS curve is almost certain to be erroneous. Suspect data points have been boxed in Fig. 5.3.

Cabbeling

The lines of equal σ on a TS diagram are slightly curved downward, as well as being inclined to the coordinate axes (Fig. 5.4). Thus, when two water types of different salinity and temperature lie side by side and have precisely the same density – as indicated by points A and B on Fig. 5.4 – their mixture will be represented by a point on the straight line joining their positions on the TS diagram. If they mix in equal proportions, the mixture would be represented by the point C.

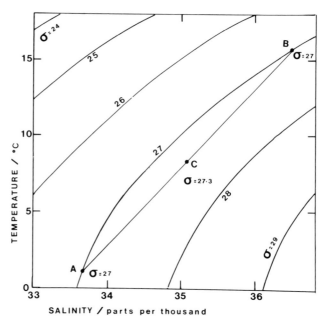

FIG. 5.4. *Cabbeling consists of mixing waters of equal density (A and B) to produce a mixture of greater density (C) which then sinks.*

Because all points on the line joining A and B lie on the concave side of the isopycnal line of constant σ, the mixture must be slightly more dense and so heavier than either of the two parent water types. It tends to slowly sink. Sinking due to this mixing process is known as cabbeling or caballing and we may note that in those areas where it occurs, it will help to maintain a discontinuity between the two different water types and hence maintain a sharp front between them.

5.5 Dissolved Gases

Breaking waves at the sea surface aerate the water and dissolve atmospheric gases into it. The most important of these are oxygen (O_2) which comprises 21% of atmospheric gases, nitrogen (N_2) which comprises 78% of the atmosphere and carbon dioxide (CO_2) which is 0.03% of the atmosphere.

Dissolved oxygen (DO) supports life in aquatic systems and fish have special structures, the gills, for extracting it. The solubility of oxygen in water depends on both the salinity and the temperature, as depicted in Fig. 5.5, with a normal range of 7×10^{-6} to 14×10^{-6} (mg of O_2 per kg of water). Hot water can hold less oxygen, which is why air bubbles form in a heated saucepan of water.

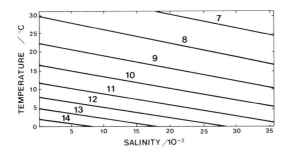

FIG. 5.5. *The saturated dissolved oxygen concentration in terms of mg O_2 per kg of water as a function of salinity and temperature.*

Water can be either supersaturated, with DO values higher than those of Fig. 5.5, or undersaturated with lower values. Air and still water will eventually reach an equilibrium which defines the saturation DO. Vigorous stirring will supersaturate the water, a problem that has bedevilled laboratory determination of the correct saturated DO values. A series of experiments reported in 1955 (and still extensively quoted) claimed significant discrepancies between their results and the classical results upon which Fig. 5.5 is based. Subsequent work confirmed the classical results.

However, in natural water supersaturation is virtually always a result of plant photosynthesis. This process converts carbon dioxide into oxygen. As it can only take place in sunlight, there is a daily noon time maximum of DO in heavily vegetated waters, such as those of estuaries, followed by an evening minimum.

Departures from saturation are expressed as per cent saturation:

$$\% \text{ saturation} = 100 \times DO/(DO)_s,$$

where DO is the observed value and $(DO)_s$ is the saturation value. Alternatively, oxygen consumption or apparent oxygen utilisation (AOU) is defined as

$$AOU = (DO)_s - DO.$$

Extremely low values of dissolved oxygen, below 4 ppm, are a cause for environmental concern. They arise where sewage or other wastes with high biochemical oxygen demand (BOD) pollute estuarine waters and induce high bacterial action. The bacteria multiply rapidly to reach enormous abundance, thereby depleting the water of oxygen faster than it can be replaced by either plants or the atmosphere. A quantitative measure, referred to as BOD-5, is obtained by the controlled incubation of the water sample at $20°C$ for 5 days after a suitable bacterial "seed" begins the decomposition process. Generally BOD-5 values greater than 5×10^{-6} (5 ppm) indicate polluted water because there are few waters that can sustain a DO drop of this magnitude and still support aquatic life. Low BOD values are less of a problem for sewage discharged directly into the sea for the majority of fresh water bacteria soon perish in salt water.

Dissolved nitrogen in water seems to be unaltered by biological changes, and is considered to be a conservative constituent of the water. Nevertheless, under unusual conditions fish appear to suffer from nitrogen-induced disease and juvenile chinook salmon are killed at 127% saturation. This occurs where spillway water, such as that of a large dam or power station, plunges into a deep pool.

The concentration of dissolved oxygen and dissolved nitrogen at saturation obeys Henry's Law. This states that the dissolved concentration of a gas is directly proportional to the partial pressure of the gas (which is in turn proportional to the atmospheric pressure), provided the temperature and salinity remain constant. The constant of proportionality in Henry's Law is called the saturation coefficient and, for example, oxygen in fresh water at $0°C$ has a saturation coefficient of 6.93×10^{-10} Pa^{-1}. According to Henry's Law this means that at standard atmospheric pressure (101.3 kPa) the saturated DO value will be

$$\underset{A}{[6.93 \times 10^{-10}]} \times \underset{B}{[0.21]} \times \underset{C}{[1.01 \times 10^{5}]}$$

where

A   = saturation coefficient,
B   = proportion of oxygen in the atmosphere,
C   = atmospheric pressure,
B X C = partial pressure of oxygen,

when the calculations are done to three decimal places the result, 14.7×10^{-6}, agrees with the curves of Fig. 5.5.

Carbon dioxide dissolved in seawater does not follow Henry's Law. It has a very complicated chemistry that favours the formation of bicarbonates. The standard measure of gaseous carbon in natural water is the pH, which is a direct measure of the acidity or alkalinity of a liquid. Pure water has a pH of 7. Values of pH below 7 denote acids, the lower the value the stronger the acid, whereas pH values above 7 correspond to alkaline solutions.

The pH of seawater at the surface is very stable, usually ranging between 8.1 and 8.3 with a direct relation between salinity and pH. From Fig. 5.6 we see that

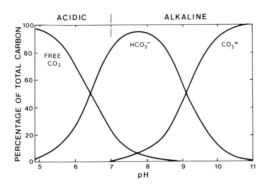

FIG. 5.6. *Percentage of dissolved carbon dioxide (CO_2), bicarbonate (HCO_3^-) and carbonate $(CO_3^=)$ as a function of pH.*

this implies a dominance of bicarbonate in seawater. In shallow waters and rock pools the range is greater; plants utilise carbon dioxide and raise the pH, while the respiration of organisms acts in the opposite direction. The pH of an estuary depends on the nature of the river water flowing into it, which in turn depends on the terrain over which the river has flowed before meeting the sea, on biological activity in the river and on the strength of the currents (which effectively mix air into the water and gases within the water).

Streams transporting large quantities of humic material in colloidal suspension are slightly acid. Upon meeting seawater the colloidal particles are coagulated (a process known as flocculation) and the pH shifts towards the alkaline. East Bay, Texas, receives considerable runoff from organically rich salt marshes, and during summer the pH ranges from 6.9 in the bay to 7.8 near the mouth where it discharges into the Gulf of Mexico. Gulf waters during the same period gave a pH value of 8.0. Highly acid streams occur primarily on low marshy or swampy terrain, on poorly drained sandy "flatwoods" or under special conditions – such as the discharge of sulphurous hot springs. These streams are usually stained brownish and support a relatively meagre biota.

The oceanic uptake of carbon dioxide is important for global environmental reasons. Since 1958 there has been a well-documented increase in atmospheric carbon dioxide from 3.15×10^{-4} to 3.33×10^{-4}. This steady increase is attributed, firstly to the burning of coal and other fossil fuels to generate the developed world's energy requirements; and secondly to the destruction of vast tracts of tropical forests, so that there are less trees available to use up the carbon dioxide and photosynthesise it to oxygen.

There is great concern that continued increases in atmospheric carbon dioxide levels will raise the world's temperature. If this should indeed happen and the icecaps melt, then the resulting rise in sea level would destroy all the coastal cities of the world. Whether this will, or will not, occur depends in part on the ability of the oceans to absorb excess atmospheric CO_2. If the oceans were well-mixed reservoirs and were able to maintain equilibrium with the atmosphere, much of the increased atmospheric CO_2 would be absorbed. Present indications are that the oceans as a whole respond only slowly to changes in atmospheric carbon dioxide, mainly because of slow rates of mixing within the sea.

5.6 Nutrients

Life depends on the availability of carbon, oxygen, nitrogen and phosphorus, as well as water. Nitrogen is utilised in amino acids, which make up proteins, whereas phosphorus is used in compounds such as ATP (adenosine triphosphate) that are important for energy transfer within organisms. In the oceans these constituent elements are available in solution as dissolved bicarbonate, phosphate and nitrate.

All life in the oceans depends on photosynthesis. This fixes carbon from the atmosphere and stores it as plant tissue. It requires light and carbon dioxide as well as an adequate supply of water and nutrients. The relative proportions of nutrients used in photosynthesis are determined from their plant tissue concentrations. Studies of these have led to photosynthesis being characterised by a chemical equation of the form

$$106\ CO_2\quad +\quad 90\ H_2O\quad +\quad 16\ NO_3\quad +\quad 1\ PO_4\quad +\quad Energy$$
$$\text{(carbon dioxide)}\quad\text{(water)}\qquad\text{(nitrate)}\qquad\text{(phosphate)}\qquad\text{(light)}$$
$$\longrightarrow 154\ O_2 + \text{protoplasm.}$$

The standard rule of thumb is that 5.40×10^9 J of incoming light energy produces 3.258 kg of protoplasm in the proportions of 106 C, 180 H, 46 O, 16 N, 1 P. When this protoplasm is burnt it releases 5.4×10^7 J of heat energy.

Carbon, nitrogen and phosphorus are extracted from solution in the top hundred metres of the ocean where enough light penetrates for photosynthesis. This is called the euphotic zone. Coastal waters, except those near river mouths or those comprising upwelling areas, tend to be depleted in dissolved nutrient elements because they are "locked up" in plant matter. Upwelling regions rework nutrients that drop to the bottom as organic detritus, whereas rivers carry nutrients from dissolved humus.

In recent decades the nutrient load of rivers has increased greatly. Increased urbanisation has led to increased nutrient loads through increased sewage. Rural rivers have not been spared. The "green revolution" has led to widespread over-application of fertilisers with the excess running directly into waterways after a rainstorm. This produces either high nitrogen loads if urea-based fertilisers are responsible, or high phosphorus loads from super-phosphate fertilisers. We shall see in Chapter 10 that these large nutrient loads lead to problems of eutrophication in estuaries.

The ratio between carbon, nitrogen and phosphorus in planktonic diatoms varies considerably, though a mean value of C:N:P = 106:16:1 is representative. The ratio of nitrogen to phosphorus in naturally growing aquatic plants is similar to the ratio of these elements in available form in the water in which they grow. In addition, the N:P ratio of plants is very similar to that of zooplankton animals. This indicates that the plants and animals evolved so as to make maximum use of the scarcer nitrogen and phosphorus nutrients.

5.7 Rivers

We have already noted the remarkable constancy in the ionic composition of seawater in regions free from river discharge. However, as shown in Table 5.2, the dominant ions in river water are bicarbonates and the relative proportions vary greatly between localities depending on the properties of the soil washing into the particular river. The practical salinity definition, exemplified in Fig. 5.2,

TABLE 5.2. *Ionic Concentrations (mg l^{-1}) of World River Waters*

River	Cl	Na	SO$_4$	Mg	Ca	K	HCO$_3$
World	8	6	11	4	15	2	58
N. America	8	9	20	5	21	2	68
S. America	5	4	5	2	7	0	31
Europe	7	5	24	6	31	2	95
Asia	9	5	9	6	18	2	79
Africa	12	11	13	4	13	0	43
Australia	10	3	2	3	4	2	32
Seawater ($g\,l^{-1}$)	19	11	2.5	1	0.5	0.5	0

is invalid in coastal areas subject to strong river influences and in those regions it is more sensible to retain measurements of conductivity in electrical conductivity units. For example, the World Health Organisation standard for drinking water sets 0.083 S m^{-1} as the highest desirable salinity.

Rivers generally meet the sea in an estuary (Chapter 10) and the circulation in estuaries can be quite complicated. The circulation will depend on the density and quantity of the river water, both of which will vary seasonally. The circulation will, in turn, determine the nutrient distribution. It is because of the nutrient-rich run off from the land that bays, estuaries and inshore coastal waters are far richer in marine life than mid-ocean waters.

One concern, mentioned in the previous section, is that of excess nutrients being deposited in estuaries. These lead to scum-like algal blooms. A completely different concern arises in regions that have dammed their rivers to such an extent that the coastal nutrient supply is depleted. Small quantities of sewage discharged into such coastal waters may lead to bioenhancement. This is enhancement of the biological quality of receiving waters and is measured in terms of numbers of organisms and numbers of species of plankton and fish. Of course, bioenhancement is critically dependent on the quantity and nature of the effluent discharged. If it is too toxic, or if there is too much, it will degrade the environment.

Rivers with a particularly large discharge will produce a freshwater plume that penetrates into the coastal waters. A river such as the Amazon carries 0.2×10^6 m^3 s^{-1} of fresh water into the ocean. This produces a substantial current in its own right and the coastal circulation at the mouth of the Amazon is controlled by the river flow. Observations of the Amazon plume, and the plume of the Burdekin river flowing into the Great Barrier Reef Lagoon, indicate that they do not spread uniformly but pinch off to form isolated lenses of relatively fresh water. The seasonal circulation in the Adriatic Sea is strongly influenced by outflow from the Po River and drainage from Italy and Yugoslavia.

5.8 Water Quality

Wastewater disposal must not impair the beneficial uses of coastal waters, even when they are under heavy industrial and urban pressure. To ensure that this is indeed the case, a coastal zone manager must determine what the beneficial uses are. To do this he will need to weigh political, economic, social and scientific factors, but once it has been done he can define a set of water quality criteria for the constituents of a given discharge. Water quality criteria become water quality standards, when they are given some formal and enforceable standing.

There are two possible approaches. One is to define effluent standards, thereby insisting that only suitably treated wastewater is disposed. The other approach is to define receiving-water standards. This generally allows a local mixing zone within which various determinands — such as clarity, temperature, biochemical oxygen demand, etc. — could dilute to concentrations consistent with the criteria.

Obviously the above process is greatly dependent on local conditions and it is impossible to give a single universally applicable set of parameters defining good water quality. Water quality standards for an industrial area will differ from those of a heavily urbanised area. Furthermore, as additional knowledge is gained about the response of receiving waters to specific inputs of determinands, new criteria can be adopted and the legally enforceable standards modified accordingly.

The open circles in the matrix of Table 5.3 indicate the inter-relationships between water quality criteria and beneficial uses for Cockburn Sound, the major coastal industrial area for Perth, the capital of Western Australia. As the state government specifically wished to keep this industrial area suitable for fishing, swimming and recreational boating, as well as for commercial shipping, it commissioned an intensive three-year study which advocated the water quality

TABLE 5.3. *Relationships between Water Quality Determinands and Beneficial Uses*

Water quality determinand	Aesthetic enjoyment	Seafood processing	Industrial cooling water	Shipping	Water contact recreation	Fish passage	Crustacea, fish & molluscs for food	Aquatic ecosystem maintenance
Grease, oil, floatables	X	O	O	O	O	O	O	O
Suspended & settleable solids	X				O			X
Colour, odour & turbidity	O				X	O		O
Fine solids		O	O			O	X	O
Light penetration	O				X			
Barriers*						X	X	O
Temperature		O	O			O	X	O
pH		O	O	O	O	O	X	X
Hydrocarbons		O				O	X	O
Salinity		O				O	O	X
Dissolved oxygen		O				O	X	O
Arsenic and heavy metals		O				O	X	O
Pesticides, PCBs		O				O	O	O
Phenolic compounds		O				O	X	O
Surfactants	O	X	O	O	O	X	X	O
Cyanide		O				O	X	O
Fluoride		O				O	X	O
Total chlorine residual		O				O	X	O
Hydrogen sulphide		O				O	X	O
Ammonia		O				O	X	O
Nutrients (N & P)	X		O	O		O	O	X
Faecal coliforms		O			O		X	
Radionuclides		O		O	O		X	

O Indicates beneficial uses upon which water quality parameter has an impact.
X Indicates the use which controls the nature of the water quality criteria given in Table 5.4.
* Barriers to flushing and fish passage.

criteria of Table 5.4 for the most sensitive beneficial uses. In general, however, it is preferable to express water quality criteria in a probabilistic form, i.e. a mean or a median and a second value which is to be met a high percentage of the time. The use of probabilistic criteria is a more rational approach than to require waste management systems to be designed to meet the "once-in-a-lifetime" event.

It is worth specifically commenting upon heavy metals. Because of the ability of shellfish and molluscs to process seawater and to concentrate heavy metals in their tissue, it is vital that recreational or commercial oyster beds be separated from chemical wastewater. Though some trace elements are necessary in small

TABLE 5.4. *Water Quality Criteria for Cockburn Sound*

Determinand	Criteria
Grease, oil, floatables	No visible evidences of wastewater origin
Suspended & settleable solids	No visible evidences of wastewater origin, no deposition
Colour, odour, turbidity	No noticeable or objectionable change in natural conditions
Fine solids	Less than 80 mg l^{-1}
Light penetration	Secchi disc visible for 2-m depth
Barriers	No construction or chemical barriers
Temperature	No change greater than $\pm 1°C$ from normal
pH	Within 6.5 – 8.5 range; no change greater than 0.2 units
Hydrocarbons	Soluble aromatics 1 μg l^{-1}, fuel oil 3 μg l^{-1}, kero ⟩ 5 μg l^{-1}, crude oil 10 μg l^{-1}
Salinity	No long term change greater than $\pm 2\%$ of normal
Dissolved oxygen	No reduction below 6 mg l^{-1} or decrease greater than 10% of normal
Arsenic and heavy metals	Values in seawater depend upon individual metals Concentrations in seafood not to exceed values given below
Pesticides	Values depend upon individual pesticide
Polychlorinated biphenyls	Maximum concentration 0.001 μg l^{-1}
Phenolic compounds	Median less than 300 μg l^{-1}
Surfactants	Maximum concentration less than 1% of 96 hr LC_{50} *
Cyanide	Median less than 5 μg l^{-1}
Fluoride	Median less than 2 mg l^{-1}
Hydrogen sulphide (undissociated)	Maximum less than 2 μg l^{-1}
Ammonia (expressed as N)	Median 0.6 mg l^{-1}
Nutrients (N & P)	Reduce total nitrogen inputs to 1000 kg d^{-1}
Faecal coliforms	Median less than 15 org/100 ml for mussel areas; 150 org/100 ml for recreation uses
Radionuclides	Maximum 10 pCi l^{-1}
Heavy metals in seafood	Microgram of the element per g of wet body weight
Cadmium	5.5
Zinc	40.0
Copper	30.0
Lead	2.0
Nickel	5.5
Chromium	5.5
Cobalt	5.5
Mercury	0.5
Arsenic	1.5 (based on As_2O_3)

* LC_{50} is the concentration found lethal to 50% of test organisms as a result of 96-hr exposure.

amounts for human health and wellbeing, others, such as lead, mercury or cadmium, are dangerous in themselves. Cadmium does not occur naturally and the only foods that contain more than negligible amounts of cadmium are shellfish collected from waters near to zinc smelters. Another source of wastewaters rich in both heavy metals and radioactivity are tailings from uranium mining. Substantial amounts of this form of contaminated water were released to the sea, generally via rivers, in the 1950s, but modern control strategies are based upon total containment of the tailings.

Heavy metal poisoning produces what is called Minimata disease. It acquired this name from the severe poisoning that afflicted fishermen and their families round Minimata Bay in Japan when it was polluted by effluent from a factory. Inorganic mercury in the bay waters was converted into methylmercury by micro-organisms in the water and it then moved up the food chain. The mercury became more concentrated as it passed through plant-eating small fish to carnivorous large fish, like tuna, sword fish and pike.

Further Reading

The current definitions of oceanographic quantities are given in a report by a working group of IAPSO (International Association of Physical Sciences of the Ocean) known as the *Sun Report*, and issued in December 1979. It is IAPSO Publication Scientifique 31 and is available from IUGG Publications Office, 39 ter, rue Gay-Lussac, 75005 Paris, France.

Much of the material on the physical aspects of this chapter is dealt with in greater detail by

O. I. MAMAYEV: *Temperature–Salinity Analysis of World Oceans,* Elsevier, Amsterdam, 1975.

and more specialised recent work on salinity will be found in

E. R. LEWIS and R. G. PERKIN: Salinity: its definition and calculation, *J. Geophys. Res.* 83, 466–478, 1978.

The chemical aspects of oceanography are detailed in the two-volume set

J. P. RILEY and G. SKIRROW (eds): *Chemical Oceanography*, Academic Press, London, 1965.

A classic work on the interaction between micro-nutrient elements and phytoplankton is

H. W. HARVEY: *The Chemistry and Fertility of Sea Waters*, Cambridge University Press, 1960.

Considerations about water quality will be found in

UNITED STATES ENVIRONMENTAL PROTECTION AGENCY: *Water Quality Criteria, 1972* (EPA.R. 73.033, available from the US Govt. Printing Office).

B. T. HART: *A Compilation of Australian Water Quality Criteria*, AWRC Technical Paper no. 7 Aust. Govt. Publishing Service, Canberra, 1974,

whilst heavy metals are exhaustively documented by

U. FOERSTNER & G. T. W. WITTMAN: *Metal Pollution in the Aquatic Environment*, Springer-Verlag, Berlin, 1979.

CHAPTER 6

Water Circulation

6.1 Introduction

This chapter aims to provide an introduction to the dominant forces that move water from place to place. The scientific study of these forces is called hydrodynamics. Our specific interest is in those forces that provide mean flows, or currents, that are reasonably steady for at least a month. These surface currents are important to maritime transport, and mariners need to be aware of their locations, their fluctuations and the reasons for them.

These quasi-steady currents can be categorised as follows:

(a) Currents generated by the large-scale, world-wide wind system which are then modified by the effects of the Earth's rotation. These currents exist as a weak equatorward flow on the eastern side of an ocean (e.g. the California current, the West Australian current) and a strong poleward flow on the western side of the ocean (the Gulf Stream, the Agulhas current, the East Australian current). They are connected by currents in the tropics and the poles.

Though these currents are well defined on the edges of ocean basins, they are strongest on the seaward side of the shelf break. Figure 3.8 demonstrates this in the case of the Agulhas current. Figure 6.1 maps these major surface currents, whilst Table 6.1 lists typical transports within them.

(b) Currents for which the continental shelf acts as a boundary layer. The concept of a coastal boundary layer will be expounded in Chapter 7. An example of this type of flow occurs on the northeastern seaboard of America, with steady southwestward flows of about 10 cm s^{-1}. This type of circulation is driven by the large-scale currents shown in Fig. 6.1, but modified by the presence of the coastline and a shallow bottom in such a way that the mean circulation is in the opposite direction to the Gulf Stream.

(c) Currents induced by the run off of large river systems. These have been discussed in Chapter 5.7.

(d) Coastal circulation is also affected by the intermittent encroachment of deep sea phenomena onto the shelf. An example of this is discussed in Chapter 8.6.

The general characteristics of major currents are amenable to scientific study. This chapter, and the next two, lay the basis for this study by explaining the

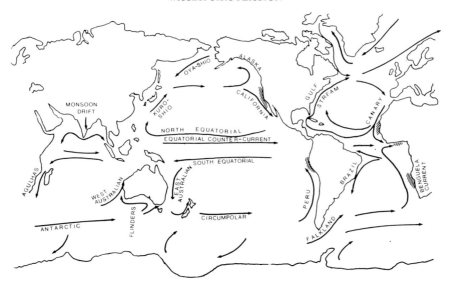

FIG. 6.1. *Major surface currents of the world oceans. The monsoon drift of the North Equatorial Current near India flows westward from November to March. Currents on the western boundaries of ocean basins are stronger than those on the eastern boundary. Currents on the eastern boundaries are weaker and upwelling may occur. Upwelling regions are shaded.*

TABLE 6.1. *Flows in Major Oceanic Currents*

Current	Flow* ($m^3 \ s^{-1}$)
Gulf Stream	100×10^6
Agulhas	40×10^6
Kuroshio	65×10^6
California	12×10^6
West Australian	10×10^6
East Australian	20×10^6
Antarctic Circumpolar	200×10^6
Peru	18×10^6
Benguela	15×10^6
Equatorial undercurrent	40×10^6
Brazil	10×10^6
Equatorial countercurrent	25×10^6
Pacific North Equatorial	30×10^6
Pacific South Equatorial	10×10^6
Flinders	15×10^6

*Both hydrologists and oceanographers often use non-standard terms when referring to flows. Hydrologists call 1 $m^3 \ s^{-1}$ a cumec and oceanographers call $10^6 \ m^3 \ s^{-1}$ a Sverdrup.

nature of the four dominant physical mechanisms responsible for circulation and mixing. These are fluid pressure forces (Ch. 6.2), the effects of the Earth's rotation (Ch. 6.3), diffusion (Ch. 6.4) and viscosity (Ch. 6.5). The next two chapters then apply these physical ideas to coastal waters.

6.2 Pressure Forces

In order to explain the motions of seawater we need to be aware of the forces that act on a drop of water and their relative importance. Once we have this understanding, then the mathematical description of these forces can be incorporated into Newton's second law of motion — that the acceleration of a drop of water is proportional to the sum of the forces acting on the drop. Within a fluid this is written mathematically as

$$F = \rho a$$

FORCE PER UNIT VOLUME = DENSITY × ACCELERATION

where the acceleration represents a velocity increase with time, so that over a small time interval, which we represent by dt,

$$a = \text{change in velocity/time taken}$$

$$= \frac{dU}{dt}.$$

Water is usually in equilibrium with gravity. This is called hydrostatic equilibrium and leads to the hydrostatic equation that relates pressure and depth. Departures from this hydrostatic equilibrium do occur, but are very small. Thus even though gravity is the single most dominant force acting on the oceans, we will not need to explicitly consider it. Gravity is not a direct driving force for coastal circulation — though it plays an important indirect role.

Water will flow under the influence of pressure differences if there is a region of high pressure at one location, and a region of low pressure at another location. This pressure difference can occur either as a result of density differences between the waters of the two regions, or possibly as the result of height differences due to water being piled up at one location.

To write this mathematically we should recall (Ch. 5.1) that the pressure p at a depth z is given by

$$p = \rho g z$$

and that the pressure represents the force acting per unit area of surface. At the sea bottom, at a depth H, the pressure will be $\rho g H$ and it produces a force that acts equally in all directions.

(i) Density difference (Fig. 6.2a)

The excess pressure due to two water masses, one of density ρ_1 and the other of density ρ_2 separated by a distance L is given by the difference of the two pressures, and this excess pressure is equal to the force per unit area acting on a fluid element

$$\text{Force per unit area} = (\rho_2 - \rho_1)gH,$$

so that the

$$\text{Force per unit volume} = (\rho_2 - \rho_1)\frac{gH}{L}.$$

(a)

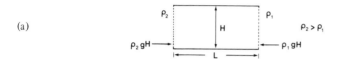

(b)

(c)

(d)

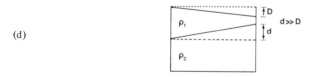

FIG. 6.2. *Pressure gradient forces arise from: (a) density differences between water masses; (b) height differences; and (c) internal density stratification. Case (c) is idealised. In practice the surface slopes gently opposite to the thermocline slope, as in (d).*

(ii) *Height difference (Fig. 6.2b)*

The excess pressure between water masses of equal density, but one having a depth H and the other having a slightly greater depth $H + D$, is the difference between them, namely $\rho g D$, so that in this situation

$$\text{Force per unit volume} = \rho \frac{gD}{L},$$

where $\rho g D/L$ is the pressure gradient along the bottom. The term D/L is the gradient of the sea surface (i.e. the slope of the sea surface). We may then rewrite the equation as

$$\text{Acceleration} = g \times \text{gradient of sea surface.}$$

(iii) *Baroclinic effects (Fig. 6.2c)*

There is often a height difference within a layer of water comprising two different water masses, such as occurs at the thermocline. To simplify this discussion, let us imagine the situation is as shown in Fig. 6.2c – a flat surface, called the rigid lid, with a pycnocline (a line of sharp density variation) displaced a distance d. In this situation all the pressure gradient forces occur in the bottom layer, and at the very bottom it may be shown, by adding the pressure together, that the pressure excess is $g(\rho_2 - \rho_1) d$, where d is the elevation of the boundary between the light and heavy fluids.

Since all the pressure gradients occur in the bottom layer, we find that the pressure gradient force per unit volume is

$$\rho_2 a = g(\rho_2 - \rho_1) \frac{d}{L}.$$

Thus

$$a = \frac{[g(\rho_2 - \rho_1)]}{\rho_2} \frac{d}{L}$$

$$= g' \frac{d}{L}.$$

The term $g' = g(\rho_2 - \rho_1)/\rho_2$ is called the modified gravity, or the reduced gravity, and plays an important role in the dynamics of internal waves. Alternatively, some prefer to think in terms of the equivalent depth, H_e, which was defined in Chapter 3.7.

In fact, Fig. 6.2c is unrealistic because baroclinic motions actually do move the sea surface. The sea surface and the pycnocline slope in opposite directions. If the pycnocline is elevated by a distance d on the right, then the sea surface is depressed by a small distance

$$D = d \, (\rho_2 - \rho_1)/\rho_2.$$

The fact that large pycnocline or thermocline displacements are associated with small surface changes is not just an interesting curiosity. It profoundly affects nearshore flow. To see this, consider it from another viewpoint. If a wind blows over the surface of a layered body of water near a coastline, then this wind will produce a small change in the sea surface. This, as will be shown in Fig. 8.10, can produce enormous pycnocline fluctuations which alter the surface flow.

Western Current Separation

At some location along its path a western boundary current (i.e. one on the western side of an ocean basin, such as the Gulf Stream or the East Australian current) will leave the coastline and become an interior oceanic current. In the case of the Gulf Stream this separation occurs at Cape Hatteras, with the current south of it often being referred to as the Florida current. Separation of the East Australian current occurs just north of Newcastle. The reason for this separation is that oceanic motions are baroclinic. Western boundary currents comprise a warm layer overlying a colder one. At the equator, tropical easterly (i.e. westward) winds "pile up" warm surface water at a western coastline such as the Caribbean. This, in turn, produces a pressure gradient along the western boundary from the equator poleward and generates a strong current stream.

But we know from the above discussion on baroclinic effects that the equatorial pile-up will produce a slope in the opposite direction in the lower, colder water layer (Fig. 6.3). Thus the warm surface water does not lie uniformly over

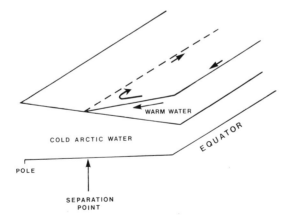

FIG. 6.3. *Schematic illustration (not to scale) of a westward boundary current separating from the coast, so that the current, which is restricted to the upper layer of water, moves into the middle of the ocean.*

the colder layer, but forms a wedge with a distinct separation point. The current, which is restricted to the upper layer of water, has no option but to move into the ocean interior.

6.3 The Coriolis Force

Oceanographers and meteorologists must take account of the effects of the Earth's rotation when studying the dynamics of large wind or ocean current systems. These effects are called Coriolis effects, after Gaspard Coriolis (1792–1843), a French mathematician who first realised their importance.

The Coriolis effect is that of a force which acts only on moving particles. For example, if you make a straight scratch from the centre of a gramophone record to the needle whilst the record is rotating on the turntable, then you will find a curved line on the gramophone record when you stop the turntable and examine it (Fig. 6.4). Any observer in the reference frame of the surface of the gramophone record would have reasoned like this:

We know that Newton's first law tells us that bodies move in a straight line unless some external force acts upon them. The body making the scratch did not move in a straight line so that apparently some external force, which we shall call the Coriolis force, must have been acting on the body that made the scratch.

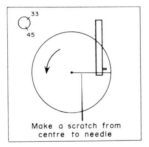
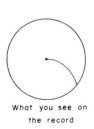

Make a scratch from
centre to needle

What you see on
the record

FIG. 6.4. *The Coriolis force at work. The rotation of the turntable simulates the Earth's rotation direction when viewed from above the North Pole.*

Notice that an observer rotating on the gramophone record is rotating about his vertical axis, but the Coriolis deflections are produced in the horizontal plane. However, the Earth is not a flat disc but a sphere. Consider the rate of rotation of a horizontal rod placed along a meridian, so that its ends are at slightly different latitudes. If we consider the difference in movement of the two ends in a small time, we can show that the rod takes $(24/\sin \phi)$ hours to rotate about the vertical, where ϕ is the latitude of the midpoint of the rod. In fact a horizontal rod pointing in any direction will rotate at the same rate.

The direction of rotation is clockwise (looking down) in the Southern Hemisphere. It is anti-clockwise (looking down) in the Northern Hemisphere. At the equator itself (latitude $\phi = 0°$) there is no rotation about the vertical, which means that it takes an infinitely long time for a rod to rotate about the vertical there.

The magnitude of the acceleration that deflects water moving on the Earth's surface is proportional to the speed of the current, and inversely proportional to the time of rotation about the local vertical. Dimensionally, a velocity $[LT^{-1}]$ divided by a time $[T]$ produces an acceleration $[LT^{-2}]$ so that our ideas are indeed dimensionally consistent. In the Northern Hemisphere a moving particle deflects to the right of its direction of motion. In the Southern Hemisphere a moving particle deflects to the left of its direction of motion.

Inertial Motions

Figure 6.5 depicts a series of observations made in the Baltic following the passage of a line squall. It shows a succession of rotary oscillations superimposed on a steady northward drift of water. There were nine full turns each completed in a period

$$T_i = 12/\sin \phi \text{ hours,}$$

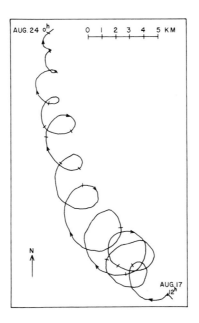

FIG. 6.5. *Inertial oscillations depicted by a progressive vector diagram of current observations in the Baltic.*

where T_i is called the inertial period at a latitude ϕ. At the latitude of these observations, the inertial period was 14 hr and 8 min.

They are called inertial oscillations because inertia keeps the water mass moving after the initial impulse (e.g. the line squall) has passed — provided friction is small. They are very common in ocean current observations in both deep and shallow waters. Inertial oscillations are one of the many oceanographic manifestations of the Earth's rotation.

I used to find it puzzling that the inertial period at the poles is 12 hr, yet we know that the Earth rotates every 24 hr. To understand this I used a geometric construction to map out the trajectory of a water particle undergoing inertial oscillation when viewed from a non-rotating reference frame. (Say, a spaceship directly above the pole.) Assume that a flatlander on a disc rotating once every 24 hr moves a water particle towards the pole with a velocity equal to his rotational velocity. The water then moves clockwise around the centre of the inertial circle which is due east of the flatlander's location. But from the spaceship we see that the inertial circle is itself rotating in an anticlockwise circle about the pole.

The resulting trajectory of the water particle, from our vantage point, is an ellipse as shown in Fig. 6.6. Each dot represents a 40-min interval, and the numbers beside every third dot denote elapsed hours. From our viewpoint it is evident that only half of the elliptical motion has been completed. However, as far as the flatlander in the rotating frame of reference is concerned, the motion repeats after 12 hr when the water particle returns to his location with the same poleward and eastward motion.

Inertial oscillations can be mathematically described as a balance between the inertial forces (i.e. the force producing an acceleration) and the Coriolis force.

This may be written

$$\text{acceleration} = \frac{dU}{dt} = \frac{2\pi U}{T_i},$$

but if the motion is circular, then the Coriolis force must provide the centripetal force that is necessary

$$\frac{U^2}{r_i} = \frac{2\pi U}{T_i}$$

to give the radius of inertial oscillations as

$$r_i = \frac{UT_i}{2\pi}.$$

Because the inertial period appears so often in conjunction with the 2π, the quantity

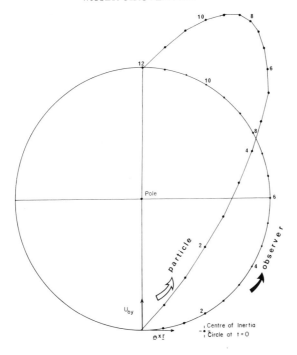

FIG. 6.6. *An inertial oscillation at the North Pole is a circular motion with a 12-hr period for a rotating observer, but is an elliptical motion of 24-hr periodicity when viewed from outside the rotating system, as in this diagram. The centre of the inertia circle is always on the tangent to the observer's path and an equal distance to his right as he faces the pole. Radii of the inertia circle can be constructed by marking the centre of the inertia circle and joining it to the corresponding point of the particle's trajectory.*

$$f = \frac{2\pi}{T_i}$$

is known as the Coriolis parameter.

Geostrophic Motions

A pressure gradient force will arise between water masses of different densities (Chapter 6.2). Water will try to equalise the pressure by moving from a region of higher pressure into a region of lower pressure. However, a parcel of water moving from a region of higher pressure will suffer a deflection due to the influence of the Coriolis force, so that the end result is that the large-scale water motion moves parallel to the pressure gradient, rather than perpendicular to it. Large-scale water motions follow isobaric surfaces, slowly swirling around regions of high pressure and regions of low pressure. This also occurs in the atmosphere where the prevailing wind is parallel to the isobars.

The pressure gradient force produces an acceleration gD/L, where D/L is the sea surface slope. This slope is measured by reference to a plane, known as the geoid, which is perpendicular to the gravitational force, as measured by a plumb line. If we set this pressure gradient force equal to the acceleration produced by the Coriolis force we obtain an equation for geostrophic equilibrium

$$gD/L = 2\pi U/T_i = fU,$$

which enables us to find the geostrophic current speed as

$$U = gDT_i/2\pi L = gD/fL.$$

The speed of the geostrophic motion, U, will depend on the inertial period T_i (or alternatively, the Coriolis parameter f) and the sea surface slope.

Newspapers reproduce the daily weather map which shows regions of high and low atmospheric pressure and plots the isobars connecting points of equal atmospheric pressure. One aspect of a temperate latitude weather map is that the prevailing wind blows parallel to the isobars, with its direction determined by the Coriolis deflection. In the Northern Hemisphere fluids move clockwise around a high-pressure system and anticlockwise around a low-pressure region. In the Southern Hemisphere they move anti-clockwise around a high-pressure system and clockwise around a low-pressure region.

Oceanographers also have maps of pressure surfaces, but they call them geopotential topographies. The method by which these are computed is somewhat complex, but they represent the depth of water between two pressure surfaces. If the water is light, then its value will be large. For example, Fig. 6.7 depicts the geopotential topography between the surface and 13 MPa (1300 decibars). There is a region of heavy water at 39°S, 114°E and two regions of light water at 36°S, 112°E and 39°S, 116°E.

The geopotential topographies of Fig. 6.7 arose from a multi-disciplinary study of the western rock lobster larvae, *Panulirus longipes cygnus*. Environmental cruises were made in the waters near the southern part of Western Australia. Hydrology stations were occupied and sea surface characteristics continuously recorded. Current meters were moored at selected sites and, in addition, satellite-tracked free drifting buoys were released.

The buoy trajectory is in general agreement with the shape of the geopotential topography, but the instantaneous currents seem much more variable. This indicates one major problem of oceanic current measurements; they are extremely variable. They fluctuate in speed and direction and the only way to determine the mean and the variation with time is to make frequent measurements for a sufficient period of time (probably several months at least). The geostrophic

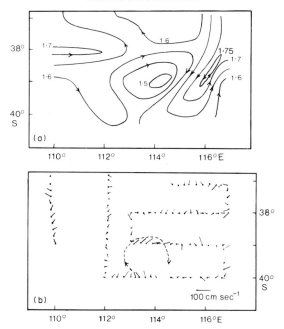

FIG. 6.7. *(a) The geopotential topography (in units of dynamic metre = 10 m² s⁻²) of the sea surface relative to the 1300 decibar (13 MPa) reference surface for an area near the south coast of Western Australia. (b) Simultaneous current measurements by Eulerian (bars) and Lagrangian (dashed lines) techniques confirm that the flows are basically parallel to the geopotential contours. The length of a bar denotes the speed and its orientation with respect to the dot gives its direction.*

method of current computations utilising geopotential topographies effectively averages over a large area and hence is representative of the average current. The geostrophic method requires information on the distribution of density in the ocean and it is much easier to obtain this information than it is to measure currents directly. Unfortunately, geopotential topographies are of limited value over the continental shelf because the sloping bottom hinders their interpretation.

6.4 Diffusion

All fluids are composed of molecules which are in continual random motion known as Brownian motion. Molecules collide during the course of this motion and these collisions equalise the fluid properties. This means that if there is a large concentration of substance at one location, and less of it elsewhere, the random intermingling of colliding molecules will equalise the concentration. Even though the fluid may be motionless, the molecules within it are moving about (Fig. 6.8).

Because molecules and their motion account for the amount, momentum and temperature of a fluid, all these three quantities diffuse. It is generally assumed that the flux (the quantity passing through a cross-sectional area in a unit time) of a substance, such as salt, is proportional to the gradient of the concentration of the substance. The constant of proportionality is called the diffusion coefficient or the diffusivity.

Figure 6.8 illustrates a simple laboratory experiment to determine the molecular diffusivity of salt in water. A column of water was made with a saline solution (35 g salt per kg of water) under fresh water. Two floats were constructed and calibrated so as to mark the 4×10^{-3} ($4^o/oo$) and 27×10^{-3} ($27^o/oo$) isohalines respectively. As the salt diffused from the bottom layer into the top layer the floats separated. The diffusivity is proportional to the rate at which the square of the separation distance increased. By measuring the separation of the two floats over a 3-week period (Fig. 6.9) the diffusivity was found to be 1.5×10^{-8} kg m^{-1} s^{-1}. It is very common to divide this quantity by the fluid density. The result is the kinematic diffusivity and has units of m^2 s^{-1}. In general, both quantities are loosely referred to as the diffusivity (or the diffusion coefficient) and one has to examine the units to pinpoint the intended one. The kinematic diffusivity of salt in tap water is 1.5×10^{-11} m^2 s^{-1}.

Look at this value carefully. It takes of the order of 10^{11} s (3000 years!) for salt to diffuse 1 m by molecular action alone. But we know this is unrealistic. Freshwater discharge from a river does not remain as freshwater for thousands of years when it reaches the sea. The reason is that actual diffusion in estuaries and seas occurs through turbulence, not through molecular motions. This effectively stirs and mixes seawater.

Much of the present-day work on turbulence is based on what is called "the similarity approach". This argues that the eddies and swirls that occur in turbulent motion transfer their properties in the same random way as molecules, and their movement is analogous to the mean free path of molecules. This approach enables us to use identical equations to represent turbulent diffusion, but with the molecular diffusion coefficients replaced by eddy diffusion coefficients (also known as Austausch coefficients). Eddy coefficients are anywhere from 10^2 to 10^{10} times as big as molecular coefficients.

Turbulent eddies in seawater have horizontal scale sizes that range from centimetres to kilometres or more. Thus a wide range of eddy coefficients can be expected. Density stratification inhibits the vertical transfer of these properties, so that vertical eddy diffusion coefficients are much smaller than horizontal eddy diffusion coefficients.

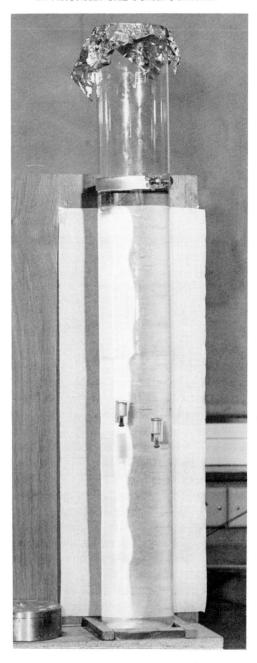

FIG. 6.8. *Laboratory diffusion experiment in progress. The floats mark the 4 × 10⁻³ and 27 × 10⁻³ isohalines respectively. Initially freshwater overlay 35 × 10⁻³ salinity salt water.*

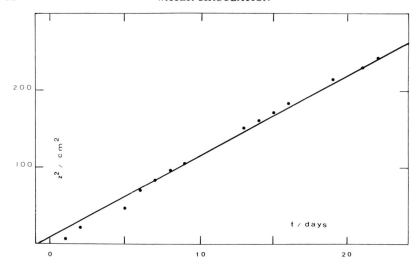

FIG. 6.9. *Results of the experiment shown in Fig. 6.8. The square of the floats' separation distance varied linearly with time. The separation times are so long that they indicate molecular diffusion is not significant in coastal and estuarine waters.*

6.5 Viscosity (Fluid Friction)

Consider a high-speed jet pumping subsurface wastewater into the sea. Each molecule will have a large momentum because the jet is moving fast. However, turbulent eddies will transfer momentum sideways. Patches of high momentum molecules will be transported out of the jet and impart their momentum to the surrounding water. Simultaneously the jet will take in − entrain − patches of low momentum molecules from the surroundings. There are two effects. The jet slows down as if it were acted upon by a fluid frictional force, but at the same time the surrounding water speeds up as if it had a force driving it. This force is known as the viscosity.

Viscosity represents the sideways transfer of momentum arising from velocity differences in the fluid. This effectively produces a "momentum pressure" though technically it is called a shear stress. Nevertheless, this shear stress is actually very like a pressure. It has the same units and dimensions as pressure, and it generates forces through stress gradients which are completely analogous to forces generated by pressure gradients.

In non-turbulent laboratory situations shear stresses arise because random molecular motions transfer momentum. In this case the coefficient of molecular dynamic viscosity, μ, is defined as the proportionality constant that links shear stress and velocity gradients

Shear stress = Flux of momentum = $\mu \times$ (gradient in velocity)

and the molecular kinematic viscosity is μ/ρ where ρ is the fluid density. Eddy viscosities, which we shall designate by η, far exceed molecular viscosities in coastal and oceanic waters and it is usual to use a vertical eddy viscosity that ranges from 0 to 10^2 kg m^{-1} s^{-1} and a horizontal eddy viscosity that ranges from 10^4 to 10^7 kg m^{-1} s^{-1}. Generally, vertical velocity gradients are much larger than horizontal velocity gradients, so that in practice vertical shear stresses are more important than horizontal shear stresses, despite the difference between the magnitudes of the coefficients of eddy viscosity.

There are many problems with the use of eddy viscosities. The vertical eddy viscosity is not a constant, but seems to depend on the local temperature gradient. There are phenomena which require negative eddy viscosities to explain them. Though there is nothing mathematically wrong with this, it indicates that our physical understanding of turbulence is still very poor.

Further Reading

The basic concepts of this chapter are also applicable to meteorology. Any text in physical oceanography (see further reading list of Chapter 1) or dynamic meteorology will give a fuller exposition of this material. Suitable meteorological texts would be

S. L. HESS: *Introduction to Theoretical Meteorology*, Holt, Rinehart & Winston, 1959.
J. R. HOLTON: *Introduction to Dynamic Meteorology* (2nd edition), Academic Press, N.Y., 1979.

The theory of ocean circulation is dealt with by

A. S. MONIN, V. M. KAMENKOVICHE, V. G. KORT: *Variability of the Oceans*, New York, John Wiley & Sons, 1977,
M. E. STERN: *Ocean Circulation Physics*, Academic, N.Y., 1975,

and its particular application to the Gulf Stream is given by

H. STOMMEL: *The Gulf Stream* (2nd edition), University of California Press, 1966.

The role of fluid forces in water circulation is dealt with by most fluid dynamic textbooks. Unfortunately these are usually directed at engineers or mathematicians and their relevance is not immediately apparent.

I. MICHELSON: *The Science of Fluids*, Van Nostrand Reinhold Co., New York, 1970,

is an intermediate level text emphasising geophysical phenomena. At a more sophisticated level one can refer to

G. K. BATCHELOR: *Introduction to Fluid Dynamics*, Cambridge University Press, 1967.

The classical reference on this is

H. LAMB: *Hydrodynamics* (6th edition), Dover, N.Y., 1945.

An elementary treatment of kinetic theory and the molecular transfer of fluid properties is given by

F. W. SEARS & G. L. SALINGER: *Thermodynamics, Kinetic Theory and Statistical Thermodynamics*, (3rd edition 1975) Addison-Wesley, Reading, Mass.,

with a more detailed account by

R. B. BIRD, W. E. STEWART & E. N. LIGHTFOOT: *Transport Phenomena*, John Wiley and Sons, New York, 1960.

In addition

V. P. STARR: *Physics of Negative Viscosity Phenomena*, McGraw-Hill, N.Y., 1969,

is highly recommended reading.

Details on the geostrophic method and geopotential topographies can be found in advanced physical oceanography texts (see Chapter 1 again). A book devoted to the topic is

L. M. FOMIN: *The Dynamic Method in Oceanography*, Elsevier, Amsterdam, 1974.

CHAPTER 7

Boundary Layers

7.1 Introduction

An oceanic boundary layer, as the name suggests, is that portion of the sea that is directly affected by a boundary. Near such boundaries, the laws of heat, momentum and mass transfer need to take account of the boundaries' presence, and the resulting fluid motions are then determined by these laws. The fluid near the water surface and the fluid near the sea floor are two examples of oceanic boundary layers.

Consider, for example, the effect of a uniform wind on the surface of a body of water. It will set the surface water moving, which means that some of the momentum carried by the molecules of the moving air will have been transferred to the surface water molecules. There is a transfer of momentum downwards and the flux of this momentum is called the wind stress. Experimental observations indicate that the wind stress, τ, increases as the square of the wind velocity and it is often estimated in terms of the wind speed, W measured by an anemometer conventionally situated 10 m above the water surface, as

$$\tau = \rho_a C_D W^2 \tag{7.1}$$

where ρ_a is the density of air (1.3 kg m^{-3}) and C_D is the drag coefficient, whose exact value depends on atmospheric conditions but is about 1.4×10^{-3}.

The topmost part of the water, in which the wind stress acts directly, is called the surface layer and within the surface layer there is a substantial velocity gradient known as a current shear. The topmost part of the water moves faster than the layers beneath it. Nevertheless, the wind effects are transmitted downwards into the interior of the fluid by a combination of turbulence, convection and rotational effects. The turbulent fluctuations in the body of moving water generate viscous stresses, or shear stresses, as described in the last section of the previous chapter. These are called Reynolds stresses (in honour of the pioneer of turbulence measurements) and in this particular case they transfer momentum downwards through the body of turbulent water.

If the ocean were initially at rest, then a constant wind stress at the surface would generate a mixed layer, whose thickness would increase linearly with time. Within this mixed layer the mean water density and temperature remain constant and there is a sharp jump in density and temperature below it. If the wind stops, the heat diffuses out of this mixed layer and it becomes stratified so that when the wind starts up again it generates a new mixed layer than propagates downward from the surface. The details of mixing and convective processes will be discussed in Chapter 8. Figure 7.1 serves as a reminder of these dominant boundary layer forcing terms.

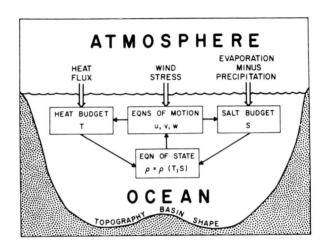

FIG. 7.1. *A schematic diagram showing the inter-actions between the various elements of oceanic circulation.*

The effects of wind stress and Reynolds stresses are akin to those of friction, and there is at present great interest in the best way to characterise, or as people usually say to parameterise, the turbulent stress effects in terms of the mean flow variables. One method of doing this is to assume that the turbulent momentum flux is carried by turbulent eddies in the same way that the random motion of molecules transfers momentum in non-turbulent laminar flow. In this case the stress is directly proportional to the vertical gradient of horizontal velocity.

$$\tau = \eta \frac{du}{dz} ,\qquad (7.2)$$

where η is the turbulent counterpart of the coefficient of viscosity. η is referred to as the vertical eddy viscosity or sometimes as a vertical Austausch coefficient.

It should be emphasised that equation (7.2) is mainly used because it is simple and convenient. It has many disadvantages which include the fact that the "constant" η is certainly not a constant, but will vary with depth and with flow conditions. We must therefore remember that eddy viscosity terms in the above form are just an interim measure, to represent one of the effects of turbulence, until we understand this feature of fluid motion well enough to represent it more exactly.

7.2 Ekman Layers

When a steady wind blows for a length of time much greater than the local inertial period, then there is a boundary layer flow generated in which the effects of turbulent viscosity and the Earth's rotation are balanced. This is called an Ekman layer in honour of the Norwegian oceanographer V. W. Ekman (1874–1954) who used this idea to explain the observation in the Arctic Ocean, that when the wind blew steadily for a period of time, drifting ice did not move downwind but at an angle of $20°$ to $40°$ to the right of the wind.

The wind stress acting on the surface of the water starts it moving in the downwind direction, but within the time span of an inertial period the Coriolis force deflects the motion to the right in the Northern Hemisphere and to the left in the Southern Hemisphere. The angle of deflection depends on the water depth, and on the depth dependence of the eddy viscosity, but in deep water it is $45°$. The surface water moves the layer of water underneath it through viscous interaction, but this subsurface water moves a bit slower, and is also deflected by the Coriolis force. This combination of viscous interaction and Coriolis deflection continues downward until either the bottom is reached (in shallow water) or the strength of the current is negligible.

If we assume that the forces due to the wind stress and internal Reynolds stresses are exactly balanced by the Coriolis force, then the equations of horizontal motion equate the stress gradient forces with rotational forces. They are

$$\frac{d\tau_x}{dz} = \rho\, f v$$

$$\frac{d\tau_y}{dz} = -\rho\, f u$$

(7.3)

where u and v are the currents in the x and y direction and τ_x and τ_y are the two components of the stress. The Coriolis parameter is represented by f. When equation (7.3) is solved, then the resulting horizontal current within the Ekman layer comprises a logarithmic spiral, illustrated in Fig. 7.2. This figure is actually a photograph of a model Ekman spiral that was constructed for classroom demonstrations. The length and orientation of each horizontal brass rod represents the current speed and direction. The first rod is at $45°$ to the wind direction and to the left of it, in order to keep Australian students happy. Going downwards in equal depth intervals each successive rod is to the left of the previous one and shorter.

The Ekman layer depth is usually arbitrarily taken as the depth where the direction of the flow becomes opposite to that at the surface — in which case its

FIG. 7.2. *A demonstration model, built in a workshop, of the Ekman spiral of water flows in the Southern Hemisphere. These result from a balance between the frictional effects and the Coriolis deflection. Horizontal rods represent the speed and direction of the water movement.*

speed will have dropped to 0.04 of its value at the surface. This depth, D_E, will vary with latitude (because the inertial period and Coriolis parameter vary with latitude), and indirect arguments indicate that it is likely to vary linearly with the surface wind speed.

If the eddy viscosity is treated as a constant, then a dimensional argument will indicate that as D_E depends only on the eddy kinematic viscosity term (η/ρ) with units of $m^2\ s^{-1}$ and on the Coriolis forces, which are characterised by the inertial period with units of seconds, then D_E will vary as the square root of both (η/ρ) and T_i. An exact calculation reveals that

$$D_E = \sqrt{\frac{\eta \pi T_i}{\rho}} = \pi\sqrt{2\,\eta/f\rho}. \qquad (7.4)$$

For a surface wind speed of 10 m s^{-1}, the Ekman layer depth in deep water ranges from 100 m at 10° latitude to 45 m at 80° latitude.

The Ekman layer depth is often equated with the mixed layer depth. Though the two are likely to be reasonably similar in the open ocean, different effects generate them. A short period of very strong winds will influence the mixed layer depth, but is unlikely to affect the Ekman layer. In this case the mixed layer depth would exceed D_E. Conversely, if a steady uniform wind is somehow suddenly switched on, the Ekman layer will form in the space of a few inertial periods, whereas the mixed layer will only progress downward a short distance in that time. In addition, the mixed layer depth can be influenced by factors other than wind. Extreme surface cooling produces denser and heavier surface water which mixes as it sinks.

Upwelling

The total mass transport in the Ekman layers of the water turns out to be exactly perpendicular to the wind direction. To the right of the wind in the Northern Hemisphere and to the left in the Southern Hemisphere. The reason for this is that over the whole depth of the Ekman layer the upper parts which have velocity components in the downwind direction are exactly balanced by components in the opposite direction at lower levels. Summed from top to bottom there is no total movement parallel to the wind.

An equatorward wind near the east coast of an ocean basin produces an Ekman drift that induces upwelling. Colder subsurface water rises to the surface, cooling the surroundings and bringing nutrient-rich deep water to the surface. Areas of upwelling in the world oceans — the Californian coast, the Peruvian coast, the Senegal coast — are regions of high fishing yield (or were areas of high fishing yield before they were overexploited). As nutrients rise to the surface, so do plankton which feed on the nutrients; fish which feed on the plankton; and fish which feed on other fish. The food chain is then completed by humans who feed on fish, and they do so in this instance because the fish are close to the surface and easy to catch.

The physical mechanism by which the upwelling operates is depicted in Fig. 7.3 for a Southern Hemisphere situation. A northward (southerly) wind produces an Ekman drift of surface waters away from the coast. These waters are replaced by cooler upwelled water flowing up the continental shelf. At greater depth there is a subsurface compensation current, whereas at the surface there is a sinuous boundary of eddies between upwelled coastal water and oceanic surface water. This boundary is an upwelling front.

In general, upwelling occurs in the eastern boundary region of weak oceanic current flows where the surface wind can significantly affect the mean water drift. Surprisingly, there is no evidence for any upwelling on the Western Australian coast, even though the offshore Ekman transport inferred from mean wind stress charts would indicate strong coastal upwelling. The reason for this lack of up-welling remains a mystery.

Upwelling also occurs at equatorial and tropical locations where the Coriolis

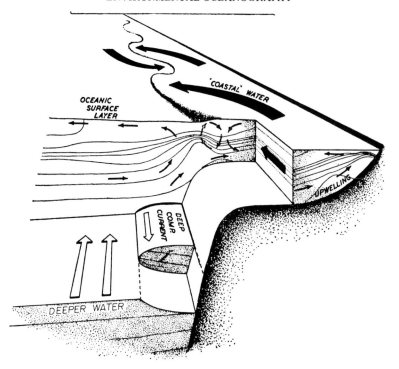

FIG. 7.3. *Hydrographic structure during upwelling of the Benguela current. Northward (equatorward) winds generate the upwelling.*

force is small. At the equator this is a result of surface waters diverging due to the westward (easterly) tropical trade winds deflecting tropical waters poleward through Coriolis effects on either side of the equator. The equatorial waters rise to make up for this poleward loss of surface water on both sides. At other times tropical cyclones (hurricanes) induce a localised upwelling on the continental shelf. There are also other imperfectly understood mechanisms at work.

Shallow Water

Ekman layers in shallow water are more complex than the deep water spiral of Fig. 7.2. For a start, the horizontal angle, α, between the wind and the surface drift is no longer 45°. It depends on the ratio between the depth of the sea H, and the depth of frictional influence D_E. If H/D_E is small, then the angle will be small and the surface current flows nearly parallel to the direction of the wind. As H/D_E increases, the angle is alternately a little smaller and larger than 45°. For instance, if $H = D_E$, then $\alpha = 45°$. Table 7.1 shows some deflection angles, α, for different values of H/D_E less than unity.

TABLE 7.1

H/D_E	0.25	0.5	0.75	1
α	21.5°	45°	45.5°	45°

Secondly, for shallow depths when H/D_E is significantly below 0.5, then the logarithmic spiral of velocity vectors becomes strongly distorted. Furthermore, the assumption that η is a constant becomes suspect, since there are compelling theoretical reasons to believe that very close to the surface η will start out at zero and increase with depth, before starting to decrease as the bottom is approached. The effect of a decrease of the eddy viscosity coefficient towards the bottom in shallow water is illustrated in Fig. 7.4. This figure presents observa-

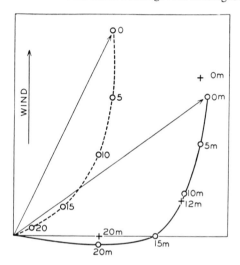

FIG. 7.4. *Wind-induced current in shallow water, assuming a constant eddy viscosity (dashed curve) or an eddy viscosity that decreases toward the bottom (full curve). Observed currents are indicated by crosses.*

tions of wind drift currents on the North Siberian shelf over a water depth of 22 m compared to (i) computations on an Ekman spiral in which η remained constant, with a value of 20 kg m^{-1} s^{-1}, and (ii) one in which it decreased towards the bottom. There is no doubt that the assumption of an eddy viscosity coefficient varying with depth agrees much better with observations than that of a constant η.

Langmuir Cells (Windrows)

About 20 min after the onset of wind speeds greater than 3 m s^{-1} windrows appear on the surface of the sea. These are lines of particulate matter, such as seaweed or oil films, and correspond to the surface convergence zone of a set of helical roll vortices (Fig. 7.5) known as Langmuir cells. They are named after Irving Langmuir (1881–1957) who was the first to systematically investigate them.

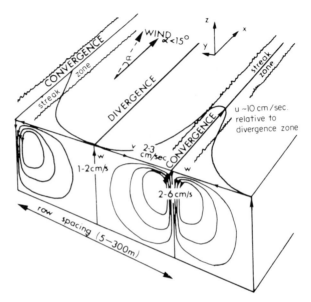

FIG. 7.5. *The Langmuir circulation consists of a helical trajectory combining downwind motion in convergence zones (windrows) with subsequent downwelling, divergence and upwelling.*

Langmuir cells, and their associated windrows, exist whether surface pollutants make them visible or not. They are aligned virtually parallel to the wind, or at least at no more than $15°$ to the wind direction. The surface velocity in the direction of the wind is larger in the convergence streak zones — the windrows — than out of them. The depth and spacing of the vortices is in dispute. The width of the cells is generally several times greater than the depth, but the factors that control these two variables are uncertain. It has been suggested on the basis of oceanic observations that $b = 4.5W$, where b is the distance (in metres) between windrows and W is the wind speed in m s^{-1}. However, the depth of the vortex is apparently limited by the depth of the mixed layer; thus in the presence of shallow mixed layers near the coast the width never approaches the value of $b = 4.5W$.

There is an inadequate theoretical understanding of Langmuir circulations, and objections can be found to all of the existing theories. A similar phenomenon exists in the atmosphere when cloud streets — long rows of cumulus clouds — are produced, and in the atmospheric case this has been shown to be an instability of the Ekman spiral. The main difference between the atmospheric and oceanic case is that in the atmosphere the growth time for the instability is of the order of the inertial period, whereas in the sea it is much shorter.

7.3 Benthic Boundary Layers

In the previous section we discussed eddy viscosity and internal friction. Of considerably greater importance in shallow coastal waters is the effect of an external friction, namely bottom friction. At the bottom of the sea we have a benthic boundary layer over which the horizontal velocity changes from a particular value, say U, to zero since the bottom itself is stationary. This large velocity shear has associated with it a large bottom frictional stress, τ_b which is generally modelled (or parameterised) by a quadratic rule

$$\tau_b = \rho B_D U^2 . \tag{7.5}$$

The drag coefficient, B_D depends on the roughness of the boundary and has a typical magnitude of 10^{-3} to 10^{-2}.

If the bottom shear stress becomes too large, then part of the bottom sediment will suspend and start to move with the fluid. This produces distinctive wavelike patterns on the sediment floor whose explanation still remains somewhat of a mystery. Attempts to classify these structures in terms of bulk flow parameters concentrate on the Froude number – Fr – which is a non-dimensional number that is the ratio between the current speed and the speed of waves that can occur:

$$Fr = U/\sqrt{gH},$$

where H is the depth of water. As the current speed, U, increases, patterns are formed which may be classified as follows:

(i)   Flat bed ($Fr = 0$) – no sediment movement.
(ii) Ripples ($Fr \ll 1$) – a three-dimensional pattern of small irregularities.
(iii) Dunes ($Fr < 1$) – larger irregularities in both length and height with an asymmetric shape of smooth rises and sharp drops in the direction of the current.
(iv) Wavy ($Fr \sim 1$) – sinusoidal dunes.
(v)   Antidunes ($Fr > 1$) – dunes with sharp rises and smooth downslopes in the direction of the current.

More recent studies of these structures have concentrated on their boundary-layer aspects rather than on their wave aspects. These use a friction velocity u_* defined in terms of the dominant stress (bottom stress in this case) as

$$u_* = \sqrt{\tau/\rho}. \tag{7.6}$$

A more definite classification for bed features can be obtained by using non-dimensional numbers in which the current speed is replaced by the frictional velocity.

In addition to the benthic boundary layer generated by bottom friction, there will also be a benthic Ekman layer set up if the water currents are sufficiently steady and if there is sufficient depth of water. Recent attempts to introduce realistic eddy viscosities suitable in shallow seas also use a friction velocity u_* defined in terms of the dominant stress (be it wind stress or bottom friction). Reasonable success has been achieved with a constant eddy viscosity.

$$(\eta/\rho) = u_* H/20 \tag{7.7}$$

in shallow water and

$$(\eta/\rho) = u_*\, 2/200\, f \tag{7.8}$$

in deeper water, with the transition occurring when

$$H = 0.1\, u_*/f. \tag{7.9}$$

7.4 Coastal Boundary Layer

One form of boundary layer that has received far less attention than those previously mentioned is the coastal boundary layer. This may be defined as that band of water within which relatively persistent alongshore flow dominates. Outside the coastal boundary layer inertial motions and other flows with little directional preference predominate. The width of the coastal boundary layer depends on both the depth of the water and the variation of this depth with distance, and is equal to the width of influence of trapped continental shelf waves and edge waves. It is generally of the order of tens of kilometres in mid-latitude shelf waters.

Numerous observations of the movement of drogued buoys (i.e. floats with a drogue, such as a parachute, attached) indicate that near a straight shoreline the primary currents generated by local winds are directed within a few degrees parallel to the shore virtually whatever the wind direction. Figure 7.6 indicates this phenomenon in 10-m depth of nearshore waters north of Perth in Western Australia. The buoy deflection *is in the wrong direction* to be a Coriolis deflection, so that the trajectory can have little relation to an Ekman spiral. The subsurface flow is nearly parallel to the shoreline, though the surface flow seems to register the combined effects of the subsurface current and the wind.

During March the winds in south-western Australia are predominantly easterlies (i.e. they blow towards the west). After a period of time this depresses the water level near the coast and produces an offshore pressure head that would drive a shoreward subsurface current, were it not for the Coriolis deflection, which moves it northward. Thus the observed northward flow is actually a geostrophic current set up in response to wind-generated onshore—offshore

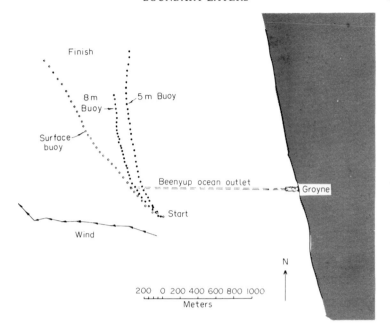

FIG. 7.6. *Trajectories of drogued buoys at surface, 5-m and 8-m
depths in 10-m depth of water near the shoreline. The wind was
dominantly offshore, but the drogues moved predominantly
alongshore.*

pressure gradients. If the wind is sufficiently regular for a sufficiently long period
of time, then the resulting alongshore current may be strong enough to be considered a coastal jet.

Cross-flow

Given the separation of shelf waters into a coastal boundary layer and an
outer region, the dispersal of effluents discharged at the shore may be imagined
to take place in two steps: (i) within the coastal boundary layer; (ii) between it
and the outer region. Once mixed with the large mass of outer shelf water, most
effluents cease to be of concern. The mass exchange process between the coastal
boundary layer and the outer region is thus of crucial interest in pollution studies.

The mass exchange between these two regions is governed by what we might
think of as a secondary flow in the onshore–offshore direction superimposed on
the dominant coastal jet-like flow. This secondary flow is called cross-flow and it
generally occurs in the transition period after a new wind regime, during which
time the ocean is trying to set up its own new geostrophic and Ekman balances.

The establishment of onshore–offshore pressure gradients requires at least
some onshore–offshore displacement of water. It takes very little water to

change surface elevations by the small amounts necessary (a few centimetres), but internal adjustment of the water density often involves vertical thermocline movements by tens of metres over nearshore regions about 5 km in width. For example, a change from a downwelling to an upwelling, or vice versa, can involve nearly a complete exchange of water from the coastal boundary layer. Since a given sense of thermocline elevation (upwelling or downwelling) accompanies a given direction of a coastal jet, on a reversal of this jet's flow direction – following, for instance, on a reversal of the wind direction – there is a switch from downwelling to upwelling or vice versa. At the same time there is a substantial exchange of mass through cross-flows.

Further Reading

The concept of a boundary layer originated in aerodynamics and the classical reference work on laboratory boundary layers is

H. SCHLICHTING: *Boundary Layer Theory*, McGraw-Hill, New York, 1960 (647pp).

There are many similarities between oceanic and atmospheric boundary layers and there are a number of books which deal with the latter.
A particularly readable account is given by

T. R. OKE: *Boundary Layer Climates,* Methuen, London, 1978 (372pp).

whereas the detailed mathematics is given by

E. J. PLATE: *Aerodynamic Characteristics of Atmospheric Boundary Layers*, US Atomic Energy Commission, Oak Ridge, 1971 (190pp).

and by

G. A. McBEAN (ed.): *The Planetary Boundary Layer*, Technical Note 165, World Meteorological Organisation, Geneva, 1979 (201pp).

Of more relevance to coastal waters are:

O. M. PHILLIPS: *Dynamics of the Upper Ocean,* 2nd edition, Cambridge University Press, Cambridge, 1977 (336pp).

and

E. B. KRAUS (ed.): *Modelling and Prediction of the Upper Layers of the Ocean*, Pergamon Press, Oxford, 1977 (325pp).

An extensive review of upwelling is given by

R. L. SMITH: Upwelling, *Oceanogr. Mar. Biol. Ann. Rev.* 6, 11–46, 1968.

The structure and behaviour of the coastal boundary layer is still a field of active research. Recent reviews include a three part article

G. T. CSANADY: Circulation in the Coastal Ocean, EOS (*Transactions of the American Geophysical Union*), 62, 9–11, 41–43, 73–75, 1981.

which is a simplified version of material from

G. T. CSANADY: *Circulation in the Coastal Ocean*, D. Reidel, Dordrecht, 1982 (274pp).

More mathematical expositions may be found in

G. T. CSANADY: The coastal jet conceptual model in the dynamics of shallow seas, in E. D. Goldberg *et al.* (eds.), *The Sea*, vol. 6, John Wiley, New York, pp. 117–144, 1977.

C. D. WINANT: Coastal circulation and wind induced currents, *Ann. Rev. Fluid Mech.* 12, 271–302, 1980.

J. S. ALLEN: Models of wind-driven currents on the continental shelf, *Ann. Rev. Fluid Mech.* 12, 389–434, 1980.

The bottom boundary layer, of great concern to sedimentologists, is dealt with in detail by

A. J. RAUDKIVI: *Loose Boundary Hydraulics*, Pergamon Press, Oxford, 1967 (331pp).

CHAPTER 8

Mixing

8.1 Turbulence

In the late nineteenth century Osborne Reynolds (1842–1912) studied the flow, at various speeds U, of various fluids of density ρ and viscosity μ in pipes of radius r. He found that this motion was smooth and laminar when the dimensionless quantity $\rho \, r \, U/\mu$ (nowadays called the Reynolds number) was less than 4000, but turbulent when it exceeded this value. The molecular kinematic viscosity of water, μ/ρ, is 1.4×10^{-6} m^2 s^{-1} and U is typically 1 cm s^{-1}, so that water bodies deeper than about 1 m will be turbulent. This form of turbulence, sometimes called Reynolds number turbulence, is always present in rivers, oceans and coastal waters. What this means is that the fluid properties (momentum, heat, salt, etc.) are not transferred by the random collisions of molecules as is the case in laminar flow, but are transferred on a much larger scale by the motion of the fluid. The similarity approach to turbulence argues that this large-scale transfer is accomplished by eddies and swirls whose random motions and interactions are analogous to those of molecules.

In turbulent flow, the fluid properties are interchanged through their fluctuations (or perturbations) about the mean value. To measure these fluctuations (e.g. the sudden gust of wind; the short, sharp burst of current) is very expensive and time-consuming. Routine environmental investigations only measure mean values, so that much of the study of turbulence has been directed towards methods of using mean quantities to describe turbulent effects. The simplest way to do this was discussed in Chàpters 6 and 7. Assume that the flux of the fluid property of interest is proportional to the mean concentration gradient of that property. The constant of proportionality is the appropriate eddy coefficient. In the case of horizontal momentum, its flux is given by the vertical gradient of mean horizontal velocity as $\eta \, du/dz$, where η is the vertical eddy viscosity.

The size of the eddy, l, determines the magnitude of η, since it determines the mixing length over which the masses travel before imparting and attaining their momenta. These are related by dimensional analysis as

$$\eta/\rho = l^2 \left| \frac{dU}{dz} \right|. \tag{8.1}$$

Unfortunately, there is no single size characterising oceanic eddies. They exist in all sizes from globs of water a few centimetres in size to large eddies associated with boundary currents that can be 200 km across. As a general rule the momentum cascades from the larger eddies to the smaller ones, or as L. F. Richardson (1881–1953) expressed it:

> Big whorls have little whorls
> which feed on their velocity;
> and little whorls have lesser whorls,
> and so on to viscosity.

The major exception to this rule are the large eddies in the ocean which manage to transfer significant amounts of their energy back into the even larger-scale gyres of the temperate latitude current systems. This is an example of a negative viscosity phenomenon.

To further complicate an already complex situation, the strong hydrostatic equilibrium introduces different eddy sizes in the horizontal and in the vertical. This distinction is particularly significant where the density of the water increases strongly with depth, because such an increase influences horizontal and vertical turbulence in a different manner. Where the density of seawater increases strongly with depth, vertical random motion is impeded, since a mass that is brought to a higher level will be surrounded by lighter water and sink, though horizontal motions are not impeded. Turbulence in this type of stratified system will be considered in further detail in the next section.

Turbulence transfers heat and salt as well as momentum, and the same reasoning is applied to the eddy thermal conductivity and the eddy diffusivity. The vertical transfer of heat and salt is much slower than that of momentum, so that the vertical eddy diffusivity and conductivity are much less than the vertical eddy viscosity. However, as it is the same whorl system that transfers all three properties horizontally, the horizontal eddy conductivity, diffusivity and viscosity are all equal.

Stratified Turbulence

Fluids in which there is a marked density stratification, with light fluid on top of dense fluid, are very stable. If one attempts to move the fluid vertically it will suffer a buoyancy force that returns it to its original position. The greater the density stratification, the more stable the system.

Let us imagine the situation of two layers of fluid, a light one sitting on top of a dense one. If there is relative motion between the two layers, then the boundary between the two will deform (Fig. 8.1). If the relative motion is strong, then the boundary may become unstable and turbulence ensues. Basically, the density gradient and gravity act as stabilising forces; the current shear acts as a destabilising force. The ratio between these two effects is called the Richardson number, and is given by

$$Ri = \frac{-\,(g/\rho)\,(d\rho/dz)}{\left|\dfrac{dU}{dz}\right|^{2}}.$$

(8.2)

If the current shear dU/dz is very strong, or if the stratification $d\rho/dz$ is very weak, and the Richardson number falls below $1/4$, then billows will form (Fig. 8.1) and produce turbulent rotors, wherein the fluid from one layer gets mixed into the other layer. This form of turbulence is sometimes called Richardson number turbulence.

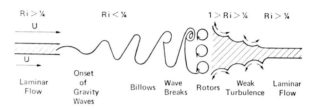

FIG. 8.1. *The cycle of turbulence in stratified flows. When the velocity shear is large the Richardson number,* Ri, *drops below its critical value and turbulence ensues.*

8.2 Convection

When water in a kettle is heated the bottom water warms first. As its temperature increases, the density drops and it will rise to the surface. At the surface, the water near the edges of the kettle cools most rapidly, is thus relatively more dense and is displaced by warmer water. It sinks to the bottom whereupon the cycle begins anew.

This process of a vertical circulation being driven by vertical density differences is known as convection. It is controlled by buoyancy forces, and is to be contrasted to the process of advection which refers to the horizontal circulation of water from one place to another.

Convection occurs in lakes, and in the oceans, when the air temperature drops below the surface temperature of the water. The surface water cools and sinks and is replaced by subsurface water which also cools and sinks. As we have shown in section 5.2, the mechanics of the process vary between high and low salinity waters, but the water may continue to convect until it freezes.

Thermohaline Convection

In the deep ocean a thermocline separates warm salty water from the colder less saline water underneath it. Figure 5.3 shows an example of this. If the surface waters could be cooled, or if the deep waters could be heated, then there would be a massive convection generated as the cold salty surface waters sink, or as the warm, fresh bottom waters rise.

Imagine a long pipe maintained vertically in the sea with its top in the upper mixed layer and its bottom in the cold deep waters. If a pump were started that pumped the cold deep waters up from the bottom, then as soon as these waters had started to reach the top of the pipe, the pump could be turned off and the circulation would continue by itself (Fig. 8.2). The cold fresh water, as it rises

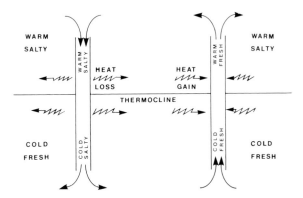

FIG. 8.2. *The salt fountain mechanism. Because heat diffuses faster than salt, the same phenomenon can occur on a small scale even when the pipe is absent.*

up the pipe, would be heated by the warm water surrounding the pipe and become buoyant. As it rose higher it would continue to become warmer, and hence continue to spontaneously rise until it reached the top of the pipe. In fact the mechanism will work in either direction. If the initial pumping started the flow downwards, then the topmost saline water would cool, become more dense, and continue to fall as it travelled down the pipe.

Double Diffusive Convection

The salt fountain mechanism described in the previous section is an example of a class of motions generically known as double diffusive convection. The second case consists of cold fresh water overlaying hot salt water. The layer above the interface becomes lighter than that above it and tends to rise, whilst water below gets heavier and tends to sink. This phenomenon is called "layering" and may lead to fairly homogeneous layers separated by thinner regions of high gradients of temperature and salinity.

Double diffusion utilises molecular diffusion to drive convection. The molecular diffusivity of heat is one hundred times greater than the molecular diffusivity of salt so that solid or sharp boundaries are not essential for either the thermocline salt fountain or the layering instability. Both motions can be set up in the interior of a fluid, and it is in no way necessary to have pipes connecting the two fluids.

Figure 8.3 is a photograph of salt fingers produced by thermohaline double diffusion at the interface between stratified solutions of sugar and salt of equal density. The two solutions were originally side by side in a laboratory tank, separated by a barrier. As the barrier was removed, the two solutions intruded and vertical layers of salt and sugar solutions formed through double diffusive processes.

Such layers are liable to occur whenever one fluid intrudes into another stratified fluid at the depth where the two densities are equal.

8.3 Turbulent Entrainment

We saw in section 8.1 that a stratified fluid can become turbulent within a thin layer if there is a velocity shear across this layer. This phenomenon can give rise to an interesting effect, known as turbulent entrainment, when there is a strong density gradient − a pycnocline − between two fluid regions, one of which is turbulent.

If there is a turbulent layer of lighter fluid overlaying a stable layer, then the velocity fluctuations at the interface will produce small-scale billows and rotors that entrain the non-turbulent fluid into the turbulent one. As the quantity of stable fluid decreases, and the quantity of turbulent fluid increases, the pycnocline moves downwards at a velocity U_e, known as the entrainment velocity.

Turbulent entrainment is responsible for the formation and maintenance of thermoclines in the upper layers of the ocean. Wind, acting on the sea surface, stirs the upper layer of the ocean − the well-mixed layer. This layer entrains cold water from beneath the mixed layer, provided the wind imparts sufficient energy. If the wind is sufficiently energetic it both entrains some cold water and then mixes it throughout the well-mixed layer. This produces an upper layer of more or less constant temperature, sharply separated from the lower regions in which the temperature decreases with depth. This separation region constitutes a thermocline.

The thermocline progresses downwards until the energy that the well-mixed layer receives from the wind is insufficient to entrain and completely mix the lower waters. This happens when the wind drops. It also happens when the mixed layer becomes deep. Detailed examination of the upper layers of the ocean can reveal a stepped thermocline structure. This occurs when a prolonged windy period, which has generated a deep thermocline, is followed by a long calm period. The upper layers become quiescent during the calm period and the near surface waters are further warmed by the sun. A new spell of windy weather will mix the warm upper waters and create a new thermocline above the previous one.

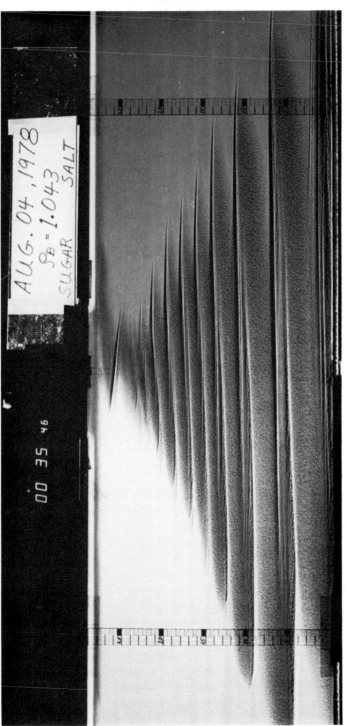

FIG. 8.3. *Mixing of stratified waters of equal density but different properties through double diffusion.*

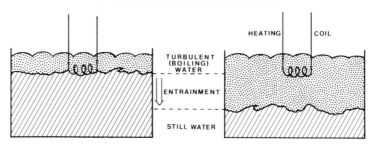

FIG. 8.4. *Turbulent entrainment occurs when an upper layer of water is boiled. In the sea the upper level stirring is provided by the wind.*

All of these effects can be easily demonstrated in the laboratory. Figure 8.4 illustrates the turbulent entrainment process, in which an electric heating element (rather than the wind) provides the surface stirring. The heating element is placed near the top of a beaker of water and produces an upper turbulent layer of warm (and hence light) water which proceeds to entrain the lower layer of water. The sharp interface between the topmost boiling water and the bottom water is easily seen, as are its distortions.

This interface progresses downwards and will eventually reach the bottom. When this happens there is a dramatic increase in the boiling intensity of the water because energy no longer needs to be supplied to entrainment and can all be supplied to the boiling water. Alternatively, if the experiment is run for a while, switched off for a while, and then restarted, the stepped thermocline structure described above becomes evident. What can also be seen is that if the surface stirring continues, the top thermocline progresses down and eventually assimilates the old thermocline.

8.4 Dispersion

Dispersion is the general name given to the process whereby particles of water, or particles of a soluble pollutant, are scattered. In still water, the physical mechanism that accomplishes dispersion is molecular diffusion. In this case, if a slug of soluble pollutant is quickly inserted into the water, it will diffuse (or disperse) so that its concentration at various distances from the injection point will be a Gaussian normal curve. With time, the peak concentration decreases and the effects of the pollutant begin to appear at greater distances from the injection point (Fig. 8.5). In this non-turbulent case, as has been discussed in section 6.4, the flux of pollutant is proportional to the gradient of concentration of the pollutant, with the coefficient of molecular diffusion being the proportionality constant.

The great English fluid mechanician, Sir Geoffrey Taylor (1886–1975), found that the flow of dissolved contaminants in a pipe full of a moving turbu-

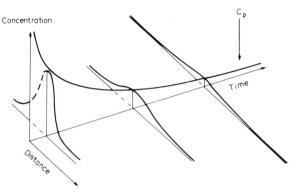

FIG. 8.5. *Concentration–distance curves for an instantaneous slug of pollutant undergoing molecular diffusion. As time proceeds the curve spreads out, the peak concentration declines and the variance increases.*

lent fluid possessed the remarkable property that the flux of the contaminant in the direction of flow was proportional to the gradient of the mean concentration of the contaminant. This was true even though the spread of the contaminants was caused primarily by the velocity profile in the cross-section; flows with velocity gradients are often referred to as "shear flows" and the mechanism that Taylor analysed is often known as the shear effect. Taylor's work was a great boon to the mathematical analysis of dispersion, for it meant that in the situation that he analysed a diffusion equation could be used to describe dispersion and the resulting dispersion coefficient, Λ, was a constant for a particular flow regime and pipe radius.

The dispersion coefficient can be related to the statistical properties of the concentration distribution curve, when it is plotted as a function of distance. This curve grows wider with time (Fig. 8.5) and a measure of its width is the variance, generally written as σ^2. For a Gaussian curve the variance is the width between the points where the concentration is reduced to 0.368 ($=1/e$) of its peak value. If the dispersion coefficient is constant, then it means that the variance grows linearly with time

$$\sigma^2 = 2\Lambda t \tag{8.3}$$

or

$$\Lambda = \frac{1}{2} \frac{d\sigma^2}{dt}$$

There has been a widespread tendency to extend the diffusion equation approach into environments for which it was not specifically derived. One of the earliest attempts to illustrate this measured the separation distance between two parsnips floating on Loch Ness. The square of their separation distance (an approximate measure of σ^2) when divided by the elapsed time was not a constant but increased as the 4/3 power of the distance between them. Since that time numerous experiments have confirmed that the ratio is not constant, and the increase ranges from a power law of 8/7 to one of 4/3. Most of these experiments used a fluorescent dye as a tracer instead of parsnips. The results of a host of estuarine and coastal investigations are depicted in Fig. 8.6 from which it can be seen that σ^2 increases as the 7/3 power of the time. (This favours an 8/7 power

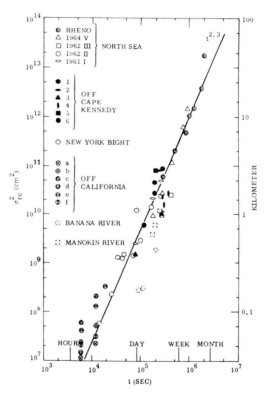

FIG. 8.6. *A summary of the results of many dispersion studies shows that the variance grows as the 7/3 power of the time.*

law for σ^2 versus time as a function of separation distance.) The dispersion co-efficient, being the time derivative of the variance, must increase as the 4/3 power of the time. The fact that it is not a constant also means that the diffusion equation is not an adequate description for dispersion in coastal waters. Having said this, there is nothing better available as yet and so we are forced to continue to use it.

Most dispersion studies use the dye Rhodamine WT since it can be detected accurately in minute concentrations by a fluorimeter. The dye is relatively stable in seawater and does not decompose too quickly from the effects of light or from chemical reaction with other substances in the water. It is thus possible to simulate the motion and dispersion of a soluble pollutant in the water by dumping a barrel of the dye solution and tracing the dye for a number of days.

Wastewater released from a coastal city, or heated water discharged from a coastal power plant, relies on turbulent dispersion to mix and dilute the effluent and minimise its environmental impact. Mixing can be enhanced by artificial means, one of which is an outfall diffuser system. This produces rapid mixing by means of a manifold containing many discharge ports along a line. For example, the 3-m diameter, 8.3-km long outfall built by the Orange County (Los Angeles) Sanitation district has a 1.8-km long diffuser at the end with 500 equally spaced discharge ports. The choice of the best diffuser for a particular application rests with the design engineer who must base his choice upon the desired discharge rate, length of diffuser, depth of discharge, ambient currents and density stratification. In addition, the structural design must ensure that the outfall will not be damaged by catastrophic events (e.g. extreme waves or earthquakes) which may occur once or twice in the life of the structure.

Effluent disperses rapidly and its peak concentration decreases quickly. If it is discharged from the side of a boat and mixes on its way down, then it will form a line from top to bottom — or from top to thermocline. According to diffusion theory the peak concentration, C_p, is given by

$$C_p = \frac{m/H}{2\pi\sigma^2} \tag{8.4}$$

where m is the mass discharged, H is the relevant depth and σ^2 is obtained from Fig. 8.6. For example: if 5 tonnes of cyanide is thrown into 100 m of water, how long before its concentration drops below the recommended 5 μg l^{-1}? The main difficulty in answering this question is getting all the physical quantities into the same units. As Fig. 8.6 is in (cm)^2 let us work in kg and cm. Firstly 5 tonnes is 5000 kg; 100 m is 10^4 cm and 5 μg l^{-1} is 5×10^{-12} kg cm^{-3}. Substituting into (8.4) we find that the requisite dilution is achieved when $\sigma^2 = 1.6 \times 10^{11}$ cm^2. From Fig. 8.6 we see that the variance attains this value in about a week. Dispersive processes render this enormous quantity of toxic poison harmless in about a week by spreading it over a large area.

8.5 Oceanic Fronts

So far in this chapter a number of mechanisms have been mentioned, all of which will tend to mix waters of different properties. Yet at the same time one is continually reminded of the fact that water masses with quite distinct properties co-exist. At the boundary between water masses one often finds a visible line of demarcation, with peculiar ripples or waves which is known as siome. Flotsam accumulates along the siome convergence line. Often this includes detritus such as dust, foam and the whole food chain from phytoplankton up through zooplankton, molluscs, fish, birds, insects, dolphins and whales. Thus the siome becomes a productive fishing area.

The boundary between adjacent water masses of dissimilar properties is known as a surface front. It can be termed an oceanic front, a coastal front or an estuarine front depending on its location. In general, the frontal zone is a region of intense motion and mixing. Vertical velocities may be thousands of times larger than typical open ocean values, double diffusion can be strongly operative and turbulence can be intense. The exact mechanism by which the front maintains its identity against all these strong mixing processes is still uncertain.

Fronts can conveniently be classified into six categories:

(1)   large-scale open ocean fronts;

(2)   fronts representing the edge of major western boundary currents; these fronts are associated with the intrusion of warm, salty water of tropical origin into higher latitudes (e.g. Gulf Stream, Kuroshio);

(3)   shelf break fronts formed at the boundary of shelf and slope waters, such as are found in the Middle Atlantic Bight;

(4)   upwelling fronts, essentially the surface manifestation of an inclined pycnocline, commonly formed during a coastal upwelling. Figure 8.7 illustrates the time evolution of this process in the Northern Hemisphere in the presence of a pycnocline separating two distinct water masses. A steady northward wind depresses the coastal surface elevation through an Ekman drift. This raises the pycnocline elevation at the coast through a subsurface return flow which partially helps to minimise the pressure gradient (as a general rule: if the surface of a two-layer fluid tilts, the thermocline will tilt in the opposite direction). If the wind continues, the pycnocline breaks the surface producing an upwelling front with an associated coastal jet at the frontal boundary;

(5)   plume fronts at the boundaries of riverine plumes discharging into coastal waters (e.g. Amazon, Columbia, Hudson Rivers);

(6)   shallow sea fronts, formed in continental seas and estuaries, and around islands, banks, capes and shoals; these are commonly located in boundary regions between shallow wind and tidally mixed near-shore waters and stratified, deeper offshore waters; these fronts are delineated by a sharp change in sea surface temperature and show up well on satellite infra-red photographs.

A convenient measure of shallow sea fronts is the stratification parameter

$$S_H = \log_{10}(H/U^3),$$

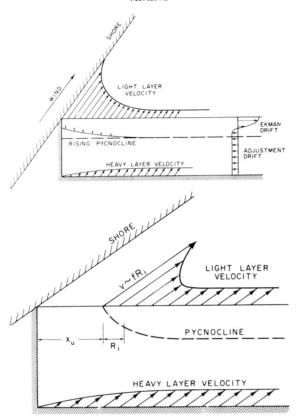

FIG. 8.7. *Evolution of an upwelling front and
offshore coastal jet in the Northern Hemisphere.*

where H is the water depth in metres and U is the surface tidal stream in m s^{-1}
at mean spring tides. This parameter is a measure of the ratio of energy necessary
to maintain well-mixed conditions (which is proportional to the depth) to the
energy dissipated by tides (which is proportional to U^3). Low values of S_H
denotes vertically well-mixed (and hence colder) water. Contours of S_H for the
British Isles are shown in Fig. 8.8. Infra-red images and ship observations indicate
that frontal regions between well-mixed and stratified conditions do indeed
reflect the shape of these contours and fronts have been observed along the
$S_H = 2$ contours.

8.6 Large-scale Mixing

Gyres

The temperature latitude ocean circulation is dominated by gyres of anti-

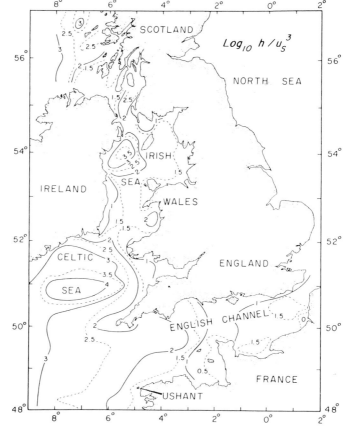

FIG. 8.8. *The stratification parameter* S_H *can be used to determine the shape of shallow sea fronts, whose boundaries lie along contours of constant* S_H.

cyclonic vorticity (clockwise in the Northern Hemisphere, anticlockwise in the Southern Hemisphere). The currents at the western boundaries of these gyres are stronger and more intense than those in the middle or at the eastern boundaries of the gyre (Fig. 6.1). Yet in the earlier parts of this chapter we have seen how large currents (i.e. large velocities) can lead to turbulence, either through the Reynolds number becoming so large that the whole flow becomes turbulent, or through the Richardson number being reduced at the edges of the current where the current shear will be strong. There are also other ways in which instabilities, such as meanders in current positions, can be generated, but once again these are more likely to occur in fast flows than in slow ones. These instabilities also mix water but on a much larger scale.

Rings

The Gulf Stream in the western mid-Atlantic is one of the best known and most widely studied of the western boundary currents. It, along with the Kuroshio on the east coast of Japan, is a relatively narrow current that forms wandering loops, called meanders, after leaving the coastline. These meanders pinch off (Fig. 8.9) and fuse to form a circular ring of relatively rapid current. Such a ring is typically 150–300 km across and extends downward 2500–3500 m, almost to the ocean bottom. They occasionally intrude onto the continental shelf and strongly affect the shelf circulation when they do so.

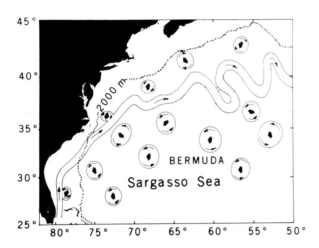

FIG. 8.9. *Representation of Gulf Stream meanders and the distribution and movement of rings. The shelf circulation changes markedly when a ring intrudes onto the shelf.*

Because the Gulf Stream separates the warmer Sargasso Sea on the south from the colder water to the north, the seawater in the core of the ring differs considerably in temperature from the water around it. A meander pinching off on the southern side encloses cold water and forms a cold core ring in the warm Sargasso Sea. A meander to the northern side forms a warm core ring in the cold water between the Gulf Stream and the coast. These differences in temperature allow a ring to be readily located and tracked. Rings move at a speed of about 3–5 km per day and can persist from 1 to 3 years before being reabsorbed into the initiating current.

Rings have also been spawned from the Antarctic circumpolar current, though they are smaller and rotate less rapidly than the average Gulf Stream ring. Thus each of these strong currents generates very strong, very visible, large-scale turbulence which busily transfers salt, heat and kinetic energy from one part of the ocean to another. They also carry with them a distinct biological community which in many respects is distinct from that outside the ring. These organisms, and their chemical and physical environment, are typical of the water mass from which the core of the ring was derived. In the case of a ring to the south of the Gulf Stream, the cold water community in its core must attempt to cope with its slowly changing environment as the ring dissipates and gradually loses its identity.

Rings may contain pollutants dumped by authorities with simplistic ideas of ocean circulations. In the future they may also harbour submarines. Sound detection is the primary means used to track submarines. But the temperature and salinity variations in a ring can bend and distort the sound sufficiently to hide submarines.

Eastern Boundary Eddies

We have already seen in section 7.2 that eastern boundary currents are often a source of upwelling near the coast and that this can lead to a complex circulation with coastal countercurrents, sometimes at the surface, but more often beneath the surface at a depth of 100–200 m. Detailed studies of currents such as the California current do not show a simple unidirectional flow, but rather a series of large eddies superimposed on a broad weak equatorial movement. Though it has been suggested that this complex structure may itself be a result of the upwelling process, recent detailed work on the West Australian current – a region in which upwelling does not occur – shows it to be strongly composed of eddies. (Remember: strong currents spawn rings, all else are eddies.) Figure 8.10 is a schematic diagram of the West Australian current's summer circulation pattern and the symbiosis between the current and its eddies is apparent. The eddies rotate in the same direction as the current and are thus not a product of looping and meandering. This form of eastern boundary current eddy circulation can exhibit negative viscosity phenomena – in which it is the eddies that drive the mean circulation.

Though Fig. 8.10 indicates a southward circulation, at other times the eddies have an equatorward drift, and there is an equatorward flow outside of the eddy structure. To differentiate between the two situations, the equatorward flow of Fig. 6.1 is called the West Australian current whereas the southward flow of Fig. 8.10 is called the Leeuwin current.

Further Reading

An engineering perspective on the contents of this chapter is given by

H. B. FISCHER, E. J. LIST, R. C. Y. KOH, J. IMBERGER & N. H. BROOKS: *Mixing in Inland and Coastal Waters*, Academic Press, New York, 1979,

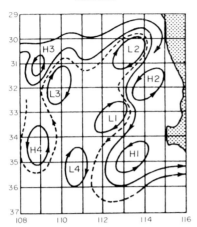

FIG. 8.10. *The circulation of the West Australian current is dominated by eddies. The southward flow shown here, now known as the Leeuwin current, is seasonal and often absent.*

and

F. S. SHERMAN, J. IMBERGER & G. M. CORCOS: Turbulence and mixing in stably stratified waters, *Ann. Rev. Fluid Mech.* 10, 267–288, 1978,

with a more scientific approach emanating from

G. T. CSANADY: *Turbulent Diffusion in the Environment,* D. Reidel, Dordrecht, 1973.

A detailed exposition of the fluid mechanics of convective effects is given by

J. S. TURNER: *Buoyancy Effects in Fluids,* Cambridge University Press, Cambridge, 1973,

and

K. N. FEDEROV: *The Thermohaline Finestructure of the Ocean,* Pergamon Press, Oxford, 1978.

Coastal fronts are dealt with by

M. J. BOWMAN & W. E. ESAIAS (eds.): *Oceanic Fronts in Coastal Processes,* Springer-Verlag, Berlin, 1978.
Journal of Geophysical Research, Issue No. C9, September 20, 1978 (Ocean Fronts).

In addition, the *Journal of Geophysical Research,* Issue No. C6 of June 20, 1978 was devoted to micro-oceanography.

CHAPTER 9

Coastal Meteorology

9.1 Introduction

The boundary between air and sea has many unique and interesting features. Wind blowing over the water surface produces waves. Pressure changes in the atmosphere raise or lower sea level. Both media are fluids — a liquid in the case of water and a gas in the case of air — and they may both form boundary layers at the air—sea interface. At the air—land—sea boundary the interactions are even more interesting and form the major topics in this book. This chapter specifically concentrates on the coastal atmosphere.

An astute observer can gain prior knowledge of coming weather by watching the sea. Heavy swell precedes fronts and storms on the western coasts of continents situated in temperate latitudes. The Gilbertese population of the Pacific island of Kiribati use the shellfish nimatanin (*Nerita plicata*) as their most reliable barometer. This fish is found in the shallows of the island's reefs. It surfaces in fair weather, and great numbers of them indicate a long spell of fine weather. If it remains in reef crevices it is an infallible sign of bad weather. The deeper it hides, the worse the weather.

Coastal meteorology essentially revolves around two considerations. The nature of water vapour and particulates in the air, and the effects of wind on the coastal waters.

9.2 The Hydrological Cycle

The hydrological cycle is a useful, if academic, point from which to study the overall transfer of water. This cycle (Fig. 9.1) begins with the evaporation of water from the oceans. The resulting vapour is transported by moving air masses. Under the proper conditions, the vapour is condensed to clouds, which in turn may precipitate. The rain which falls upon land disperses in several ways, with the greater part being cycled through plants. A portion of the water finds its way over and through the surface soil to stream channels, while other water penetrates farther into the ground to become part of the earth's groundwater supply. Gravity moves both surface streamflow and groundwater downhill and they may eventually discharge into the ocean. The region in which coastal

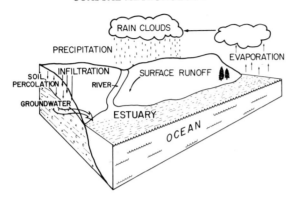

FIG. 9.1. *The hydrological cycle traces the flow of water through air, sea and land.*

waters and riverine waters interact is known as an estuary and forms the basis of the next chapter.

The hydrological cycle serves to emphasise the four basic phases relevant to coastal waters: precipitation, evaporation, surface stream flow and groundwater exchange with the oceans. The last of these is small on a global scale but can have important localised pollution effects. Septic tank systems tend to leak sewage into groundwater which can then flow into estuaries. Large holiday towns on the shores of poorly flushed estuaries can then indirectly pollute their adjacent waters.

Precipitation

In general, rainfall is heaviest near the equator and decreases with increasing latitude until about 30°. At this latitude there is a region of strong subsidence (downward air movement) which encompasses all of the major deserts of the world. Poleward of 30° the amount of precipitation again rises. However, any detailed study of rainfall isohyets (lines joining points of equal precipitation) indicates that geographic factors are even more important than just distance from the equator.

The main source of moisture for precipitation comprises evaporation from the surface of large bodies of water. Therefore precipitation over land tends to be heavier near coastlines, since the air in their vicinity will often be laden with moisture. Local effects can then augment the coastal precipitation. Frictional effects over land are greater, and hence retard winds more strongly, than frictional effects over water. In regions of prevailing onshore winds the sudden slowing of the wind as it hits land produces convergence which leads to ascent and enhanced precipitation. This will be reinforced if there are mountain ranges close inshore — such as the Welsh mountains or the Southern Alps of New Zealand.

Accurate estimation of the quantity and distribution of precipitation at sea has only been possible with satellite-based remote sensing techniques, especially microwave radiometers to be discussed in Chapter 11. These results confirm the dominant rainfall in the tropics – especially at the inter-tropical convergence zone. Yet it is clear that the sea surface temperature exerts a powerful influence on a region's climatology. Areas of persistently low sea surface temperature – such as the strong upwelling region off Peru – have consistently lower rainfall in comparison with other locations at the same latitude. Conversely, areas of warm sea surface temperature encourage large-scale convergence of air masses, vertical ascent and hence precipitation.

Tropical cyclones may form when the sea surface temperature exceeds $27°C$. These intense rotating storms are known as hurricanes in the Atlantic and as typhoons in the North Pacific and Indian oceans. They produce a large area of strong winds and intense rainfall, with rates that can exceed 20 mm hr^{-1} over 4000 km^2. They can be tracked by standard airport radars provided they are sufficiently close, because rain reflects radar signals. Figure 9.2 depicts the radar picture of Tropical Cyclone Joan which caused considerable damage to the Western Australian town of Port Hedland in December 1975. After Joan crossed the coast she produced 600 mm of rain in a 30-hr period, over an area that is otherwise a desert. Rivers and drains were unable to cope with such large discharges and flooded, damaging railway lines and roads.

Evaporation

There is a continual exchange of water molecules at the sea surface. They move backwards and forwards between the water and the atmosphere. Evaporation takes place when more molecules leave the water than return to it. This increases nett water vapour in the atmosphere, and evaporation is the nett loss of water by this molecular motion. On the other hand, if more molecules are moving from air to water, then condensation occurs.

You measure evaporation with a ruler. The amount of water that has disappeared from a standard, vandal-proof, container is the evaporation; provided you have made allowance for any rain that fell in the interim. The most common standard container is a cylindrical pan of unpainted galvanised iron 122 cm in diameter and 25.4 cm deep. This is known as a Class A evaporation pan and usual practice is to fill it to a depth of 20 cm every day, after noting the daily evaporation rate. Many people have investigated whether this measured evaporation rate represents open water conditions. The consensus is that it does not, and that the pan measurement must be multiplied by a coefficient, known as the pan factor, to truly represent open water conditions. The value of this coefficient varies with location and time of year, but is generally about 0.7 in temperate climates. It has been estimated that the oceans lose the equivalent of a 1.25-m layer of water per year through evaporation.

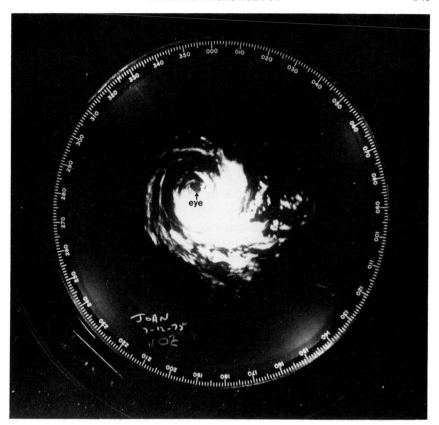

FIG. 9.2. *A tropical cyclone as seen by an airport radar just before the cyclone destroyed it. Areas of active rainfall reflect radar signals and show up as white patches. The heaviest rainfall is in the forward left quadrant (in the Southern Hemisphere) just ahead of the eye.*

The heat energy lost by evaporation is the largest of the three principal oceanic sources of heat loss, being about 97 W m^{-2} (watts per square metre) on average. The other two sources are long-wave radiation — mainly in the infra-red (and hence used in remote estimation of sea surface temperature) — which averages 63 W m^{-2} and sensible heat loss (a term used to cover conduction and convection) which averages 10 W m^{-2}.

Evaporative heat transfer pumps heat energy into the lowest portion of the atmospheric boundary layer. The boundary layer is turbulent and so the energy flux must depend on turbulent fluctuations in specific humidity, q', and in vertical velocity w'. If these two quantities are correlated then the evaporative heat loss can be expressed as

$$E = \rho_a q' w'$$

where $q'w'$ is the mean value of the cross product of the fluctuations, and ρ_a is the air density (Fig. 9.3). This way of considering evaporative energy loss is the turbulent boundary layer approach. Though theoretically attractive, the complexity and cost of instrumentation and analysis prevents this approach being routinely used. Numerous empirical formulas have been derived which express evaporation as a function of atmospheric elements and which parameterise the turbulent transport in some way. Many of these are based on Dalton's law of partial pressure and the form most commonly used in oceanography gives the evaporation loss as

$$E_a \text{ (mm day}^{-1}) = 0.143(e_w - e_a) \, W/100, \tag{9.1}$$

where e_a and e_w are the vapour pressure (in pascals) in the air at ship height (10 m) and at the water surface respectively; and W is the wind speed in m s^{-1}. Equation (9.1), which represents the mass transfer approach, applies only to moderate and strong wind conditions ($W > 5$ m s^{-1}), for if the wind drops to zero, evaporation continues to take place, albeit more slowly. The extension of (9.1) to this situation will be dealt with subsequently.

If water is warmer than the air above it, then the water will heat the air and cause turbulence. Evaporation will also take place and the greatest evaporation occurs when cold air flows over warm water. If the air is very much colder than the water (a situation that can only occur near the coast) then the air becomes saturated and steam fog forms.

When the sea surface is colder than the air above it, both turbulence and evaporation are suppressed. Warm moist air passing over a cold sea surface induces condensation which brings heat energy into the water surface. This

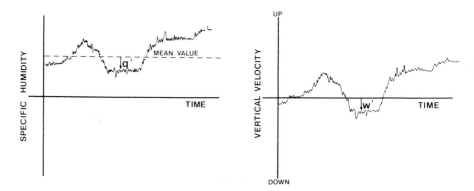

FIG. 9.3. *The turbulent boundary layer approach treats evaporation as a consequence of the fact that humidity fluctuations (q') about their mean value are correlated with vertical wind velocity fluctuations (w') so that wet patches move up whilst dry patches move down.*

situation can also lead to a type of fog, known as advection fog, when contact with the sea lowers the air temperature to dew point.

Maximum evaporation outside of the tropics occurs in winter. This seems contrary to experience that evaporation is greatest from heated water. This is, however, not quite correct. Evaporation is greatest when a water surface is warmer than the air above it. In winter the sea surface outside of the tropics is much warmer than the air and hence evaporation is then a maximum.

Energy Budgets

A third way of studying evaporation is to consider the energy budget required to maintain it. As 2.46×10^6 joules of heat energy are lost with each kilogram of evaporated water, one should be able to calculate evaporation from a knowledge of the heat input and its subsequent transformations.

Energy is imparted to the sea by sunlight (see Chapter 11), with most of the insolation energy being in the visible spectrum. Let us call this Q_S. A certain proportion of this will be reflected — as if the sea surface were a grimy distorted mirror. The total reflected energy we shall represent by AQ_S where A, the proportion reflected, is called the albedo. Finally, lesser amounts of heat energy can reach a particular location through advection, which is transport by streams, currents, rain, snow, and so on. The income of energy to the water, Q_{in} is then

$$Q_{in} = Q_s (1-A) + Q_a \qquad (9.2)$$

which is illustrated in Fig. 9.4a.

Energy is removed from the sea by conduction, convection, radiation and evaporation. A more detailed discussion of insolation and radiation will be deferred until Chapter 11, but for a known water temperature the radiative loss, Q_b, can be calculated. It will be proportional to the fourth power of the absolute temperature. The expenditure of energy is then

$$Q_{ex} = Q_b + Q_e + Q_h, \qquad (9.3)$$

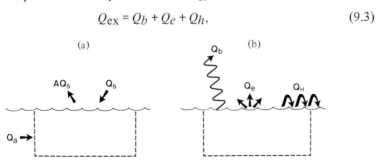

FIG. 9.4. *The energy budget approach to evaporation treats a balance between incoming energy sources:* Q_s *(solar insolation) and* Q_a *(advected heat) and outgoing energy losses:* AQ_s *due to reflection,* Q_e *(evaporation),* Q_h *(sensible heat loss) and* Q_b *(radiation).*

which is schematically illustrated in Fig. 9.4b. Q_e is the energy used in evaporation, and Q_h is the heat energy transferred to the atmosphere by conduction and convection. Q_h which is called the sensible heat, is notoriously difficult to measure.

The most common way to deal with the sensible heat loss is to note that the factors controlling sensible heat transfer are the same as those controlling evaporative heat loss. The ratio between the amount of heat given off to the atmosphere as sensible heat and that used for evaporation is called Bowen's ratio, B, and is often approximated by the formula

$$B = Q_h/Q_e = \gamma\,(T_w - T_a)/(e_w - e_a). \tag{9.4}$$

This formula is trying to make the reasonable point that the conduction and convection processes subsumed into Q_h will depend on the temperature difference, $T_w - T_a$, between water and air, whereas evaporative heat losses, Q_e, depend on the vapour pressure as in equation (9.1). γ is called the psychrometric constant and is generally taken as 64 Pa K^{-1}.

The energy approach to evaporation then equates equations (9.2), (9.3) and (9.4), to obtain an estimate of Q_e. This is then related to the evaporation E, (in m day^{-1}) through the latent heat of vaporisation, L, and the density of water, ρ, as

$$Q_e = \rho LE. \tag{9.5}$$

The latent heat of vaporisation varies slightly with temperature, salinity and atmospheric pressure but is near 2.46×10^6 J kg^{-1}.

Penman Equation

The Penman equation combines the mass transfer and energy budget approaches, to produce a form which can use climatological data to estimate evaporation. It assumes that the total evaporation is due to an energy component, E_n, which is determined solely from incoming and outgoing radiation; and an aerodynamic term, E_a, as given in equation (9.1). The Penman equation combines them to give the total evaporation from the water surface, E, as

$$E = (E_n \Delta + \gamma E_a)/(\Delta + \gamma), \tag{9.6}$$

where γ is, once again, the psychrometric constant and Δ is the vapour pressure gradient at air temperature. These two quantities appear in the definition (equation 9.4) of the Bowen ratio, since $B = \gamma/\Delta$.

The term E_n is the evaporation due solely to radiation:

$$E_n = [Q_s\,(1-A) - Q_b]/\rho L, \tag{9.7}$$

with its units adjusted to agree with those of E_a given by (9.1). The Penman equation sums the aerodynamic and radiative evaporations with weighting factors γ and Δ respectively.

9.3 Winds

When winds blow over the surface of the water they generate waves. This has been discussed on a number of previous occasions, in which we have seen that an anemometer at 10 m height has become the standard wind speed measuring instrument. Since most anemometers are not set to this height, it is necessary to "correct" their readings to an equivalent 10-m reading, W_{10}. This can be done by assuming a form for the vertical velocity profile on the basis of viscous boundary layer theory, but a more convenient form, adequate for most purposes, is to assume

$$\frac{W_{10}}{W} = \left[\frac{10}{z}\right]^k,$$

where z is the anemometer height (in metres) and W is the observed wind speed. The exponent k varies with terrain and atmospheric stability but a rough value of $1/7$ is adequate for most purposes.

In the absence of an anemometer it is possible to estimate the wind speed through the Beaufort Wind Scale (Table 9.1). Recordings of the Beaufort number are surprisingly useful and should not be neglected during a field experiment.

Sea Breeze

Coastal dwellers are well aware of sea breezes. In Perth, Western Australia, the local sea breeze is popularly called the Fremantle Doctor, because on uncomfortably hot summer days it brings relief in the form of a sudden drop in temperature associated with its afternoon arrival from the direction of the Port of Fremantle. The origin of a sea breeze lies in this strong temperature contrast. During daylight hours the land is more rapidly heated and this causes air over land to rise. The cooler air, originally situated over coastal waters, moves in to replace the vertically ascending air over land. This intrusion proceeds gradually and a sea breeze front forms (Fig. 9.5).

Strong sea breeze fronts occur along the Gulf Coast of Texas, along the Australian coastline and, to a lesser extent, in Britain. On large tropical islands the sea breezes coming in from opposite sides often converge towards the centre, resulting in an afternoon maximum of rainfall. The rainfall on Viti Levu, the major island of Fiji, exhibits this pattern. Outside of the tropics the Coriolis deflection causes the onshore sea breeze to turn (clockwise in the Northern Hemisphere; anticlockwise in the Southern Hemisphere) so that eventually it

TABLE 9.1. *Beaufort Scale of Wind Force*

Beaufort number	Wind speed m s^{-1}	Wind description	State	Sea state		Wave height (m)
0	< 0.5	Calm	Still	Mirror-like		0
1	0.5–1.5	Light air	Smoke moves, wind vanes still	Wavelet-scales	Calm seas	
2	2–3	Light breeze	Wind felt on face, leaves rustle	Short waves, none break		0–0.1
3	3.5–5	Gentle breeze	Light flags extended	Foam has glassy appearance, not yet white	Smooth seas	0.1–0.5
4	5.5–8	Moderate breeze	Dust and papers moved	Longer waves with white areas	Slight seas	0.5–1.25
5	8.5–10.5	Fresh breeze	Small trees sway	Long pronounced waves with white foam crests	Moderate seas	1.25–2.5
6	11–13.5	Strong breeze	Large branches move	Large waves, white foam crests all over	Rough seas	2.5–4
7	14–16.5	Moderate gale	Whole trees move	Wind blows foam in streaks		
8	17–20	Gale	Break twigs off trees	Higher waves	Very rough seas	4–6
9	20.5–23.5	Strong gale	Some houses damaged	Dense foam streaks		
10	24–27.5	Whole gale	Trees uprooted	High waves with long over-hanging crests	High seas	6–9
11	28–33	Violent storm	Extensive damage	Ships in sight hidden in wave troughs	Very high seas	9–14
12	> 33	Hurricane	Devastation	Air–sea boundary indistinguishable		over 14

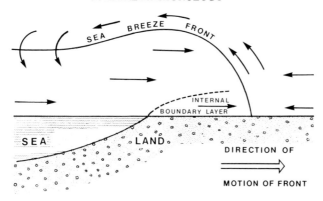

FIG. 9.5. *The vertical structure of a sea breeze front.*
There is a marked change in wind direction and an
abrupt drop in temperature across the front.

blows more or less parallel to the shore. Analogous lake breeze systems develop adjacent to large inland water bodies such as the Great Lakes.

A typical sea breeze has a height of about 1 km and a speed of advance that is related to the temperature difference between the two air masses. They may penetrate 50 km inland, though their strength depends on the terrain over which they travel. Extensive exposed mud-flats attenuate the strength of the front, whereas hills and mountain ranges can enhance it by funnelling the sea breeze through valleys. Figure 9.6 depicts the wind roses for Port Augusta, South Australia. This industrial town is at the head of Spencer Gulf, which has low mountain ranges on both sides. The high ground channels and enhances the sea breeze so that late summer (December to February) afternoons always have strong southerly (northward) sea breezes. These disappear during winter. The seaward extent of a typical sea breeze is unknown, though microwave results, to be shown in Fig. 11.11, suggest that it may be several hundred kilometres.

At night the temperature contrast between land and sea reverses and the air over the sea is warmer. This generates a land breeze that blows in the opposite direction to the sea breeze. Land breezes tend to be weaker, with typical velocities of about 2 m s^{-1} compared to sea breeze velocities of 4–7 m s^{-1}. A significant wind due to other causes can completely mask the land breeze. However, land breezes can sometimes have significant effects. On the coast of the western Mediterranean, particularly near the Straits of Gibraltar, land breezes drive banks of fog out across the coast. These are observed early in the day and are sucked inland and evaporated during the morning.

Storm Surge

The height of high tide and low tide is affected by weather. This produces

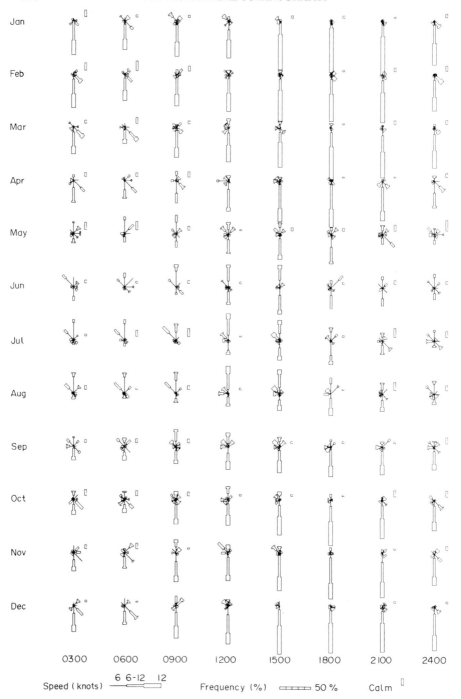

FIG. 9.6. *Average 3-hourly wind roses for Port Augusta, South Australia, based on 2 years of record. The southerly (northward) sea breeze is strongest between 1800 and 2100 in January (summer) but is much weaker in winter.*

the most significant discrepancies between predicted and actual heights of high water and low water at ports and seaside piers. Two major factors are responsible: pressure changes and strong winds. Unfortunately the two effects often come in tandem. Low pressures, which raise the sea surface level, are characteristics of bad weather and storms which are, in turn, always accompanied by strong winds. Onshore winds (i.e. a wind blowing towards the coast) pile up water on the shore and the two effects can pile up sufficient water to cause severe flooding. Very strong offshore winds can occasionally lower the sea level sufficiently to ground vessels in port.

Standard sea level air pressure has been defined as 101.325 kPa. It is due to the weight of the column of air that we know as the atmosphere. During calm periods, with fine weather, a barometer measures air pressure higher than the standard; whereas during severe storms air pressure drops very much lower.

Changes in sea level induced by these barometric changes are small but nevertheless measurable. We can use the hydrostatic equation

$$p = \rho g z$$

to notice that 100 kPa corresponds to 10 m of water, thus for every change of 0.1 kPa (= 1 millibar) there will be a 1-cm change in water level. Because this manifests itself as a rise when the barometer falls, and a sea surface drop when the barometer rises, the link between sea level and atmospheric pressure is sometimes called the inverse barometer effect.

Figure 9.7a shows the barometer trace from Townsville, North Queensland, when the town lay directly in the path of Tropical Cyclone Althea. The pressure

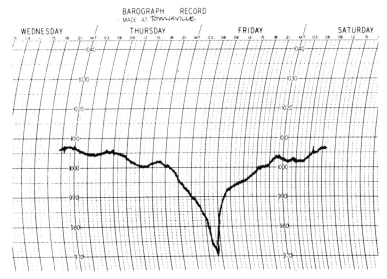

FIG. 9.7(a). *The pressure trace at Townsville whilst it played host to Tropical Cyclone Althea. The maximum storm surge occurred 1 hr after passage of the eye.*

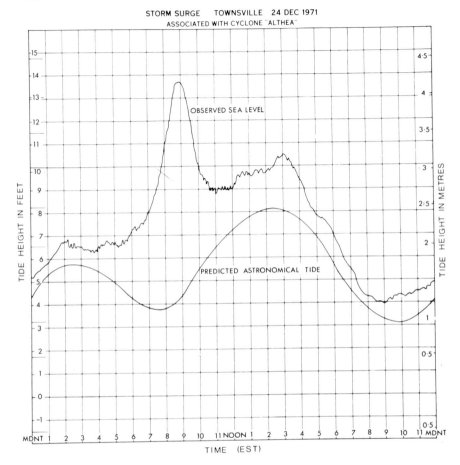

FIG. 9.7(b). *The observed and predicted sea level at Townsville whilst it played host to Tropical Cyclone Althea. The maximum storm surge occurred 1 hr after passage of the eye.*

dropped by 35 millibars, which raised sea level by 35 cm. Figure 9.7b reproduces the Townsville harbour tide gauge record of that day. There was a substantial water pile up, known as a storm surge, when the tropical cyclone crossed from sea to land.

A tropical cyclone is an intense rotating storm of high winds, with a well developed centre (the eye) in which there are very low pressures. In the American region they are known as hurricanes, whereas they are known as typhoons in the Orient. Figure 9.7a shows that tropical cyclone Althea had a minimum pressure of 97 kPa (970 millibars). Compare this to the lowest ever recorded surface pressure of 87 kPa (870 millibars) in a Pacific typhoon.

Northern and Southern Hemisphere tropical cyclones rotate in different directions. Looking down on a tropical cyclone, as in Fig. 9.2, they rotate anticlockwise in the Northern Hemisphere and clockwise in the antipodes. Regions of onshore winds are most dangerous, for it is they that contribute greatly to storm surge. Thus when a tropical cyclone is heading directly towards a coast, prime storm surge candidates lie to the right of the hurricane's direction of motion in the Northern Hemisphere, and to the left of the direction of motion in the Southern Hemisphere.

A tropical cyclone moves at a speed that ranges from 0 to 15 m s^{-1} and it can set up a resonance with the wind waves it generates if the cyclone speed matches the wave speed $\sqrt{gH}$. Thus as well as the water pile-up and the short period wind waves being generated inside the tropical cyclone (waves of greater than 20 m height have been reported in tropical cyclones) there is always the possibility of a swell wave resonance.

The storm surge is the combination of some or all of these effects: (i) the inverse barometer effect during the cyclone's low pressure, (ii) the wind-induced water pile-up produced by the tropical cyclone's very strong winds (iii) the possible resonance of swell waves; and (iv) the effects of wave set-up.

If these occur during an unusually high tide, then the resulting flooding can be devastating of property and of lives. In the Indian subcontinent 300,000 people perished when a typhoon produced extensive flooding in low-lying areas. In the United States, 6000 people died in Galveston, Texas, at the turn of the century due to storm surge induced flooding following the passage of a hurricane.

Sailing Ships

Commercial cargo-carrying sailing ships are reappearing on the oceans. Advances in engineering have made it possible to drive sails mechanically and control them automatically or remotely with a computer. This means that the extensive rigging of old sailing ships is now unnecessary and many problems associated with those old sailing ships have disappeared.

The world's first wind-assisted tanker, the tiny 1600 tonne *Shin-Aitoku Maru* has already entered coastal service in Japan, and it is to be joined by a number of other ships and barges in which both engines and wind power will be jointly used. In strong winds the *Shin-Aitoku Maru* can cruise up to 15 knots (7.2 m s^{-1}) under the sole power of its two 12-m by 8-m plastic sails. In lesser winds it will operate mainly with engines and sails combined for maximum fuel economy. The sails use a vertical furling system along with a hard rectangular sail of aerofoil wing section with symmetric camber. The driving system for the sails consists of two small hydraulic pumps and hydraulic actuators tied into an automatic control system relying on wind sensors and a gyroscope.

One of the greatest boons to the future development of ocean-going sail-powered ships has been the development of weather satellites. A ship equipped with real-time satellite reception can chart its course so as to take advantage of the most favourable wind conditions.

9.4 Aerosols

When waves break, bubbles of air are trapped to produce a characteristic white foam. These bubbles provide the major source of oxygen, carbon dioxide, sulphur dioxide and other gases dissolved in the ocean. Further, their bursting at the sea surface causes droplets of water to be ejected upwards several centi-metres into the atmosphere. When winds are strong, they are joined by plumes of spray torn from wave crests.

Large droplets do not stay airborne for long and small droplets soon evaporate. However, the salt particles which remain in the air after the water has evaporated (and been wafted away) are lifted by turbulence and convection and transported great distances by wind. They participate as condensation nuclei in the hydro-logical cycle and hence encourage rain which returns them to the ocean. Salt encrustation during hurricane force winds is a little appreciated consequence of this. Large areas of Perth, Western Australia, were blacked out during the south-ward passage of Tropical Cyclone Alby when the equipment at the city's major power station (situated on the coast) became completely clogged up with salt.

Salt spray is composed of comparatively huge particles. Much more common are very tiny particles less than one-tenth of a micrometre in diameter. For every "giant" dust or salt particle more than 1 m across there may be a thousand or more very tiny ones. All of these particles, salt, smoke, dust, that are larger than molecular size are called aerosols. They are of particularly meteorological interest because of their effects on clouds, and hence, possibly, climate.

The majority of small aerosol particles consist of ammonium sulphate or sulphuric acid (acid rain). In heavily populated regions of the United States and Europe most of them derive from industrial pollution. There are a number of other natural sources, the most important of which are intertidal areas along the coast. Aerosols form from dimethyl sulphide gas given off by drying marine algae exposed at low tide. Part of the evidence for this is the large increase in aerosol particle numbers over the Australian Great Barrier Reef.

Coastal Air Pollution

Of course, the aerosol contribution from major industrial centres far exceeds that from natural sources. The smoke from large chimneys is a major producer of sulphur dioxide and hence of acid rain. Usually the smoke plume from a large stack is carried downwind and is dispersed laterally by random air motions in a similar manner to the turbulent dispersion of water particles. However, smoke from stacks located in coastal areas will be dispersed by the sea breeze in ways which are, as yet, poorly understood. One problem, for example, is that the apparent ventilation effects of a morning land breeze or other offshore wind are spurious. The pollutants carried out to sea in the morning will be returned by the sea breeze in the afternoon.

Another form of air pollution, unique to coastal locations, is known as shoreline fumigation (Fig. 9.8). During sea breezes, or other onshore winds, the air over the water will be cool and relatively stable. As soon as it arrives over land it is heated by the warmer land and starts to convect. This forms a turbulent coastal internal boundary layer, which will spread pollutant throughout its volume. This type of spreading is known as fumigation — the name given to a plume which disperses downwards but not upwards. Localities situated downwind of a coastal stack, and some distance from it, are thus likely to suffer larger air pollution than those quite close to the stack.

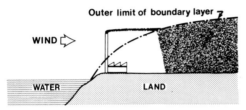

FIG. 9.8. *Intense air pollution episodes, known as fumigation, may arise from a coastal internal boundary layer formed during onshore winds. Smoke from an industrial stack spreads to the ground as soon as it penetrates the boundary layer.*

9.5 Oil Spills

Accidental oil spills have occurred quite frequently and have received much public attention. Table 9.2 lists a selection of spills over 2000 tonnes (1 tonne = 1000 kg) between 1967 and early 1979. The damage that results from oil spilled from ships or platforms is usually local and of limited duration. However, the effects of exceptionally large spills; such as those from the *Amoco Cadiz* or *Torrey Canyon*, which led respectively to spillages of 230,000 and 117,000 tonnes, can persist for several years. Damage to fish, plankton, sea birds and other organisms may result. This leads in turn to the impairment of fishing and shellfish farming. These spills may also result in damage to beaches and shorelines leading to losses in the hotel and tourist trades and in amenities.

Although the probability of tanker accidents throughout the oceans is relatively low, the risk increases considerably where traffic is heavy. Moreover, the damage is likely to be serious if accidents happen close to coasts where economic activities are concentrated. This is the case in the Channel, the North Sea, and along the United States eastern seaboard, all of which are important centres of fishing and tourism. Prevention, in the form of agreements on navigation, is

TABLE 9.2. *Selected Large Oil Spills in Coastal Waters*

Year	Polluter	Amount of oil released tonnes	Affected area	Type of accident
1967	Torrey Canyon	117,000	UK/France	Went aground
1967	R. C. Stoner	20,000	North Pacific	Went aground
1968	Ocean Eagle	12,000	USA (Puerto Rico)	Went aground
1969	Santa Barbara Platform	6000	USA (west coast)	Blew out
1970	Texaco Oklahoma	31,500	USA	Went aground
1970	Polycammandeur	16,000	Spain	Went aground
1970	Arrow	10,000	Canada (east coast)	Went aground
1970	Chevron Platform	10,000	USA (Mex. Gulf)	Caught fire
1970	Pacific Glory v. Allegro	6300	United Kingdom	Collided
1970	Ocean Grandeur	2500	Australia	Went aground
1971	Juliana	7000	Japan	Went aground
1971	Oregon Standard	3000	USA (west coast)	Collided
1973	Javvackta	16,000	Sweden	Went aground
1974	Mitzushima Refinery	8000	Japan	Leaked
1974	Yuyo Maru	3000	Japan	Collided
1974	Universe Leader	2500	Ireland	Terminal Oper.
1974	Saglek	2000	Canada (east coast)	Terminal Oper.
1975	Spartan Lady	20,000	North Atlantic	Sank
1975	Showa Maru	7000	Singapore Straits	Went aground
1975	Olympic Alliance v. HMS Achilles	2100	United Kingdom	Collided
1975	Allied Chemical Barge	2000	USA (east coast)	Sank
1976	Urquiola	100,000	Spain	Exploded
1976	Argo Merchant	25,000	USA (east coast)	Went aground
1976	Boelhen	10,000	France	Went aground
1976	Sealift Pacific	4200	USA (Alaska)	Went aground
1976	Barge in Chesapeake Bay	2700	USA (east coast)	Sank
1977	Grand Zenith	32,000	Canada (east coast)	Sank
1977	Ekofisk Platform	21,300	North Sea	Blew out
1977	Irenes Challenge	19,000	North Pacific	Sank
1978	Amoco Cadiz	230,000	France	Went aground
1978	Heleni V v. Roseline	4000	United Kingdom	Collided
1979	Andros Patria	60,000	Spain	Caught fire
1979	Betelgeuse	35,000	Ireland	Terminal Oper.

increasingly seen as the best means of dealing with pollution from tanker accidents.

Although spills are often dramatic, land based sources of oil pollution are much more significant. These include operations at terminals and in ports and also oily water discharges from off-shore platforms. Such discharges, because they take place constantly, can cause major changes in affected areas.

Fate of an Oil Spill

When oil is spilled, its rate of dispersion is a function of air–sea dynamics, chemical and physical properties of the oil and the magnitude of the spill. At

least two major effects — the motion of the oil, and its evaporation — are controlled by meteorological factors. There are eight primary processes that occur
following a spill:

(i) *Spreading and motion*

If a large quantity of oil is discharged into the water it spreads out, on the
water's surface, into a large slick. There are three stages (Fig. 9.9) in this spreading
process. In the first stage the spread is driven by gravity as the original thick
patch of oil spreads into an even layer. A second stage is reached during which
viscous forces dominate. This stage continues until the oil is a monomolecular
slick when surface tension effects control its spread.

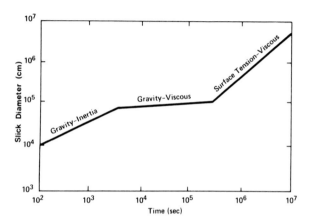

FIG. 9.9. *The three phases of oil slick spreading
based on a 10,000-tonne spill. The duration of
each phase depends on the amount spilled.*

During all three of these spreading phases, the shape and direction of movement of the oil slick depends upon the wind, surface currents, waves and
Langmuir cell circulations. As a very rough first approximation, the velocity,
U_O, of the centre of mass of the oil moves as the vector sum of the surface
current U_c and a fraction, ζ, of the wind velocity W:

$$U_O = U_c + \zeta W.$$

The fraction ζ is the wind factor, whereas the wind-induced drift ζW is called the
leeway. We can obtain a rough estimate for the wind factor from some simple
fluid dynamical reasoning. Assume that the wind stress is continuous across the

surface of the oil and that the drag coefficients on both media are identical. We can equate stress equations of the form of equation (7.1) to give

$$\zeta = \sqrt{\rho_a / \rho_{oil}},$$

where ρ_a is the density of air (1.3 kg m^{-3}) and ρ_{oil} is the density of oil, which ranges from 700 kg m^{-3} to 980 kg m^{-3} depending on its composition. The wind factor, which is about 4% of the wind speed, is high enough to generally dominate the slick's motion.

(ii) *Evaporation*

The greater the rate and extent of spreading, the greater is the evaporation. Evaporation can remove about 50% of the hydrocarbons in an average light crude oil spill within 10 days so that the remains resemble a heavy crude oil.

(iii) *Solution*

Wind and wave action will also drive the low molecular weight hydrocarbons into a solution with water. The most soluble fractions are also those most toxic to marine life.

(iv) *Emulsification*

The insoluble components of petroleum emulsify into two forms: oil-in-water emulsions composed of fine particles of oil ("sweating and beading") and water-in-oil emulsions which are coherent semisolid lumps ("chocolate mousse").

(v) *Direct sea–air exchange*

Wave-produced spray and bursting bubbles will transfer petroleum hydrocarbons into the air in the same manner that salt particles are deposited there.

(vi) *Photochemical oxidation*

Sunlight-induced chemical changes harden the oil.

(vii) *Sedimentation*

As evaporation proceeds, the density of the remaining oil increases. If this heavier oil is mixed through the water column it can be deposited onto particulate sediment and settle, or alternatively it can attach onto particulate matter at the surface during rough seas in shallow water. These particles eventually settle to the bottom when the seas become calmer. It does not take too much to sink a heavy crude oil of density 980 kg m^{-3}.

Environmental Effects

There are various levels of biological effects of oil. At various places in the marine environment and at various times these will be accorded different priorities in the evaluation of their impact. These effects include the possibility of

(i) Human hazard through eating contaminated seafood.

(ii) Decrease of fisheries resource or damage to wildlife such as seabirds and marine mammals.

(iii) Decrease of aesthetic values due to unsightly slicks or oiled beaches.

(iv) Modification of the marine ecosystem by elimination of species with an initial decrease in diversity and productivity.

(v) Modification of habitats, delaying or preventing recolonisation.

In preparing environmental impact statements the risks of an oil spill need to be estimated. If possible, these should be quantified in probabilistic terms. When an actual oil spillage occurs, then a different approach is needed. There is then a great premium on accurate forecasts of the speed and direction of that particular slick as well as of its spreading rate. Based on that information the best method of clean-up has to be determined and implemented. We should add here that finding the oil once it has been spilt is not the simple task that one would first suppose. Whilst the slick is fairly thick it exhibits colour effects and there is no problem. Once it forms a monolayer, however, the best methods of detecting it rely on remote sensing techniques.

As oil moves into a bay, or onto a beach, its spreading is reversed and it tends to thicken. The reason is that onshore winds and waves will drive the oil onshore so that it continues to float in a trapped pool, part of which deposited on the beach when the tide ebbs. A large monolayer can still cause substantial pollution.

9.6 Coastal Lows

We have described the structure of a sea breeze front in Fig. 9.5. These fronts, which occur during summer in temperate latitudes, are only one type of coastal meteorological front. Meteorologists in the north-eastern part of the United States use the term coastal front to describe the winter-time phenomenon depicted in Fig. 9.10.

The two essential ingredients in the formation of the New England coastal front are the coastal low-pressure region (cyclone) which propagates up the coast and a high-pressure system (anticyclone) situated to the north of the region where the coastal front will form. This anticyclone brings cold arctic air to the New England seaboard which is banked up into a shallow dome east of the mountains in central New England. The coastal front is the boundary between this pool of cold air and the relatively warm air moving landward under the

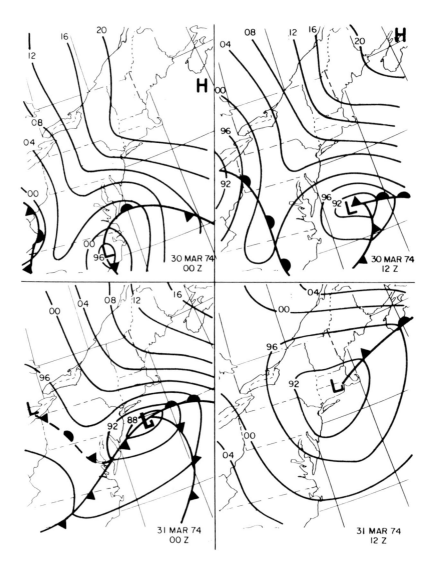

FIG. 9.10. *Surface synoptic weather maps at 12-hr intervals display the progression of a New England coastal front and its associated low-pressure system.*

influence of the low-pressure system. The front itself is marked by a substantial temperature difference and by a region of greatly enhanced rainfall.

The passage of the coastal low up the American east coast prior to the formation of the coastal front is especially interesting. A low-pressure system hugging the coast in this way is reminiscent of a Kelvin wave (Chapter 3.6) except for the embarrassing fact that it propagates the wrong way. In the Northern Hemisphere a Kelvin wave must have the coast on the right-hand side of its direction of propagation. However, a similar coastal low has been observed during South African winters that propagates down the west side of southern Africa, rounds the Cape and travels up the east side. Because this coastal low propagates in the appropriate direction it has been identified as a baroclinic Kelvin wave in the atmosphere.

The Kelvin wave is baroclinic because the coastal low occurs in conjunction with an upper level temperature inversion at a height of about 1 km. Prior to the arrival of the coastal low the region below the inversion is well mixed, well ventilated and subject only to light winds. Passage of the coastal low drops the height of the well-mixed layer which reduces its ventilation and produces enhanced air pollution in urban centres.

The propagation speed of a baroclinic, or internal, Kelvin wave is $\sqrt{gH_e}$, where H_e is its equivalent depth (Chapter 3.7) which depends on the density structure of the atmosphere. It is thus conceivable that the coastal low of Fig. 9.10 is indeed an internal Kelvin wave if the atmospheric density structure were such that H_e over the sea was very much smaller than H_e over the land. A Kelvin wave can propagate along any sharp change in depth (or equivalent depth) and in this case it propagates with the shallower region, or region of lesser equivalent depth, on its right-hand side in the Northern Hemisphere.

The Southerly buster is another coastal phenomenon that exhibits a mixture of the characteristics of coastal lows and coastal fronts. It is a front that propagates northward up the south-east coast of Australia, which means that its direction corresponds to that of Kelvin wave propagation. The inhabitants of Sydney – known for some queer reason as Sydneysiders – look forward to the Southerly buster (one of them even wrote a popular song about it) because it brings cool showery weather after hot, humid summer heat. On the other hand, an unexpected arrival of the Southerly buster causes havoc amongst Sydney harbour yacht races.

Further Reading

The inter-relation between sea and atmosphere is dealt with in a number of books. At a suitable general level there are:

A. H. PERRY and J. M. WALKER: *The Ocean-Atmosphere system*, Longman, London 1977,
J. G. HARVEY: *Atmosphere and Ocean*, Artemis Press, London 1976,

whereas advanced level texts include:

H. U. ROLL: *Physics of the Marine Atmosphere*, Academic Press, New York 1965.

E. B. KRAUS: *Atmosphere-Ocean Interaction*, Oxford University Press, Oxford, 1972.

The hydrological cycle is best discussed in hydrology or climatology texts, for example:

W. D. SELLERS: *Physical Climatology*, University of Chicago Press, Chicago, 1965.

J. P. BRUCE & R. H. CLARK: *Introduction to Hydrometeorology*, Pergamon, Oxford 1966.

R. K. LINSLEY, M. A. KOHLER & J. L. H. PAULHUS: *Hydrology for Engineers* (2nd edition), McGraw-Hill, New York, 1975.

An overview of current research activities in coastal meteorology may be obtained from the preprints of papers presented at the Conferences on Coastal Meteorology. These were held in 1976 and 1980 and the preprints are obtained from the American Meteorological Society, 45 Beacon St., Boston, Mass.

For further discussions on oil spills the reader is referred to:

NATIONAL ACADEMY OF SCIENCES: *Petroleum in the Marine Environment*, National Academy of Sciences, Washington, D.C., 1975.

CHAPTER 10

Estuaries and Reefs

10.1 Introduction

Estuaries present one of the greatest challenges to environmental scientists, managers and planners. They are important parts of the coastal ecosystem because their enclosed nature often protects them from extreme winds and extreme waves and because they provide a rich source of nourishment. Estuaries are often popular resorts for humans, whereas the high biological productivity of estuaries with marsh wetlands and mangrove swamps makes them popular breeding grounds for various fish and shellfish. Trade and industry find certain estuaries attractive locations in which to develop because they make fine sea ports. In many cases this has generated large-scale alteration of the natural balance within the estuary through dredging, which alters the general shape, or through large-scale pollution. If mankind is not to do undue damage to his environment it is essential to understand and be able to predict these effects.

Tidal variations, irregular geometry, river flow, sediment transport, chemical pollution and a specialised aquatic ecosystem interact to produce complicated mechanisms and behaviour patterns. Various classification schemes exist to try to make some sense of all these interactions. Many different schemes are possible depending on the particular estuarine behaviour under study. It is possible to classify estuaries in terms of their biology, their geomorphology, their sediment character or their hydrology, and different schemes exist within each of these categories.

It is even hard to find an acceptable definition of an estuary. One simple view is to state that an estuary is where a river meets the sea. Unfortunately, a river can meet the sea without involving an estuary. Hydrologists prefer to think of it as "a semi-enclosed body of water having a free connection with the open sea and within which seawater is measurably diluted with freshwater derived from land drainage". The weakness in this definition is that there are many estuaries in Texas and Western Australia in which low river discharge and high evaporation combine to produce hypersaline water whose salinity exceeds that of seawater. One eminent authority has even suggested that it may be more appropriate to say that estuaries are something like pornography — hard to define exactly, but we know one when we see one.

10.2 Geomorphological Classification of Estuaries

Estuaries are often grouped on the basis of geological and geomorphological criteria. This method divides estuaries into three major types: coastal plain estuaries (which includes rias), deep estuaries (fjords) and lagoon estuaries (bayous and limans).

Coastal Plain Estuaries

River deltas, drowned river valleys and embayments on the sites of submerged coastal lowlands may all be termed coastal plain estuaries. The branched inlets formed by partial submergence of deep river valleys have been termed rias, and are well exemplified by Sydney Harbour, San Francisco Bay and any other similar branched inlet.

A typical ria consists of an estuary with several tributary rivers which may form estuaries in themselves. Alternatively, one can have an estuary with a single principal river at its head gradually opening into the sea at its mouth. The head of an estuary is defined as the upper limit of tidal penetration and in certain estuaries there is an abrupt widening of the inflowing river where this occurs.

Fjords

Inlets formed by the submergence of the mouths of formerly glaciated valleys on steep coasts are known as fjords and may be found on the coasts of Canada, New Zealand, Greenland, Norway, Scotland, Chile and Siberia. Most of these consist of deep, almost rectangular, basins with a sill: that is a region at the seaward end which is shallower than both the main basin and the sea outside. River discharge is small compared with the total fjord volume so that a typical fjord will have a thin layer of freshwater overlaying a large quantity of deep, salt water.

The whole of the Baltic sea is a fjord-like estuary and it suffers from the problem of stagnant bottom water. This is associated with the blocking effects of a sill, and with strong water stability due to density variations. The stagnant water does not mix with the fluid above. This, in turn, cuts off the supply of oxygen from the aerated surface water, and the deeper layers may ultimately become completely exhausted of oxygen. This has been a progressive development in the Baltic over the past 75 years. One station, at a depth of 160 m in the central Baltic, shows an oxygen saturation decrease from 30% to near 0% during this period. There are fears that the Baltic deep water may soon become devoid of life.

Lagoons

Coastal lagoons are bar built estuaries formed by the build up, through sedimentation or wave action, of a spit, barrier island or bar. They occur all over the world in tropical and temperate climes and the term estuarine lagoon covers both a river-fed coastal lagoon and the embayments that may exist behind it, as illustrated in Fig. 10.1.

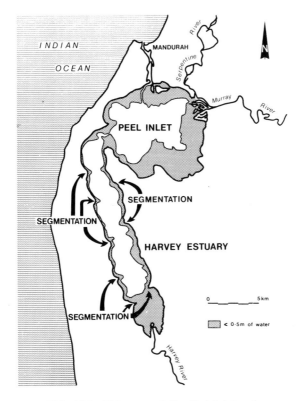

FIG. 10.1. *This map of the Peel Inlet and Harvey Estuary in Western Australia shows the process of segmentation which is dividing the Harvey Estuary lagoon into enclosed embayments.*

The configuration of lagoon entrances is the outcome of a contest between (i) the currents that flow through them, tending to keep them clear and (ii) the effects of onshore and longshore drifting of sand or shingle, which tend to seal them off. The position and dimensions of lagoon entrances change frequently in response to variations in these processes and some have been stabilised by the construction of bordering breakwaters.

The dimensions of lagoon entrances influence the extent to which tides invade a lagoon and the salinity variations within it. Changes to the entrance may, in turn, affect aquatic vegetation within it. Near the entrance, banks of sediment are exposed at low tide and the shores may be bordered by encroaching salt marshes and mangrove swamps. Away from the entrance, where the water is brackish and tidal fluctuations diminish, encroachment by salt marsh or mangrove swamp is much reduced. Mangroves, in particular, require regular tidal inundation.

Wind direction and lagoon shape interplay to control sedimentary processes within a lagoon. Winds blowing over the lagoon cause waves and currents which are related to wind direction and strength, and the lengths of fetch across which these winds are effective. Long, narrow lagoons experience strongest wave action when the wind blows along the longest dimension giving the maximum fetch. If the shores are not protected by vegetation, waves coming in at an angle move sediment to and fro along the beaches, eroding embayments and building up spits, cusps and cuspate forelands which may grow to such an extent that the lagoon becomes divided into a series of small, round or oval lagoons (Fig. 10.1). This process is called *segmentation* and is essentially an adjustment of lagoon forms to patterns more closely related to waves and currents generated within the lagoon. Currents play a part in smoothing the curved outlines of the shore in the later stages of segmentation and may also maintain the connecting straits between segmented bays. But strong tidal currents deflect spit growth and inhibit the segmentation process.

10.3 Estuarine Hydrology

From a physical viewpoint the two most important variables controlling estuarine water are the amount of mixing between fresh water and salt water and the rate at which the mixing takes place. These are, in turn, controlled by six factors: river inflow, precipitation, evaporation, tidal variations, wind strength and estuarine topography.

Figure 10.2 depicts the data obtained from weekly sampling of the Peel Inlet of Western Australia. This is a shallow estuary that is only 2.5 m at its deepest point. It is an estuarine lagoon, or actually an estuarine embayment, connected to the sea by a narrow channel. Because the tidal range on the Western Australian coast is slight, and because the narrow entrance channel chokes the tidal flows, the water in the estuary does not respond to the diurnal or semidiurnal tides, but is only affected by longer period variations in water level; such as those due to shelf waves, or meteorological perturbations. Let us now examine each of the above-mentioned six factors and see how they control the hydrology of the Peel Inlet.

Rainfall and Run Off

Figure 10.2 indicates the extreme variability of river flow into an estuary. In this particular case, long drought periods were interspersed with short, sudden

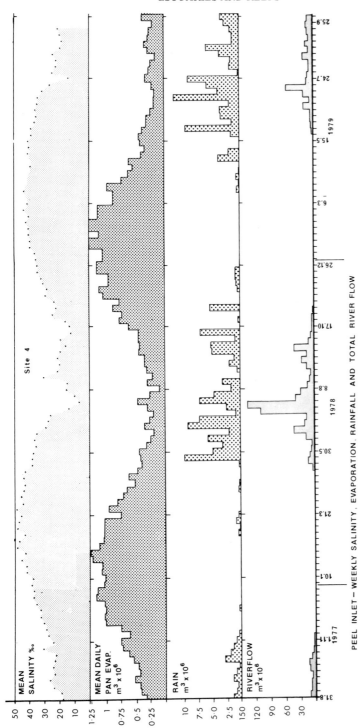

PEEL INLET – WEEKLY SALINITY, EVAPORATION, RAINFALL AND TOTAL RIVER FLOW

FIG. 10.2. *Weekly measurements of salinity, evaporation, rainfall and river flow in the Peel Inlet show marked seasonal effects between summer (dry) and winter (wet). The rainfall and evaporation measurements have been multiplied by the surface area of the inlet so that water volumes may be directly compared.*

flows. These flows are the river's response to the rainfall in the catchment area, but a river will only start to flow when the soil no longer absorbs the rain falling on it. Thus a large isolated rainstorm will produce far less run off than a succession of more modest storms that saturate the ground and fall over a large part of the catchment.

Table 10.1 lists the mean flow from some of the major rivers of the world.

TABLE 10.1. *Mean Annual Discharge and Suspended Sediment Load of Major Rivers*

River	Location of mouth	Catchment area (Mm²)	Mean flow (m³ s⁻¹)	Sediment load (Tg)
	S. America			
Amazon	Brazil	6.06	237,000	400
Orinoco	Venezuela	0.94	29,600	95
Parana	Argentina	2.28	19,500	90
	Africa			
Congo	Congo	3.97	51,000	71
Nile	Egypt	2.95	3900	122
	Asia			
Yellow	China	0.66	2000	2,080
Yangtze	China	1.92	28,500	550
Ganges	India	0.95	15,400	1,600
	N. America			
Mississippi-Missouri	USA	4.54	25,900	580
St. Lawrence	Canada	1.27	18,500	4
	Europe			
Volga	USSR	1.34	10,500	21
Danube	USSR	0.81	8000	21
	Australasia			
Fly	New Guinea	0.05	6000	118

Note	1 Mm²	= 10⁶ km²	= 10¹² m²
	1 Tg	= 10⁶ tonnes	= 10¹² g.

These flows are much smaller than typical oceanic and coastal currents so that, with the possible exception of the Amazon, river flow affects only local estuarine and coastal circulations. Furthermore, Table 10.1 masks the huge year-to-year variations in the flow of major rivers. The Danube has a minimum annual mean flow of 200 m^3 s^{-1} and a maximum annual mean flow of 19,200 m^3 s^{-1}. This range is typical enough for a large perennial river, but in general the smaller the river the greater is its flow variability.

As a river flows down into the sea it will continually displace the estuarine water and replace it with new river water. If the river flows fast this will happen quickly, whereas the displacement will be slow if the flow is sluggish. A rough measure of the time taken to replace the estuarine water is the flushing time, t_f, defined by

$$t_f = V/Q, \tag{10.1}$$

where V is the estuarine volume and Q is the river flow. It is a rough measure because it assumes that the river flows uniformly over its complete cross-section and displaces estuarine water over this whole cross-section. Genuine river flow is rarely like that, so that satisfactory ways of describing estuarine flushing remain an area of active research.

Rainfall, Evaporation and Wind

In arid parts of the world, and in the tropics where there are distinct wet and dry seasons, estuarine hydrology is influenced by daily evaporation and by the effects of rain falling directly on the estuary. Of course, when the rain is sufficiently widespread, or sufficiently prolonged, to start rivers flowing, then riverine effects dominate, but at other times the balance between rainfall and evaporation will dominate the salinity of the estuary, as in Fig. 10.2.

Wind will affect both the circulation and the salinity structure of an estuary. A sufficiently strong wind blowing long enough over all but the deepest estuaries will totally mix the water from top to bottom and will induce a windward flow at the surface and a return flow underneath. Short wind episodes can set up seiches within an estuary.

Tides

The volume of water in an estuary with an open connection to the sea will rise and fall with the rise and fall of the tides. At high tide, marshes will be covered; at low tides, mudflats exposed. The volume of water entering an estuary between low tide and the next high tide, due to tidal processes, is called the *tidal prism*. The tidal prism is approximately equal to the tidal range multiplied by the mean surface area of the estuary.

In estuaries subject to strong tides, estimates of the tidal prism can be used to estimate the extent of mixing and the resulting salinity distribution. One assumes that on the flood tide the volume of seawater entering the estuary is entirely of oceanic salinity and that it is completely mixed with a corresponding volume of estuarine water. On the ebb tide this entire quantity of mixed water is completely removed from the estuary, and on the next flood tide the process is repeated with seawater of oceanic salinity. For a given freshwater inflow and tidal prism one can then calculate the estuarine salinity.

In general we do not expect complete mixing for the entire estuary during each tidal cycle, and we also anticipate that some of the mixed water will return on each succeeding flood tide. Box models allow for this by dividing the estuary into segments, over which the mixing takes place, rather than assuming that there is complete mixing over the length of the entire estuary during each tidal cycle.

Another important characteristic of tidal flows in shallow water, but one not at all obvious to the casual observer, is that superimposed on the back-and-forth flow is a nett, steady circulation, often called the "residual circulation". Most estuaries have flood channels in which the flood current is stronger and ebb channels in which the ebb current is stronger. The process whereby a preferential direction is set up for the residual circulation is known as tidal pumping. In large estuaries (i.e. when the width exceeds the product of the inertial period and the tidal current speed) it is caused by the Coriolis deflection to the right in the Northern Hemisphere and to the left in the Southern Hemisphere. Therefore, in the Southern Hemisphere, flood tide currents are deflected toward the right bank (looking seaward) and ebb currents towards the left bank, resulting in a nett clockwise circulation.

A second cause of residual circulation is the interaction of the tidal flow with the irregular bathymetry found in most estuaries. An example is an estuarine lagoon with a narrow entrance. The flood tide is forced to enter as a narrow jet, but the ebb flow comes from all around the mouth (and, of course, produces a jet of water into the sea). Averaging within the estuary over a tidal cycle yields an inward flow in the area of the jet and an outward flow elsewhere.

Another common example of a pumped circulation is the nett flow around islands – or submerged banks – or in braided channels. An oscillatory tidal current flowing over an irregular bottom topography induces residual vortices, and various combinations of channel geometry can induce pumped gyres in most large bays.

Vertical Structure

Estuaries can be divided into four hydrographic types according to the degree of vertical mixing exhibited by their salt concentration: (a) vertically well mixed, (b) partially stratified, (c) strongly stratified and (d) salt wedge estuaries. Unlike open coastal waters, in which density differences arise predominantly from temperature changes, it is a characteristic of estuaries that the dominant density variations arise from salinity differences. The vertical stratification is one of haloclines, and the longitudinal variation of seawater at the mouth and freshwater at the head of the estuary produces a longitudinal density gradient as well. The salinity distributions in these four types are shown in Fig. 10.3 in two ways. In the left-hand column of graphs the property distributions are shown as vertical profiles of salinity, at each of four stations, between the head and the mouth of the estuary, as shown in the schematic plan view at the top. The right-hand column shows simplified longitudinal sections of salinity from head to mouth for the full depth of the estuary.

The vertically well-mixed estuary (type A, Fig. 10.3) is shallow and the water

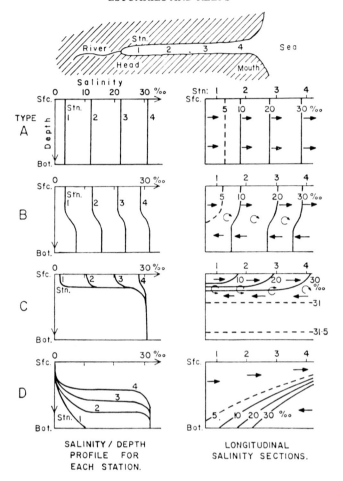

FIG. 10.3. *Typical salinity/depth profiles and longitudinal salinity sections in estuaries corresponding to A: well mixed; B: partially stratified; C: strongly stratified and D: salt wedge conditions.*

is mixed vertically by a combination of winds, tides and riverflow; so that it is homogeneous from top to bottom at any particular place along the estuary. The salinity increases with distance along the estuary from head to mouth. The river water in such an estuary flows towards the mouth while the salt progresses from the sea toward the head by means of a longitudinal dispersion. In the right-hand figure the vertical isohalines indicate the homogeneity of the water at each location, while the arrows indicate that the direction of nett water flow is seaward at all depths.

A partially stratified estuary (type B) is also usually shallow. The salinity increases from head to mouth at all depths. The water is essentially in two layers with the upper layer a little less saline than the deeper one, and a mixing layer between them. This type of estuary exhibits what has come to be thought of as the "typical" estuarine circulation in which there is a nett seaward or outward flow of the upper layer and a nett inward up-estuary flow in the bottom layer. In addition to this flow, at both levels there is vertical mixing both of fresh and salt water giving rise to the longitudinal variation of salinity in both layers. The circular arrows in the salinity section indicate this mixing.

In the highly stratified estuary (type C), of which fjords are typical, the upper layer increases in salinity from about zero, in the river at the head, to a value close to that of the outside sea at the mouth. The deep water, however, is of almost uniform salinity from head to mouth. This indicates that there is a unidirectional vertical mixing of saltwater into the upper layer. This is a characteristic of turbulent entrainment (section 8.3) and is a consequence of the stagnant deep water being entrained into the moving, wind-stirred, upper layer. Again, there is a nett outflow in the upper layer and inflow in the deeper water. In these estuaries there is a very strong halocline between the upper water and the deep water, particularly at the head where strong vertical salinity gradients may occur in summer during the period of greatest river run off whilst the snows melt.

The longitudinal section for the salt wedge estuary (type D) indicates the reason for its name. The saline water intrudes, from the sea, as a wedge below the river water. This situation usually occurs when the effects of river flow dominate tidal effects, whilst the wind is too weak to completely mix the estuary. It should be noted that, as usual, the section in Fig. 10.3 is exaggerated in the vertical direction; the salt wedge is really a very thin one so that the isohalines are, in fact, almost horizontal except at the nose of the wedge. At the nose, the point of maximum penetration, the isohalines drop sharply to the bottom. The salt wedge estuary shares many features in common with stratified estuaries. The major difference is in the lack of a salinity gradient at the surface, the water there being fresh, or nearly so, until it debouches into the sea.

10.4 Estuarine Pollution

One of the most visible manifestations of degraded water quality are "fish kills". A particularly graphic example occurred during a drought in 1951 when 500,000 eels (*Anguilla reinhardtii*) and 5,000,000 sea mullet (*Mugil cephalus*) were crammed into a 1.5×10^4 m^3 stretch of the Lane Cove River near Sydney.

At this time there were a number of factories which discharged sulphur compounds and nucleoproteins into the Lane Cove River. Natural putrefaction converted these into hydrogen sulphide (H_2S) and inorganic phosphate, whilst the process of putrefaction used up large amounts of the oxygen in the water. Also at this time, about 3 km upstream from the factories, there was a weir on the river which separated the upper reaches — composed of freshwater — from the brackish water below the weir. Lack of heavy rain decreased the freshwater overflow from the weir, until by April 1951 it was restricted to part of a small spillway. The brackish water below the weir began to emit an unpleasant odour (not of H_2S) and eels and mullet began to congregate near the weir.

As the rainless period continued and the spillway became quite dry, the fish began to die, frequently with bleeding and blackening of the gills. A few of the eels were observed to congregate near cracks in the weir as though to immerse themselves in the freshwater trickling through. Indeed, water analyses indicated that the dissolved oxygen (DO) immediately above the spillway was normal (see Fig. 5.5), whereas there was no detectable DO in the brackish waters within 5 m of the spillway.

The moral of the above tale, and one far better appreciated nowadays than it was 30 years ago, is that pollution loadings in estuaries need to be related to the flushing ability of the estuary. In many cases this is recognised by permitting liquids to be discharged in a "one in twenty" discharge. This means that waste liquid may be discharged at 1 m^3 s^{-1} when the river flows at 20 m^3 s^{-1}. The permitted discharge rate will primarily depend on the toxicity of the pollutant.

Sediments

There are seven possible sediment sources within an estuary:

(i) land erosion by rivers and streams. Table 10.1 gives estimates of these;
(ii) disposal of domestic and industrial effluents and solid wastes;
(iii) littoral drift and bank erosion;
(iv) wind erosion of coastal dunes and drying intertidal shoals;
(v) erosion of the near-shore continental shelf;
(vi) return of dredged spoil; and
(vii) decomposition and excretions of marine and river plants and animals.

In the Hjulstrom curve of Fig. 2.8 we saw that a river needs a large flow velocity for it to carry a sediment load. In fact, it is the occasional high flow episode that may only recur every 5 years or longer that brings the predominant sediment load. Because of their relative rarity, insufficient is known about these high flow events, and where the resulting sediment is deposited. But in many cases a river widens and slows down when it reaches its estuary. This deceleration often brings the flow velocity below a critical value and and sediment deposition begins.

Extrapolation of sediment loads to high flow conditions is usually done with a load—flow relationship as depicted in Fig. 10.4. This graphs the solute and suspended sediment loads for the River Avon at Melksham (UK) as well as the sum of the two loads. The standard procedure in obtaining loads is to measure

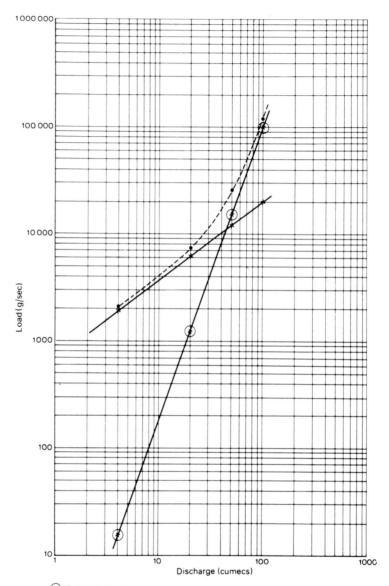

FIG. 10.4. *Load–flow relationships in the River Avon.*

the suspended sediment by filtration, the total dissolved solids (the solute load) by distillation and determine the sediment load by adding the two. The load is the product of the concentration (which is usually given in mg l^{-1}) with the flow.

Estuarine sedimentation can also occur in waters that travel fast. The reason is that small particles of clay minerals are mutually attracted and bound together in saltwater by an electrochemical process known as flocculation. If suspended sediment is present in sufficiently high concentrations, flocculation will occur rapidly when the clay particles hit saltwater. The floccules will not fall as separate units but form a fluffy mud layer on the bottom that shows up well on echo-sounders.

Aside from large construction projects or land reclamation activities, dredging and disposal of dredged materials are among the most important activities affecting estuaries. Maritime economics require that adequate navigation channels be maintained for cities situated on large tidal rivers or estuaries. Unfortunately, complete theoretical prediction of channel changes in an unsteady estuarine environment is unreliable, so that engineering works need to be based on field observations supplemented, perhaps, by hydraulic model tests (see Chapter 12).

The most common failures in the past have been associated with the return of dredged spoil from deposit grounds. On many occasions estuarine entrances have been dredged in order to increase the river flow so that it scours out and maintains the channel. In a stratified estuary the exact opposite can happen. If the surface layer of river water flows seaward faster then the subsurface saline water will also flow upstream more rapidly, bringing with it a substantial and continuing sediment load. This need not be all bad; heavy siltation of the Lune estuary in England following its dredging in the mid-nineteenth century has resulted in a splendid habitat for wading birds.

It is possible to use simple mathematics to examine this problem of siltation in stratified estuaries. Consider the situation depicted in Fig. 10.3C with a river inflow Q_R, an upper layer outflow at site 4 of Q_O, and a lower layer inflow at that site of Q_i. If we neglect rainfall and evaporation then the water mass, and hence the water volume, is conserved. The total inflow over a second will be $Q_i + Q_R$ cubic metres (provided the flow is in $m^3 \ s^{-1}$) and the total outflow is Q_O. The two are equal hence

$$Q_O = Q_i + Q_R. \tag{10.2}$$

Furthermore, salt must be conserved. The river brings no salt so that if we take S_i as the salinity of the inflowing water and S_O as the salinity of the upper layer outflow then the mass of salt $Q_i \ S_i$ coming in each second balances the mass of salt $Q_O \ S_O$ flowing out each second.

$$Q_O \ S_O = Q_i \ S_i. \tag{10.3}$$

The two equations (10.2) and (10.3) may be solved to find the dependence of the inflow, Q_i, upon the riverflow Q_R:

$$Q_i = Q_R \cdot S_o/(S_i - S_o),$$

whereas the outflow Q_o is given by

$$Q_o = Q_R \cdot S_i/(S_i - S_o).$$

If we substitute typical values, as in Fig. 10.3C, of $S_i = 31.5 \times 10^{-3}$ and $S_o = 30.0 \times 10^{-3}$ we can then see that $Q_i = 20\,Q_R$ and $Q_o = 21\,Q_R$. The surface outflow of water at the mouth of a stratified estuary can be over twenty times the river inflow. In addition, an increase in Q_R will increase the inflow by the same percentage, and possibly increase the sediment transport into the estuary. Vertical water characteristics cannot be ignored when studying estuarine circulation.

Nutrients and Eutrophication

Human activities within river catchments, particularly clearing, agriculture and sewage production, increase the nutrient content of run off entering the receiving water body. Nutrients are the basic substances essential to fish and plant life and include carbon dioxide (CO_2), nitrate (NO_3), ammonia (NH_3) and phosphate (PO_4); and any estuary that receives too much of them may be getting too much of a good thing.

The food chain relationships — or trophic relationships — in an estuary are large in number and complex in scope. But, in addition to the nutrient input, they rely on (a) autotrophic organisms such as plants and algae that can transform basic substances into living cell material by using sunlight, (b) heterotrophic organisms such as zooplankton, shellfish and fish species that use other biota as food material and (c) decomposers. Bacteria in both liquid and sediments, and fungi, are examples of decomposers.

In the absence of human activities, the trophic status of an estuary is in a balance determined by the flushing, temperature (the rate of biological activity is temperature dependent), depth and existing biota. An oversupply of nutrients — and in general nitrogen and phosphorus are the main culprits — leads to eutrophication of the estuary. This is characterised by excessive plant growth that chokes the estuary and drives out the fish.

Eutrophication is primarily a problem in lakes, but it can also occur in estuaries and especially lagoon-type estuaries. The Peel Inlet and Harvey estuary depicted in Fig. 10.1, suffer from an extensive growth of a weed called *Cladophora*. This weed floats onto what were once clean sandy beaches and emits a foul smell as it decomposes. It is very long-lived and very hardy. In laboratory experiments this particular species gaily withstood vast extremes of salt, nutrient deprivation, and had an extraordinary temperature tolerance — all of which are properties it would need to possess in order to survive the extremes in its physical and chemical environment indicated in Figs. 10.2 and 10.5. The biological cycle depicted in

Fig. 10.5 shows that phosphates and nitrates were carried down when the rivers started to flow in mid-1978. These nutrient pulses hardly affected the total bio-mass of *Cladophora* because it draws its nutritional requirements from the accumulated nutrients in the bottom sediments. What happened is that the large concentration of dissolved nutrients led to an algal bloom (as measured by the chlorophyll-a concentration) which consisted of a floating green scum of phyto-plankton. This surface scum blocked out the light and depressed *Cladophora* growth by cutting off its access to sunlight.

A more aesthetically acceptable form of eutrophication is that associated with marshlands. An estuarine marsh can assimilate substantial volumes of nutrient-rich domestic and industrial wastes because of its high plant productivity. It incorporates these wastes into the yield of organic plant material which support both hard and soft shell fisheries species. Marsh production is a major source of organic material supporting the estuarine food web in many coastal areas, as well as providing food and cover for a variety of water fowl and mammals. Deltaic marshes also serve other beneficial functions: acting as a temporary floodwater storage area, and aiding in erosion control by absorbing potentially destructive wave energy.

Estuarine Management

In order to alleviate, or at least to control, estuarine pollution it is necessary to institute management strategies. In this respect estuarine management is a part of coastal zone management (Chapter 2.6) and an overall coastal zone management body will also have control over estuaries. Nevertheless, specific estuaries have specific problems which justify the existence of a separate body to control industrial, urban, agricultural and recreational facilities on the shores of the estuary. Of course, true estuarine management should extend upstream, but it is usual for a separate authority to control rivers. In Texas this has led to bitter disputes between water supply authorities who want to dam a particular river and water quality authorities who need sufficient freshwater inflows to maintain well-flushed estuaries.

In order to develop a management strategy one needs to be able to identify the causes of pollution and the economic and political constraints that may limit possible solutions. Figure 10.6 is an attempt to identify the possible manage-ment options for the *Cladophora* problem in the Peel Inlet—Harvey Estuary system. Figure 10.6 indicates that *Cladophora* growth can be considered a result of the interactions between hydrology (wind, tides, etc.); nutrients (water-borne and sediment nitrogen and phosphorus as well as detritus); two types of phyto-plankton and various physical factors (light and temperature). Three possible management strategies are indicated by question marks on the arrows leading out of the management compartment. One could attack the *Cladophora* nuisance directly by carting away the weed (as is presently done). Or one can try to alter

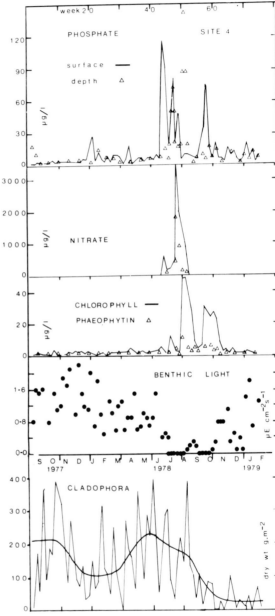

FIG. 10.5. *Weekly measurements of the nutrient loading into the Peel Inlet indicate that algal blooms follow high nutrient inputs and that their shading effect affects weed growth. Biomass measurements vary greatly and a smooth curve has been drawn through the noisy Cladophora data.*

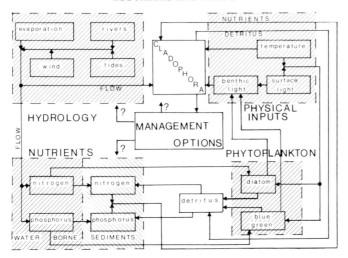

FIG. 10.6. *A systems diagram indicating the interrelation-ships between the scientific aspects and the possible management options for weed growth in the Peel Inlet.*

the hydrology of the inlet so that conditions become unfavourable for the growth of the weed (e.g. widen the channel that provides access to the sea). Or thirdly, one could attack the source of nutrients, possibly by dredging the nutrient-rich bottom sediment so that the plant will have nothing to live off. The final choice of management strategy requires scientific preparation to ensure that it will work, but from then on is a social problem to be sorted out in an open political forum.

10.5 Coral Reefs

Coral reefs, which occur in warm tropical waters, are a cemented mass of large interlocking coral and algal colonies buried in their original position by subsequent overgrowth on all sides. There are four types of reefs: (i) *Fringing reefs* edge the shores of islands and continents with no deep-water channel between them and the land. (ii) *Barrier reefs* also occur off land masses but at much greater distances and separated from them by a deep and wide channel known as the reef lagoon. The supreme example is the Great Barrier Reef of North-eastern Australia which extends for 1930 km, the outermost reefs in places over 160 km offshore. (iii) *Atolls* are not connected with any land and consist of rings of coral reef with occasional islands of purely coral formation. Within is a lagoon which, like the channel within a barrier reef, seldom exceeds 60 m in depth and varies in size between that of a small lake and of an inland sea up to 64 km across. There is usually a moderately deep opening on the lee, that is on the side opposite to the one exposed to the Trade Winds. (iv) Finally, there are *Patch reefs* which are isolated reef platforms of various shapes and sizes that grow in great numbers within the shelter of atoll lagoons or within barrier reefs.

Reefs are mainly of biological origin, built by coral polyps, small marine organisms that take up calcium carbonate from seawater and grow into a variety of skeletal forms. Closely associated with these are small plants, the pink calcareous algae, which grow in and around the coral structure. Each set of organisms assists the other, the algae drawing nutrients from coral, and utilising much of the carbon dioxide (released into the sea by coral respiration) in the manufacture of food by plant photosynthesis; this in turn replenishes the oxygen dissolved in seawater, and thus maintains a supply of oxygen for coral respiration. While coral is essential for reef building it generally forms only a small proportion of reef material. The primary reef builders are corals and red seaweeds (the algae), but there are many secondary fillers which would include certain large molluscs and a host of smaller animals and plants all with calcareous skeletons. These eventually break down to form the sand which everywhere fills in cavities and extends over the bottom, especially in the lee of reefs. There are also predators that feed on reef builders. During the early 1970s there were great fears that an infestation of the Crown of Thorns starfish would destroy the Great Barrier Reef. The crisis passed and provided yet another example of the plague and scarcity (or boom—bust) cycle in ecology.

Reef-building takes place in ocean areas where free-floating planktonic coral larvae are distributed by ocean currents and where ecological conditions permit the establishment and growth of coral and associated algae. An adequate supply of sunlight is essential for algal photosynthesis, and growth of coral is best in clear, warm water. Intensity of sunlight diminishes downward into the sea (Chapter 12), and although live corals have been found in exceptionally clear water at depths as great as 100 m, the maximum depth at which reefs are actively being built is rarely more than 50 m. How then do barrier reefs and atolls exist in waters such that their outer slopes descend to depths of hundreds or thousands of metres? This central mystery surrounding their mode of formation has attracted the attention of numerous zoologists and geologists.

Fortunately there is no such mystery surrounding the formation of fringing reefs and in their genesis one can detect a subtle interplay between physical and biological processes. Fringing reefs are often discontinuous near river mouths because the suspended sediment load reduces sunlight penetration and impedes the growth of reef-building organisms. In clear warm water with a suitable rocky bottom, corals will establish themselves and grow upwards. When they reach low water mark, upward growth ceases because corals can only tolerate very brief exposure to the air. Encrusting sheets of red coralline seaweeds occur in greatest abundance on the most exposed reef crests. The full force of oceanic surf breaking on these provides the exceptional degree of oxygenation these calcified plants need. Unable to continue upwards, the coral must grow outwards, and so the coral mass becomes broader, and also much steeper, on its outer slope.

The region immediately below water level on the outer edge of the reef is the area of most active coral growth. The reef flat, between the outer zone and the land, becomes hollowed out to form a shallow lagoon-like channel. Occasionally, when an especially deep channel has been formed in this manner, living corals may be able to establish themselves once more in this region. Patch reefs within the Great Barrier Reef are like this and the shapes of these reef platforms are related to the patterns of waves generated by the prevailing trade winds. Often they have developed a horseshoe form, with arms trailing away from the prevailing winds (Fig. 10.7).

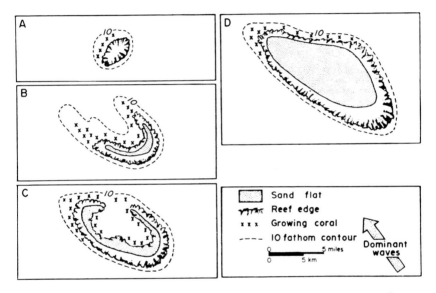

FIG. 10.7. *Initial patch reefs (A) tend to grow into forms with marginal deflection by the dominant waves as in (B) and (C). Eventually a larger reef platform may develop as in (D). A depth of 10 fathoms corresponds closely to 20 m.*

Despite its name, the Great Barrier Reef is not continuous and certainly does not present an impermeable barrier to the passage of water. Lagoon waters inside the outer reef are by no means isolated from the Coral Sea outside. To a certain extent the outer reef can be visualised as a series of horseshoe-shaped reefs of Fig. 10.7B and C. The space between two of the horseshoe arms provides a passage for Coral Sea water and, in addition, water is also exchanged through swell that breaks over the reefs. In comparison with reef biology and reef morphology, little is known about water circulation within reefs. Studies on atolls indicate that most of the water motion in the lagoon is produced by wind traction at their surfaces, though the exchange of lagoon water with that of the sea is accomplished by tides and wave action.

Figure 10.8 depicts surface, mid-depth and bottom currents from the Great Barrier Reef near Cairns. The reversals in current direction that do not tie in with changes in wind direction indicate that shelf waves propagate up the coast. At other locations (Broad Sound) the reef lagoon has macro-tides; possibly enhanced by localised seiching between the coast and the reef. To further complicate the situation, gaps in the reef system can produce localised jets of water leading to a complex topographically dominated, wind-driven circulation. Engineering works undertaken without a full appreciation of these subtleties can cause problems. Table 10.2 lists engineering works at Heron Island and their consequences. The main problem is that the boat channel built in 1945 provided an ebb channel for sediment and ever since then the beaches have been eroding.

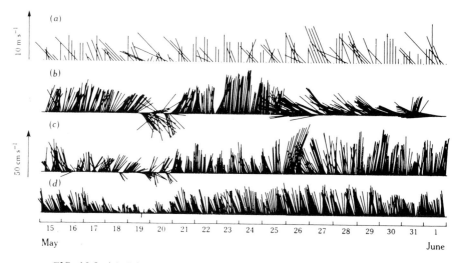

FIG. 10.8. (a) Cairns wind and current observations at (b) surface, (c) mid-depth and (d) bottom from an outlying reef. The upper current record is suspect after 25 May because of a malfunction.

Further Reading

A good introduction to estuarine physics and hydraulics will be found in:

K. R. DYER: *Estuaries: A Physical Introduction*, John Wiley & Sons, London, 1973 (140 pp.),

and

D. M. McDOWELL and B. A. O'CONNOR: *Hydraulic Behaviour of Estuaries*, Macmillan, London, 1977 (292 pp.),

whereas more detailed mathematical expositions are given by:

TABLE 10.2. *Engineering Works at Heron Island and their Consequences*

Date	Construction or event	Cause and/or consequence
1945	Gap blasted in reef rim to provide access for small boats. Wreck placed for shelter.	Ebb currents channelled around island and through gap. Beach on NW side of island commenced to erode.
1960 Aug.	First section of rock wall on NW side of island constructed before this date.	Severe erosion from cyclones of mid-1950s, and other causes continued to occur.
1965 July	Westerly extension of rock wall completed.	Beach erosion and realignment continued — sand moving across reef flat and out through gap in reef rim.
1966 Oct.	Dredging of channel and boat harbour commenced.	
1967 Feb.	Partially dredged harbour filled with sand.	Cyclone "Dinah".
1967 Oct.– Nov.	Harbour redredged and completed. Dredge spoil placed on beach on SW corner of island.	Access to island by boat improved.
	Walls approx. 1 m high constructed around harbour and entrance channel.	Ebb currents and sand transport out through gap in reef rim suppressed.
1968	Helipad constructed on dredge spoil from boat harbour.	Access to island improved.
1970 May	Timber sea wall constructed to protect helipad.	Erosion in early 1970 between end of rock wall and helipad endangered the latter.
1971 Feb.	Harbour walls breached and flattened.	Cyclones "Gertie" and "Fiona". Ebb tide now flowed out through boat channel.
1972 April	Boat harbour and channel filled with sand entering through breaches in harbour walls. Beaches eroded.	Cyclone "Emily" assisted by ebb tide currents.
1972 Oct. to 1976	Harbour redredged and spoil (20,000 m^3) placed on NW beach in front of rock wall. Habour walls *not* repaired.	Sand deposit from dredging moved westward along the rock wall under the action of waves and tidal currents and commenced to re-enter the harbour.
1976 Jan.	Harbour again filled with sediment. Sand from 1972 dredging now completely relocated to SW corner of island.	Cyclone "David" assisted by ebb tide currents (high spring tides).
1978 to 1979	Attempts made to block breaches in harbour walls with concrete blocks.	Tidal currents continued to flow through breaches and out the boat channel.
1980 Feb.	Approx. 10,000 m^3 of sediment in harbour. Erosion of NW side of island but NE side accreted.	Cyclone "Simon" assisted by ebb tide currents. Neap tides — sediment transported from reef flat onto windward side of island.

C. B. OFFICER: *Physical Oceanography of Estuaries*, John Wiley & Sons, N.Y., 1976 (465 pp.),

and

H. B. FISCHER, E. J. LIST, R. C. KOH, J. IMBERGER & N. H. BROOKS: *Mixing in Inland and Coastal Waters*, Academic Press, N.Y., 1979 (483 pp.).

Estuarine pollution and management are dealt with by:

M. G. GOSS: Effects of waste disposal operations in estuaries and the coastal ocean, *Ann. Rev. Earth Planet. Sci.* 6, 127–143, 1978.

TEXAS DEPT. WATER RESOURCES: *The Influence of Freshwater Inflows upon the Major Bays and Estuaries of the Texas Gulf Coast*, Report LP-115, 1979 (Austin, Texas).

E. P. HODGKIN, P. BIRCH, R. HUMPHRIES & R. BLACK: *The Peel–Harvey Estuarine System Study*, Report No. 9, Dept. Conservation and Environment, Western Australia. (Available from the Department of Conservation and Environment, 1 Mount Street, Perth).

For information on coral reefs one may turn to

H. J. WIENS: *Atoll Environment and Ecology*, Yale University Press, 1962.

I. BENNETT: *The Great Barrier Reef*, Frederick Warne & Co. Ltd., 1973.

G. L. PICKARD: *A Review of the Physical Oceanography of the Great Barrier Reef and Western Coral Sea*, Monograph Volume 3, Australian Institute of Marine Sciences; Australian Govt. Publishing Service, Canberra, 1977.

W. G. H. MAXWELL: *Atlas of the Great Barrier Reef*, Elsevier, New York, 1968.

CHAPTER 11

Direct and Remote Sensing

11.1 Instruments and Methods

The most direct method of obtaining information about environmental conditions in coastal waters is to go out in a boat, or ship, and make the measurements. This involves loading the boat with large amounts of measuring equipment in order to conduct *in-situ* readings; though there are occasions when samples are merely collected on the boat and analysed in a shore-based laboratory. Often the objective of the measurements is to answer questions relating to possible, or actual, man-made pollution such as: the level of trace elements in the water, the bottom and the sea animals; or the mixing and subsequent motion of waste discharges. The conduct of an environmental investigation involving fieldwork requires an acknowledged field leader who directs operations. He is the final arbiter on all scientific and personnel matters whilst the master of the vessel has absolute authority on questions of seamanship. Briefing sessions before the operation are invaluable and each team member should understand his allotted tasks by the end of them. Equipment checklists should be verified before setting out, and it is wise to check that the team members are supplied with creature comforts such as coffee and cold water, and protective clothing so that they can keep themselves, and their notebooks, dry. A typical equipment checklist is given in Appendix 2.

There are huge advantages in being able to rely on the services of divers operating either through breathing tubes connected to a shipboard air pump — known as hookahs — or with air tanks on their backs — known as SCUBA. They can take photographs of interesting phenomena, collect specimens and untangle underwater equipment. As SCUBA divers are easy to train and their equipment is inexpensive, one of the most important practical considerations in coastal work is whether SCUBA divers can easily operate at the location of interest. SCUBA diving below 50 m depth is not recommended, though if it is absolutely necessary commercial divers can be employed to penetrate deeper than this, but it will be costly.

When planning an investigation, and choosing the best instruments to use, it is wise to think ahead to the means that will be utilised to process and analyse the data that is obtained. Data reduction, statistical manipulation and plotting are all time-consuming activities that are best accomplished by a digital computer. In the best of all possible worlds each sensor is directly linked to a shipboard computer and plotter so that measurements can be analysed and displayed in real-time, and instant decisions made whether to continue the sampling, move to a new location, or deploy extra sensors. The ultimate example of this has come to be known as the zoom philosophy in which a field vessel conducts detailed intensive studies to support a large-scale monitoring and surveillance programme. The area of interest is continually narrowed as if viewed through the zoom lens of a camera. It works as follows: on the basis of transmitted aerial or satellite photographs the project director "zooms" in on an area of interest — possibly a wastewater discharge plume. He orders the field vessel into location to investigate it, which is done with regular grid transects, continually displaying the acquired data, until they strike an anomaly; perhaps a region of very low dissolved oxygen. The vessel then anchors and "zooms" in to examine this region in detail.

Navigation

Navigation, or knowing the position of one's ship, is of primary importance to oceanographic work. Most deep water navigational methods are not very accurate, but fortunately much coastal work is done within sight of land which offers a greater scope for accuracy. There are essentially five navigation systems:

(i) *Piloting*: Within visual sight of land the navigator can use a sextant to measure the horizontal angle between three well-located objects on land and use this to determine the boat's position. Alternatively, a less accurate method is to take two fixes with a compass, whereas a more accurate refinement is to use land-based theodolites.

If the bottom topography of an area is well known — using an acoustic sounder for example — and a good chart of it exists, it can be used as a navigational aid. A boat's position can be determined from the chart when the ship passes over a known feature of the sea floor.

(ii) *Dead reckoning*: This is the simplest but least accurate navigational tool. The position of a vessel is calculated from a known initial position by using the ship's speed and bearing to estimate its position at any subsequent time.

(iii) *Celestial navigation*: With a sextant, chronometer (or nowadays a radio time signal) and the astronomical ephemeris one can calculate latitude and longitude accurate to about 2 km.

(iv) *Electronic methods*: Most electronic positioning systems depend on an accurate measurement of the time required for a radio signal to travel from a transmitter at a known place on land to a receiver on a ship. Commercial systems use multiple transmitters that simultaneously emit synchronised signals at different locations. The difference in arrival time between these signals is a measure of the distance of the ship from the stations. Two or more sets of these stations provide a very accurate estimate of position. Several large-scale systems exist (Loran, Decca, Omega), though for smaller-scale monitoring one can erect one's own system.

(v) *Satellites*: Navigation satellites (NAVSAT) exist in polar orbits around the earth. The satellites emit radio waves which are picked up by a shipboard receiver. From the received information a small computer can, in a few minutes, determine a ship's position, day or night, clear or cloudy. This makes it possible to fix the position of a ship out of sight of land to within 200 m, four to six times a day.

Instruments

At the present period of time oceanographic instrumentation is undergoing rapid development and change. In part this is due to the application of new scientific principles, in part it is due to the decreasing cost of electronic components, which has led to rapid changes in the computer systems and microprocessors with which instruments are nowadays expected to interact.

Any person planning to outfit a vessel for environmental or scientific investigations should contact an oceanographic institution and reputable scientific instrument manufacturers in order to find out the range of available instruments, and the ones in common use. Table 11.1 lists a sample of the information usually needed and the type of instrument required to obtain it most efficiently. It should be emphasised that an instrument not specifically designed for sea conditions is unlikely to perform well. Seawater is a powerful corrosive that will attack metal rapidly. Oceanographic instruments offset this to some extent by installing a sacrificial anode — a lump of metal that is preferentially corroded. Even so, after any deployment and recovery an instrument must be thoroughly washed and scrubbed with clean water. It is not my aim to describe oceanographic instruments, so that the interested reader should consult the references given in the list of further reading.

Nevertheless, it is worthwhile pointing out that often more than one sensor is mounted in a single unit. A recording current meter generally also has temperature and pressure sensors attached. Combined temperature/dissolved oxygen probes are common, as are CTD probes (conductivity, temperature, depth: sometimes called STD probes since salinity is inferred from conductivity). Other common acronyms that appear in oceanographic writings include MBT or BTG for the mechanical bathythermograph, XBT for an expendable bathythermograph, which has nowadays virtually supplanted the older BTG, and AXBT to denote an XBT dropped from an aeroplane.

A bathythermograph is an instrument that measures temperature and depth. The older BTG had an ingenious arrangement of mechanical linkages that

TABLE 11.1

Characteristic	Instrument
Physical Characteristics	
Motion	Drogue; current meter
Temperature	Bathythermograph; thermistor
Salinity	Conductivity meter
Clarity	Turbidity meter (nephelometer); Secchi disc
Depth	Plumb line; echo-sounder; pressure sensor
Waves	Buoyed accelerometer ('Waverider')
Tide	Tide gauge
Chemical Characteristics	
Chemicals, nutrients	Sampling bottle; pump and tube
Dissolved oxygen (DO)	DO probe
Particulates	Settleables and floatables collectors
Bottom composition	Grab sampler; corer
Biological Characteristics	
Particulates	Plankton net; mussel buoy
Fauna	Television; baited camera; trawl
Microbes	Sterile bag sample
Meteorological Characteristics	
Radiation	Pyranometer
Wind	Anemometer
Precipitation	Rain gauge; pluviograph
Evaporation	Evaporation pan

produced an analogue record on a smoked glass slide. This was done by a stylus scratching a trace into precalibrated slides. The BTG was lowered and raised from either a stationary or moving vessel. This general idea was extended by the XBT which consists of a specially designed sensor unit, whose rate of fall is known. A thin wire is attached to the unit which relays temperature information to a chart recorder, whose speed of paper advance is geared such that it records depth linearly. After all the thin wire has played out of its spool it unplugs itself and is discarded.

There has been increasing concern in recent years over the accuracy of near-surface current meters when they are moored to record subsurface currents (Fig. 11.1). Their readings may be contaminated by surface waves and, even when this is not the case, their records need a great deal of smoothing before being useful. They are popular because a recording current meter gives a computer compatible output. However, these devices record only what happened at a single point (known as a Eulerian representation), not where the water mass

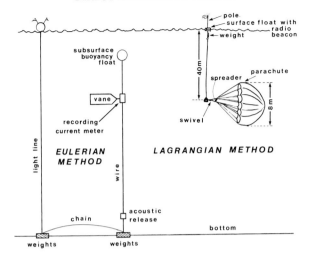

FIG. 11.1. *Subsurface currents may be measured
by Eulerian methods which moor a recording
current meter at the appropriate depth (40 m in
this case), or Lagrangian methods such as the
parachute drogued buoy. The chain in the
picture is floating to emphasise that grappling
hooks can be used to locate it if the surface
marker is lost.*

went. If the vectors from such a meter are added up, then the progressive vector
may seem to show that the water ended up several miles inland. Meter measurement, therefore, should be supplemented by drogue tracking – or even discarded
in favour of drogue tracking, which produces what is known as a Lagrangian
representation of the currents. Figure 7.6 was an example of results obtained by
Lagrangian methods.

A parachute some 8 m in diameter is a convenient form of drogue in deep
water, whereas a bucket with a hole in the bottom can be used in shallower
water (Fig. 11.1). Usually these drogues are followed for many hours or several
days – at the end of which they may either be many kilometres away or have
returned to the starting point. When calculating the currents, the aerodynamic
effects on the marker pole need to be subtracted.

11.2 Remote Sensing

Remote sensing is the term used nowadays to describe a means of gathering
physical information with instruments that are situated at a location other than
the location being examined. It is to be contrasted with the more traditional
method of *in-situ* or direct sensing in which oceanographic instruments are
lowered to the desired location and a sample or measurement made directly.

The most familiar remote sensing device is a simple camera which records the visible image of an object upon a photographic plate, or film, which is then developed into a print of the scene. An ordinary camera utilises the visible portion of the spectrum of light waves, though specialised cameras and films exist to record infra-red radiation. Visible light and infra-red are both examples of electromagnetic radiation that is of relevance to oceanography. The third form of relevant electromagnetic radiation occurs in the microwave part of the spectrum.

Remote sensing instruments have to rely on radiation, or waves, transmitting the desired information from the region under study to the instrument being used. Electromagnetic radiation is one method of doing this. Acoustic radiation, or sound waves, is another. We have already seen that sound waves can be utilised in depth sounders and in marine seismic surveys. Acoustic waves are important in the ocean because it is virtually opaque to electromagnetic radiation, but is much more transparent to sound transmission. A dramatic example of this occurred when a depth charge exploded near Australia was monitored by hydrophones near its antipode off Bermuda.

The rest of this chapter describes the nature of electromagnetic and acoustic radiation and examines some of the means by which they are used to obtain information about coastal waters. I do not want to dwell upon the instruments themselves, because this is a rapidly changing area of technology in which new instrumentation is rapidly replacing existing ones. Furthermore, I do not wish to deal with *in-situ* probes that utilise electromagnetic or acoustic radiation. Modern methods for measuring ocean current, for example, involve the use of acoustic current meters in which the nature of the sound wave is altered by the current.

Nevertheless, one should be aware of the principal dichotomy between remote sensing instrumentation. This involves active and passive remote sensing. Any device that emits light or sound, and deduces the properties of the medium from the changes between the emitted and received signals, is an active remote sensor. If the instrument consists only of a receiver, which examines the natural background radiation, then one is dealing with a passive remote sensing system.

11.3 Acoustics

Acoustic radiation transfers sound energy from one place to another by alternate wavelike compressions and rarefactions of the molecules of seawater. Acoustic radiation, or sound waves, manifests itself as small wavelike changes in pressure. These are generated by an oscillating membrane in a transducer, and are detected by hydrophones. For many underwater applications the same instrument is used for both transmission and reception.

Ocean acoustics deals with sound frequencies lying between 1 Hz and 1 MHz. Frequency denotes the number of acoustic compressions in a second and is measured in Hertz where 1 Hertz is 1 cycle per second. At high frequencies sound absorption by seawater is very high. Except for a small number of very special applications, such as acoustic image makers and side scanning sonars (a sonar is the acoustic equivalent of a radar) both of which are used for very short-range work, the use of sound transmissions is limited to frequencies less than a few hundred kiloHertz. At very low frequencies, below 1 Hz, one has great difficulty in generating sound; except with earthquakes and very large explosions.

The choice of a frequency depends on the application, and on a trade-off between low attenuation but high background noise at low frequencies, and better target definition with lower background noise at higher frequencies. Ships looking for shallow, thin gravel deposits or similar layering prefer to accept the high attenuation loss of high-frequency echo-sounders in order to get the detailed structuring of layers only a few metres thick. The small wavelength of high-frequency sound waves reveals this small structure. On the other hand, those prospecting for oil need deep penetration, which in turn requires low-frequency sound. Loss of detail is compensated by the ability to discern structures several hundred metres below the bottom. For echo-location of nearby schools of fish, one can accept high-frequency sonars, which give sufficient detail to tell the experienced observer the type of fish. Military sonars wish to find large objects, generally submarines, at long distances and thus use low-frequency sources.

Acoustic techniques have found a number of environmental applications in nearshore areas. Sewage dumped in the ocean has been tracked acoustically, as has sludge left by dredging operations. In rivers, acoustic techniques have been used to estimate the weight of suspended particulates in the water. Within estuaries, echo-sounders can be used to look at the interface between the freshwater in the upper layers of the estuary and the salty marine water at lower depths. Figure 11.2 shows part of a 200-kHz echo-sounder chart record taken during routine prawn trawling operations in the Shark's Bay area of Western Australia. The mid-water layer seen in the figure provides significant acoustic reflection which may arise from a pycnocline alone, or a pycnocline with associated scattering centres. Potential acoustic scatterers include small fish, zooplankton, phytoplankton and the small gas bubbles emitted by rotting detritus. There is evidence that zooplankton gather at estuarine interfaces, which complicates the job of interpreting charts such as Fig. 11.2.

Attenuation and Intensity

Sound intensity and attenuation is usually discussed in terms of a nondimensional quantity called a decibel (db). The reason for the introduction of this quantity is that the sound pressure varies over a range of 10^{10} and the sound intensity, which is proportional to the square of sound pressure, varies over a

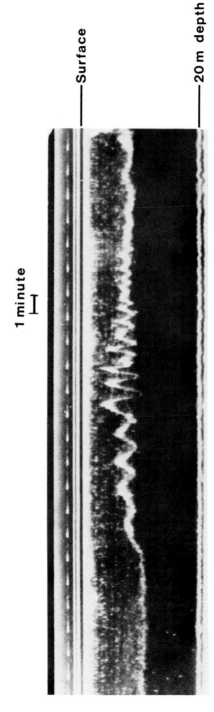

FIG. 11.2. This echo-sounder chart record, taken in 20 m depth, shows midwater layering with substantial biological activity in the top layer. Internal waves at the interface between the water layers show up very strongly.

range of 10^{20}. In order to reduce these huge numbers to manageable form, we use a logarithmic scale to define the sound level (SL) as

$$SL \text{ (db)} = 10 \log_{10} (I/I_0) = 20 \log_{10} (p/p_0) \qquad (11.1)$$

where I is the intensity of a sound wave composed of pressure fluctuations of magnitude p. The subscripted quantities I_0 and p_0 refer to arbitrarily determined reference levels. An effective reference pressure of 0.1 N m^{-2} is used for equipment associated with sonar transducers and hydrophones.

The attenuation of high-frequency sound in seawater is the result of viscous and chemical effects. Firstly, water is a viscous fluid and this viscosity acts as a frictional effect on sound waves. Viscosity dissipates their energy and converts it into heat. Viscous effects are greater at higher frequencies and, in addition, are temperature dependent. As the temperature rises, the viscosity decreases and the attenuation decreases. Experiments reveal that the attenuation for seawater is consistently higher than the attenuation for distilled water at the same temperature. This additional loss is related to an ionic relaxation phenomenon in magnesium sulphate, $MgSO_4$, salts which absorb sound energy. Below a few kiloHertz there are other chemical species whose relaxation phenomena act so as to absorb sound waves, the principal one at these lower frequencies being a boric acid relaxation. At very low frequencies, scattering by random fluctuations in the water layers will also attenuate an acoustic signal. Small temperature and salinity inhomogeneities cause this scattering.

In addition, geometric effects attenuate the sound beam. For a transducer that may be approximated as a point source radiating into a finite solid angle, the geometric drop off in intensity, or spreading loss, will be proportional to the square of the distance.

Reflection

The general idea of sonar detection is to transmit a signal and then examine the reflected signal that reaches the receiver. This reflection can arise from specific targets — submarines or schools of fish; from the physical characteristics of the water body; or from the ocean surface or ocean bottom.

Marine acousticians often use the term target strength (TS) to quantify the level of reflection. It is defined in terms of a reflection coefficient, R, as

$$TS = 20 \log_{10} \left(\frac{\text{Reflected pressure measured 1 m from target}}{\text{Sound pressure incident on target}} \right) \qquad (11.2)$$

$$= 20 \log_{10} R$$

or it can be defined in terms of a scattering cross-section, χ, as

$$TS = 20 \log \sqrt{\frac{\chi}{4\pi}}. \qquad (11.3)$$

The advantage of this second formula is that for simple geometric shapes it is possible to use physical reasoning to predict the general form for χ, the scattering cross-section. For example, for very small spherical targets within certain frequency limits, the scattering cross-section is proportional to the fourth power of the incident sound frequency.

Typical target strengths of euphausiid zooplankton (commonly known as krill) range from −90 db at 102 kHz to −70 db at 200 kHz. Copepods (another type of zooplankton) of length 1 mm have target strengths between −117 db and −110 db at 200 kHz. For prawns and small fish the fourth power law mentioned above is no longer valid at usual echo-sounder frequencies and for 50 kHz to 500 kHz sound frequencies it does not depend on frequency. Figure 11.3 shows

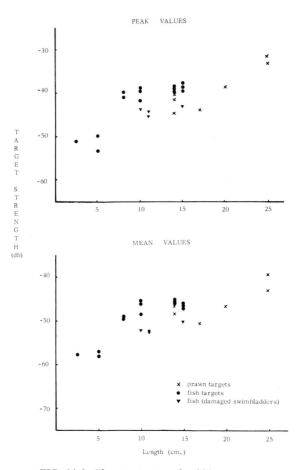

FIG. 11.3. *The target strength of king prawns and small leatherjacket fish increases with length at an acoustic frequency of 200 kHz.*

how the target strength of king prawns and small fish increases with length in this frequency range.

The presence of multiple targets, such as schools of fish, will increase the target strength. As a general rule one can add the scattering cross-section, so that for a collection of n identical scatterers the target strength will increase by $20 \log_{10} \sqrt{n}$. Thus for a distribution of targets, individually of -90 db target strength, to accumulate to provide an average combined target strength during some part of the return echo of -70 db would require $n = 100$. That is, 100 targets must be present within the appropriate volume. Certainly scattering centres which are individually below detection threshold can provide discernible echoes when a sufficient target density appears in the beam. Acoustic tracking of sludge seems to rely on this fact.

Within the ocean there can be substantial acoustic return, even in the absence of a well-defined target. This occurs most strongly when the acoustic beam hits either the surface or the bottom in a direct hit, and virtually the whole signal is reflected. However, *en route* to these perfect reflectors there is often a partial reflection of the acoustic signal due to abrupt changes in the water properties. This is described in terms of the acoustic impedance, Z, of the water where

$$Z = \rho c, \tag{11.4}$$

the product of the water density ρ and the speed of sound, c. Both ρ and c have a complicated dependence on sea temperature and salinity. For example, in an estuary there can be a layer of brackish river water lying on top of a layer of salty water. Typical densities of the two layers could be 1.01×10^3 kg m^{-3} and 1.02×10^3 kg m^{-3} respectively with sound speeds of 1525 m s^{-1} in the more salty water and 1495 m s^{-1} in the fresher water. This results in an acoustic impedance of 1.510×10^5 kg m^{-2} s^{-1} for the top layer and 1.555×10^5 kg m^{-2} s^{-1} for the bottom layer. For direct incidence reflection the reflection coefficient

$$R = \frac{\text{Pressure reflected}}{\text{Pressure incident}} = (Z_{salt} - Z_{fresh})/(Z_{salt} + Z_{fresh}) \tag{11.5}$$

so that in our example the reflection coefficient would be 0.015 and this can be related to an effective target strength of -36.5 db. This theoretical value is seldom achieved in practice because equation (11.5) assumes a perfectly sharp interface. In practice there will be substantial smearing of the interface which can lower the effective target strength by 50 db or more.

Passive Acoustic Sensing

Another important acoustical property of the ocean is the ambient noise level. This noise is partly biological in origin and partly natural. It depends upon location, position of the receiver, direction, nearby weather, and distant weather conditions.

Wind on the water surface produces sound, as do currents flowing over the bottom, breaking waves and even rainfall. Additionally, the biological noise can be strong. At certain times of the year the mating call of the toad fish drowns out most other sounds in certain nearshore regions of the US east coast. Porpoises have their own echo-location devices (usually of high frequency and therefore rapidly attenuated). Certain whales on the other hand, use low-frequency sounds, presumably for communication, and these sounds travel long distances.

Finally, of course, there are man-made sounds, such as those of acoustic signalling devices or the noise of ships. Ship noise is of two sorts — cavitation noise generated at propellers, and machinery noise generated at the motors. In general, ship noise is strongest at low frequencies due to the throb of the engine. Cavitation noise arises when the propellers are turning so rapidly that the reduced pressures in the water near the blades cause air and vapour bubbles to form. Upon leaving the vicinity of the propellers the pressure of the water returns to normal and the vapour bubbles collapse and generate a sound much like that of frying fat. At low shaft rates, cavitation noise is not present, but at higher speeds, when cavitation noise starts, it is usually the predominant contributor to the overall sound pressure level radiated by the ship.

A power spectrum of ambient ocean noise typically ranges from natural seismic noise near 0.3 Hz to high-frequency wind-generated noise at 10^5 Hz. As one might expect, because low-frequency sound is absorbed less, there are higher noise levels at lower frequencies. Typical spectral powers for the sound intensity range from 100 N^2 m^{-4} Hz^{-1} for frequency bands near 1 Hz down to 10^{-8} N^2 m^{-4} Hz^{-1} at 10^5 Hz. Though it may seem far-fetched at the moment, measurements such as these may become necessary in order to define noise pollution levels within coastal waters used extensively by divers, or used for scientific research. There is a strong movement towards the creation of marine reserves or marine parks to preserve some of the scenic and natural beauty of the underwater environment. However, the influx of tourists in their throbbing power boats produces an insidious form of acoustic pollution that will need to be carefully monitored.

11.4 Electromagnetic Radiation

Light, radio waves, microwaves and X-rays are all manifestations of electromagnetic radiation. This is a form of energy transmission in which oscillating electric and magnetic fields produce a wave that travels along, in free space, at a speed of 3×10^8 m s^{-1}. In common with all waves, it can be described either in terms of its frequency, ν, or its wavelength, λ, where the two are related through the speed, c, by

$$\lambda\nu = c \quad \text{or} \quad \lambda = c/\nu. \tag{11.6}$$

Traditionally, light waves are referred to in terms of their wavelength — red, for example, is about 0.6 μm (600 nm) and blue is around 0.4 μm (400 nm), whereas radio waves and microwaves are referred to in terms of their frequency.

The most familiar form of electromagnetic radiation is that emitted by the sun; and it is a mixture of different frequencies in well-defined proportions. The spectrum of electromagnetic radiation emitted by the sun is very close to the electromagnetic radiation that would be emitted by any hot object at 6000 K (Fig. 11.4). It has a strong peak in the visible part of the spectrum, to which human eyesight has evolved. This evolution was enhanced by the fact that various gases in the atmosphere absorb much of the wavelengths on either side of this visible window of light.

The Earth, by virtue of its own temperature (of about 300 K), also emits electromagnetic waves. These are not as strong as those of the sun, and they peak in the infra-red rather than in the visible. Any particular temperature can be characterised by a curve of the form shown in Fig. 11.4 and much of passive infra-red remote sensing relies on a measurement of radiation intensity in the infra-red part of the spectrum being convertible to an equivalent temperature.

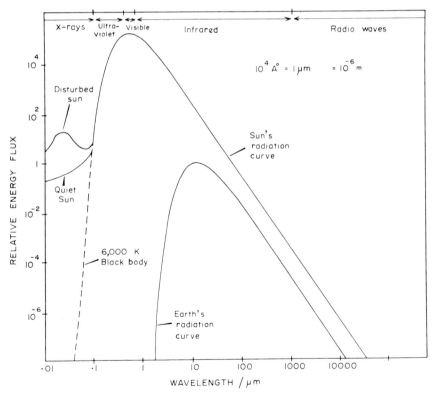

FIG. 11.4. *Idealised energy distribution curves of the sun's radiation and the approximate reradiation at the Earth's surface. (Note the logarithmic scales.)*

The curves of Fig. 11.4 are generally called the blackbody radiation curves. This is a useful concept widely used by physicists in radiation studies as a model of a perfect absorber, and radiator, of electromagnetic radiation. A blackbody is conceived to be an object or substance which absorbs all the radiation incident upon it, and emits the maximum amount of radiation at all temperatures. Although there is no known substance in the natural world with such a performance, the blackbody concept is invaluable for the formulation of laws by comparison with which the behaviour of actual radiators may be assessed. One of these is Kirchhoff's law which states that, I, the energy flux (i.e. the energy of electromagnetic radiation traversing unit area in unit of time) of a real body may be compared to the energy flux of a blackbody I_b, through their emissivity ϵ, as

$$I = \epsilon I_b. \tag{11.7}$$

The emissivity of a real blackbody would be 1, whilst the emissivity of a body absorbing none of the radiation upon it would be zero. Between these two limiting values, the greyness of real radiators can be assessed, and it is generally a frequency-dependent entity.

11.5 Marine Optics

When sunlight strikes the ocean surface, a certain percentage of it is reflected and the rest penetrates into the water. The amount reflected and the amount transmitted depend on the state of the sea surface and the angle of the sun. For a smooth sea surface, Table 11.2 shows that at normal incidence (i.e. the sun directly overhead) the reflected intensity is 2% of the incoming intensity. This increases slowly with angle up to 60°, beyond which reflection increases rapidly. The high reflection when the sun is low in the sky explains the very bright image of the sun at these times. When viewed from an aeroplane — or a satellite — calm water will produce a bright reflection, known as the specular reflection, of the sun. The occurrence of waves will break up this specular reflection into dancing glitter patterns — called sunglint — which have been used to study the statistical distribution of waves on the surface of water.

The transmitted light will either be absorbed or scattered and the total effect of these two mechanisms is called extinction, or attenuation. Biological and chemical materials dissolved in seawater and the atoms and molecules of the

TABLE 11.2

Angle between sun and zenith	0°	10°	40°	60°	80°	90°
% Reflection	2.0	2.1	2.5	6.0	34.8	100
% Transmission	98.0	97.9	97.5	94.0	65.2	0

water itself are responsible. Infra-red and red light is absorbed most strongly in the near surface layers, which heats the water and helps maintain the oceanic heat balance. Orange light lasts only about a metre deeper than red, and most of the yellow is filtered out by 10 m, leaving only greens and blues. Almost all colour, except blue, will be eliminated below 20 m.

The latitude also plays an important role in determining the total amount of radiation on the sea surface. At high polar latitudes the sun is always at low angles and an inefficient heater. During winter the number of sunlight hours can drop to zero, but during summer can rise to 24. As a general rule, the total daily radiation at a location on the Earth varies sinusoidally with a maximum value in summer (Fig. 11.5). There will, nevertheless, be variations in the curves due to local climatic effects.

Absorption

If radiation of given wavelength and intensity, I, is absorbed, then the change in intensity over a fixed distance is proportional to the intensity and to the

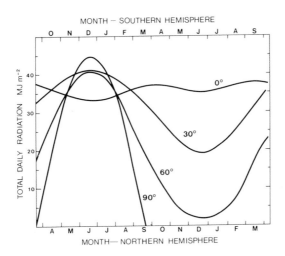

FIG. 11.5. *The total daily solar radiation received at the top of the atmosphere at various latitudes. These curves assume a radiant solar energy flux of 1.35 kW m⁻² (the solar constant) and then allow for latitude and time. Only about 55% of the total radiation at the top of the atmosphere reaches the Earth's surface. The exact percentage depends on cloudiness and atmospheric constituents.*

distance traversed. Provided that the constant of proportionality does not vary with depth, then the intensity at a depth z is given by

$$I = I_0 \exp(-\kappa z), \tag{11.8}$$

where I_0 is the intensity at the surface and κ is called the absorption coefficient. Equation (11.8) in the optical context is known as the Bouguer—Lambert law, but it is a special case of Beer's law which describes the absorption of radiation in a material. Sound absorption is also exponential in nature, and to account for this acousticians introduced the decibel. In the optical case it is usual to speak either of the absorption coefficient, or of the distance, Γ, over which light of a given intensity is reduced to 0.368 ($= 1/e$) of its original value. The quantity Γ is sometimes called the absorption distance, and it, along with κ, is strongly dependent on the wavelength of the light. The absorption coefficient and absorption distance for pure water over visible and infra-red wavelengths are shown in Fig. 11.6.

Absorption of light within natural waters is, in the absence of weeds or other large plants, attributable to four components: the water itself, phytoplankton, soluble humus-like products known as gilvin or gelbstoff ("yellow substance") and suspended inanimate particulate matter known as tripton. The extent to which these absorbing components combine to produce attenuation, or extinction, of the penetrating light also depends on scattering. Although it is the tripton, consisting mainly of mineral particles, which is the major scatterer,

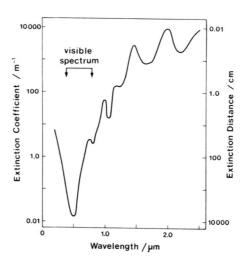

FIG. 11.6. *Idealised representation of the absorption coefficient for pure water. There is a pronounced minimum in the blue/green region of the visible spectrum.*

all four components participate in the increased light absorption. In turbid waters a light ray will scatter repeatedly and follow a zig-zag route downward. The pathlength it travels increases and the likelihood of it meeting an absorber also increases. The effects of particulate matter on vertical light attenuation are therefore complex and it is not easy to separate out its role as a scatterer from that as an absorber.

Coastal waters are generally more opaque than either pure water or open ocean regions. However, their most characteristic feature is that the wavelength of maximum transmission is shifted towards the yellow part of the spectrum. In the clearest ocean water maximum transmission is at about 465 nm (in the blue green). In the most turbid coastal waters it is about 575 nm (yellow) (Fig. 11.7), because of the optical action of gelbstoff. It does this in two ways. In the first instance gelbstoff is yellow in colour and enhances this part of the spectrum (the Yellow River in China is a classic example). Secondly, some gelbstoff exhibits fluorescence, which is an optical phenomenon in which light is absorbed at a short wavelength (generally in the ultra-violet) and re-emitted at longer wavelengths. Baltic seawater when radiated with ultra-violet light at 310 nm produces a response with a broad peak in the 430 nm to 530 nm range. This continuous conversion of light to a longer wavelength also helps push the maximum transmission towards the yellow end of the spectrum.

Gelbstoff is an important constituent for any remote sensing investigation of coastal regions. It can be detected by measuring the radiated intensity in the yellow region of the spectrum, which is the principle used in the Coastal Zone Colour Scanner (CZCS) of the NIMBUS-7 satellite. It is virtually a conservative

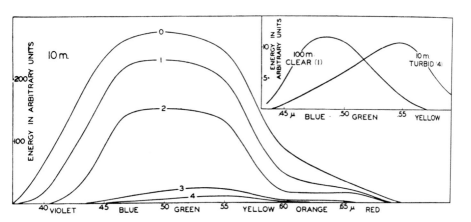

FIG. 11.7. *The energy spectra at a depth of 10 m in pure water (0), clear (1) and average (2) oceanic water and average (3) and turbid (4) coastal waters. The inset shows the shift towards the yellow in the spectrum of coastal water by comparing clean ocean water at 100 m with turbid coastal water at 10 m.*

substance, so that maps of constant gelbstoff concentrations provide information on water movement. In addition, it acts as an indirect measure of the amount of salt in the water. Figure 11.8 shows the relationship between gelbstoff and salinity in various parts of the Bothnian and Baltic seas, which indicates that a measure of gelbstoff concentration can be used to infer salinity, at least in those regions. Suspended sediment concentrations can also be deduced in an analogous way.

Despite its attractive properties as a tracer, there is still considerable controversy over the primary source of gelbstoff. One school of thought cites evidence to show that gelbstoff arrives in coastal areas via rivers. On the other hand, it can also be produced directly in the sea. Gelbstoff exists in the upwelling region west of South America, which is a region practically devoid of a freshwater supply from drainage and precipitation. In those areas it seems that phytoplankton degradation produces gelbstoff. A more detailed study of coastal

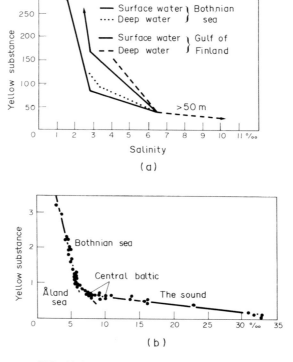

FIG. 11.8. *Gelbstoff (yellow substance) and salinity are related in northern European waters. The strong inverse relationship emphasises the coastal origin of gelbstoff.*

fluorescence may help to answer these questions because the chemical reactions involved in phytoplankton degradation produce fluorescent matter as a by-product, whereas coastal run off generally leads to non-fluorescent humic acid deposition.

However, a word of warning to intrepid adventurers, armed with fluorometers, who unthinkingly ascribe high fluorescence levels to oceanic origins. Many commercial washing powders use fluorescent dyes in order to achieve a "whiter than white" look and any coastal areas subject to large amounts of urban drain-water discharge will register anomalously high fluorescence levels. In fact, given the multinational penetration of the large soap manufacturers, and the propensity in the developing world to use rivers as a laundry, even supposedly pristine tropical rivers have been known to have astonishing fluorescence readings.

Scattering

Scattering is the name given to the effect that causes light rays to deviate from a straight line. In seawater scattering is due to two entirely different components, namely the scattering produced by the water itself and that produced by suspended particles. Scattering by pure water shows relatively small variations, affected only by changes in temperature and pressure, whereas particle scattering is dependent on the highly variable concentration of particulate matter.

The blue of the open ocean is due in part to scattering, known as Rayleigh scattering, by molecules of water. Molecular scattering increases as the inverse fourth power of the wavelength

$$\text{scattering} \ \alpha \ 1/\lambda^4$$

so that the blue end of the spectrum ($\lambda = 400$ nm) is scattered 10 times more effectively than the red ($\lambda = 700$ nm). Rayleigh scattering only occurs when particles are smaller than the wavelength of light. When particles are of the same size or larger than the wavelength, the scattering is less dependent on the wavelength, and the colour of the water depends more on the nature of the particulate material. Theoretical treatments of particulate scattering rely on a complicated electromagnetic theory to describe the interaction of an electromagnetic wave and a spherical particle. The results of this type of calculation, known as Mie scattering, are then compared with observations in order to try to determine the distribution of particles that caused the observed scattering distribution. This procedure is known as the inverse scattering problem.

There are other esoteric forms of scattering that are also named after their discoverers. An Indian physicist holidaying in the Mediterranean discovered that the deep clear blue colour of its waters was due in part to a process now known as Raman scattering. This acts in a manner slightly akin to fluorescence in that it shifts the wavelength of the incident light into a spectral peak in the blue part of the spectrum. Detailed spectroscopic examination of Rayleigh-scattered light will also reveal slight wavelength shifts due to a mechanism known as Brillouin scattering.

The oceanographic community has long tried to characterise water quality parameters by optical methods. The simplest of these is an *in-situ* method which consists of lowering a white plate about 30 cm in diameter, known as Secchi disc, overboard and noting the depth at which it is lost to sight. This depth, H_S, decreases as the total attenuation coefficient of the water (due to both absorption and scattering) increases and the two are very roughly related by $\kappa = 1.7/H_S$. More sophisticated methods rely on a knowledge of two quantities that are supposed to describe the nature of the scattering. These are the optical scattering coefficient, s, and the volume scattering function $\beta(\theta)$ at one or more angles, θ.

Another word of warning. Sophisticated, expensive methods are not necessarily the best ones to use. There are sophisticated instruments, such as nephelometers and transmissometers, that measure turbidity. Their use supposedly overcomes the subjectivity of the Secchi disc, but in practice they are delicate, temperamental machines whose measurements are not absolute because only instruments of identical optical design will give similar readings on the same sample. Where possible, use the simplest instrument, for with proper calibration it can produce excellent results. In Botany Bay, near Sydney, a Secchi disc depth of 1.2 m (the recreational water criterion of acceptability) corresponds to an approximate non-filterable residue of 6 mg per litre of water.

The volume scattering function is found by measuring the intensity of radiation at an angle θ from the forward direction of the incident light. If the volume scattering function is measured at all possible angles in a sphere around the scatterer and all the results summed together, then one obtains the optical scattering coefficient. In coastal regions, where the particle diameter, D, can range from $2\,\mu$m up to $30\,\mu$m (with most of them being about $3.5\,\mu$m), Mie scattering theory predicts that the optical scattering coefficient, s, is related to the number of scattering particles per unit volume, N, by

$$s = \pi N D^2 / 2, \tag{11.9}$$

which can be used to relate optical and water quality parameters.

Unfortunately s, the optical scattering coefficient, is a difficult quantity to measure, so that considerable research has been conducted to relate s to measured values of the volume scattering function $\beta(\theta)$, at one or more angles, θ. In the open ocean $\beta(45°)/s$ appears to be a constant, so that measurement at a $45°$ angle could be used to infer s. However, in the coastal zone the angle at which $\beta(\theta)/s$ is a constant is much smaller. There are theoretical grounds for assuming $\beta(4°)/s$ to be a constant, but coastal and harbour measurements for attenuation coefficients in the range 0.15 m^{-1} to 2 m^{-1} found $\beta(1.5°)/s$ to be the requisite constant. Further work in turbid river water in which κ ranged from 10 m^{-1} to 40 m^{-1} failed to find any angle for which $\beta(\theta)/s$ remained constant. Optical methods then yield quantitative water quality estimates provided that the pollution is not too extreme.

Photosynthetically Active Radiation (PAR)

The importance of light penetration is underscored by the fact that cells photosynthesise at a rate which depends on the absorption rate of quanta. A quantum of light of wavelength λ is energetically defined by

$$1 \text{ quantum} = hc/\lambda = 1.987 \times 10^{-25}/\lambda \text{ Joule,}$$

where $h = 6.626 \times 10^{-34}$ joule-second is Planck's constant and $c = 3 \times 10^8 \text{ m s}^{-1}$ is the speed of light. For the aquatic environment, measurements are made with a quanta meter which estimates the total quanta in the range 350–700 nm, and the results are generally given in Einstein's where

$$1 \text{ Einstein} = 6.023 \times 10^{23} \text{ quanta.}$$

The attenuation of PAR is also described by an equation of the form (11.8). There appear to be two competing influences at work. The attenuation coefficient for PAR is expected to diminish with depth because of the progressive removal of the more strongly absorbed wavelengths. On the other hand, as the angular distribution becomes more diffuse with depth so the attenuation coefficient should increase. These two tendencies cancel each other out in turbid coastal waters. Thus the PAR attenuation coefficient basically gives a measure of the euphotic zone.

The shape of the curve relating incident light and the resulting photosynthesis has been the subject of considerable study. Simple curves, of the form shown in Fig. 11.9 describe the relationship when all other nutrients are present and

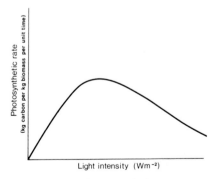

FIG. 11.9. *A typical curve relating light intensity to photosynthetic growth rate. Photosynthesis is inhibited at high light intensities.*

light is the only factor limiting biological production. However, in very shallow, clear tropical waters there may be an oversupply of light. The photosynthesis of certain plants is disrupted at very high light intensities and the curve relating photosynthesis to light intensity then has a definite peak in it.

11.6 Radar

Radar is an active sensing system in which electromagnetic waves are transmitted and reflected waves received by the same instrument. The usual radar — the type used in airports and on board ships — uses microwaves with wavelengths around 10 cm (3 GHz). These waves are strongly reflected by metal objects such as ships, aircraft or automobiles and show up as blips on a radar screen. In addition, a lot of other things show up on radar screens and in the early days of radar they were called angels because they were small blips that flew about the screen. Radar angels were subsequently found to be birds. There is substantial microwave reflection by water, and the water content of birds is sufficient for them to show up on radar screens. This is also true of the atmosphere and the more water in the atmosphere the greater the microwave reflection. Coastal microwave radar is thus an ideal way of monitoring coastal rainfall within range of the radar. Figure 9.2 depicted the radar trace showing the rainfall distribution within a hurricane about to cross the Australian coast. Careful calibration of the radar can yield quantitative estimates, in mm hr^{-1}, of the rainfall.

Recent and exciting uses of radar are in the radio wavelength part of the spectrum with frequencies between 25 MHz and 30 MHz. At these frequencies mobile coastal units can map variable surface currents out to a distance of 70 km from shore. The radar relies on a scattering mechanism known as Bragg scattering, by analogy with the diffraction of X-rays from the regular rows of atoms in a crystal lattice. The radar sifts, from the chaotic superposition of ocean surface waves, those waves travelling directly towards or away from the radar and of wavelength one half of the radar wavelength. These particular waves then return a scattered echo to the radar receiver.

The radar receiver sees the motion of the waves as a shift between the received frequency and the transmitted signal. This frequency shift is called the Doppler shift. A current beneath the surface waves represents a transport of the water mass and shifts the wave affected peaks even more (Fig. 11.10) by an amount $2U/\lambda$, where λ is the radar wavelength and U is the current in the direction of the radar. Two radar units situated about 50 km apart can then work out the complete water movement of a given patch of coastal water. Besides giving information on water motions, the same radar systems can be used to deduce information about the waves themselves. The basic idea is that the larger the waves, the larger their returned echo.

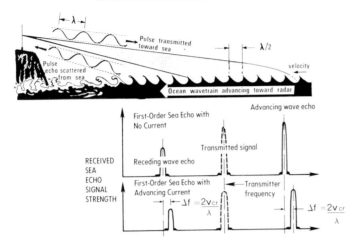

FIG. 11.10. *Sketch showing the principles of Bragg scatter from the sea, and resulting signal echo spectra without and with an underlying current.*

11.7 Satellites

Satellites observe large-scale phenomena, and there is considerable interest in their use within oceanography. A number of research satellites and operational satellites have carried instruments that produced useful oceanographic data, but the first satellite specifically dedicated to oceanographic measurements — Seasat A — was launched in mid-1978. Unfortunately a battery malfunction crippled it after 3 months, but the preliminary data that was obtained indicated an exciting future for this form of remote sensing.

In general, an instrument on board a satellite operates by scanning a small area of water, digitising the information, transmitting it to Earth and then digitising an adjacent area. The area of one scan on the ground, the footprint of the instrument, is called a pixel (an amalgam of picture cell), and a scan line is composed of a sequence of adjacent pixels. The individual pixels and scan lines show up clearly on Fig. 11.11, which displays the west coast of Australia. The sequence of scan lines can be produced either by the orbital motion of the satellite, or for those satellites that are in geosynchronous orbits and fixed over one location on the equator, by movement of the instrument on board the satellite. The forward motion of orbital satellites can be used in particularly esoteric ways in order to improve the ground resolution, and to decrease the pixel size. An instrument on board Seasat, called the Synthetic Aperture Radar (SAR), used this principle to obtain high resolution (i.e. 50 m × 50 m) information on ocean surface waves. This was an active sensor, as was a pulsed laser that Seasat carried to accurately determine sea level for tidal and geodetic studies. Most satellite instrumentation relies on passive remote sensing, because the

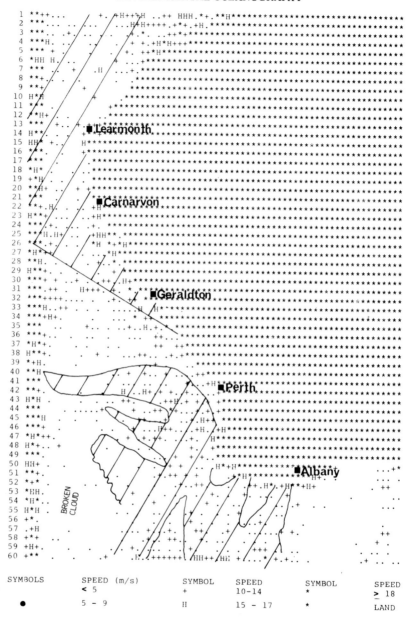

FIG. 11.11. *Ocean surface wind speeds deduced from a satellite based passive microwave sensor. Each pixel shows up clearly and represents a wind speed over water as given in the caption. Asterisks denote either very strong winds or land and the coast of Western Australia stands out strongly (especially if you look at the figure from a distance). Scan lines are numbered on the left, and the cloud distribution — deduced from another instrument on the satellite — has been shaded onto the figure with diagonal lines.*

weight and electrical power requirements of active systems are usually too great. Satellite instrumentation can be divided into three groups depending on the frequencies utilised: visible, infra-red, and microwave.

Visible Sensors

Satellite sensors operating within visible wavelengths can only relay useful oceanographic information when there is no cloud. The best known system utilising visible sensors is that on the Landsat series which produce high resolution (57 m X 57 m) pixels that can identify specific crops, map the coastline, detect and monitor visible pollution, sedimentation or erosion, and estimate suspended sediment concentrations in surface waters.

Landsat imagery can also be used for bathymetric mapping near the coast. This operates on the general principle that the deeper the water the darker it is, so that one can use the intensity of radiation to measure the depth. This technique has been used very successfully to produce updated hydrographic maps of remote coastal areas. Best results are obtained by averaging a number of the fortnightly Landsat scenes because large floating objects — such as drifting seaweed — can produce anomalous depth contours.

The orbiting research satellite Nimbus 7 carried an instrument known as the Coastal Zone Colour Scanner (CZCS) which, as its name implied, measured the colour of water in six spectral colour bands as well as an infra-red band. Since coastal composition is, as we have already seen, intimately related to the dominant colour, the CZCS system is intended to be used in determining chlorophyll, sediment, gelbstoff concentrations, and the presence of obvious colour changes (fronts) in the water on a 800 X 800 m resolution.

Infra-red Sensors

A typical infra-red sensor detects radiation at a wavelength of about 11 μm. This particular wavelength is chosen for a number of reasons. It is not absorbed by any atmospheric constituents, it can readily be detected with present technology, and at 11 μm the intensity of radiation is directly proportional to the temperature of the emitter. Infra-red pictures are widely used by weather services because clouds show up very clearly, and one can estimate the cloud top temperature. Oceanographers, however, consider clouds a nuisance when they contaminate infra-red pictures. Fortunately, clouds are much colder than seawater, so that it is generally easy to differentiate cloud from water, but they shroud the underlying water from analysis. The reason that GOSSTCOMP maps (Fig. 1.4) are only produced weekly is in order to average out the effects of clouds.

Satellite infra-red techniques will estimate temperatures to an absolute accuracy of only 1 K or 2 K, but can detect temperature changes as low as

0.1 K. The absolute accuracy can be improved if there is sufficient ground truth
— that is, independent temperature estimates for the same region — so that a
local calibration curve can be constructed. High resolution infra-red data can be
used to monitor coastal currents, because temperature differentials show up so
strongly. A tri-weekly Gulf Stream analysis (Fig. 11.12) has been used by the
oil tanker industry to save on fuel shipping costs by accurately locating the

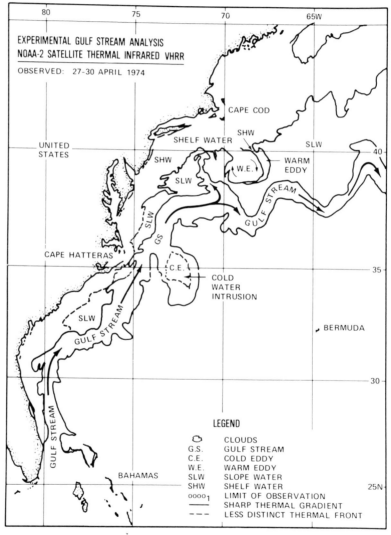

FIG. 11.12. *A simplified Gulf Stream sea surface temperature analysis
derived from results of the very high resolution infra-red radiometer
(VHRR) carried by the NOAA-2 satellite.*

warm waters of the Gulf Stream, which flows north-eastward off the US east coast.

Microwaves

The principal advantage of microwaves is that they can "see" through clouds. However, since water itself strongly affects microwaves, regions of active rainfall will show up very clearly. Global oceanic rainfall rates based upon microwave data can now be deduced for regions whose previous rainfall history was unknown, and microwaves permit us to map the detailed rainfall structure of hurricanes and other severe weather effects.

Modern passive microwave remote sensing relies heavily on measuring the emitted radiation at two different polarisations. Microwave observations of water reveal strong polarisation which diminishes as the surface wind increases. The depolarisation is apparently due to small capillary waves on the sea surface at low wind speeds and to surface foam from breaking waves at higher wind speeds. Figure 11.11 depicts coastal wind speeds deduced from microwave depolarisation. There seems to be a region of high winds near the coast for the first seven scan lines. The winds are then relatively calm from scan 7 to 20, but subsequent scans denote a windy region. The seaward extent of this windy region increases as one travels southward from scan 20, but it appears that there are winds of from 5 m sec^{-1} to 17 m sec^{-1} along most of the southern coast of Western Australia, with the notable exception of the most southeasterly parts of the scan where there is a distinct region of calm. There are edge effects of up to six pixels on both sides that should be ignored. Cloudy areas (determined from a simultaneous infra-red image) have been shaded onto the figure.

Visible and infra-red sensors are both capable of detecting ice over lakes and oceans. With microwave imagery, first-year and multiyear ice can be distinguished. The emissivity of first-year ice is close to unity in the wavelength region 0.3 to 11 cm, whereas multiyear ice has a lower emissivity.

Further Reading

Instruments

Chapter 4 of Ross's book and Chapter 6 of Pickard & Emery's book (Further Reading section, Chapter 1) give clear descriptions of the major oceanographic instruments. Those not mentioned in these books are described by:

W. BASCOM: Instruments for studying ocean pollution, *J. Env. Eng. Div. (Proc. ASCE)*, **103**, 1–8, 1977,

and

F. DOBSON, L. HASSE & R. DAVIS (eds.): *Air–Sea Interaction Instruments and Methods*, Plenum Publishing Corporation, New York, 1980.

Navigation

N. BOWDITCH: *American Practical Navigator,* US Defense Mapping Agency Hydrographic Center Publication No. 9, Washington D.C., 1977.

General Remote Sensing

There is a large literature on aspects of remote sensing – mainly dealing with electromagnetic radiation. The book by

E. C. BARRETT and L. F. CURTIS: *Introduction to Environmental Remote Sensing,* Chapman & Hall, London, 1976,

offers a good starting point, though for the latest developments one could consult the journal *Remote Sensing of Environment.*

Acoustics

Anyone requiring a general background to acoustics could do well to consult

L. E. KINSLER and A. R. FREY: *Fundamentals of Acoustics* (2nd edn), John Wiley, New York, 1962.

The major text on its oceanographic applications is

C. S. CLAY and M. MEDWIN: *Acoustical Oceanography,* John Wiley, New York, 1977.

Optics

The standard reference is

N. G. JERLOV: *Marine Optics,* Elsevier, Amsterdam, 1976.

Radar

Since most active microwave radars are related to meteorological studies, any student interested in them should consult

L. J. BATTAN: *Radar Observation of the Atmosphere,* University of Chicago Press, 1973.

The oceanographic use of HF radar systems is reviewed by

D. E. BARRICK, M. W. EVANS & B. L. WEBER: Ocean surface currents mapped by radar, *Science,* 198, 138–144, 1977.

Satellites

Articles on some of the specific sensors discussed include:

C. ELACHI: Spaceborne imaging radar, *Science,* 209, 1073–1083, 1980.
W. A. MOVIS *et al.*: Nimbus 7 Coastal Zone Color Scanner, *Science,* 210, 60–66, 1980.
TOM BEER: Microwave sensing from satellites, *Remote Sensing of Environment,* 9, 65–85, 1980.

CHAPTER 12

Data Analysis

12.1 Data Presentation

Information is processed data. The problem facing any collector of data is how to process and how to present raw data so that others can easily understand them. Raw data will be collected as an analogue trace, as a set of figures recorded in a log book, or as a set of records on paper tape, magnetic tape or punched cards. These data are hardly ever suitable for direct reproduction, as the cardinal rule in data presentation is that data should always be presented in graphical form. In the past, much data were presented in tabular form because graphing was particularly time-consuming. The advent of computer graphics systems means that this is no longer true. It also means that computing facilities with graphics equipment are as much a part of marine environmental investigations as plankton nets, current meters or CTD probes.

The choice of data to be graphed, and the manner in which they are presented, will depend on the purpose of the study. There are, for example, many graphical ways to present recorded current meter data. These include (i) current roses, which are modelled after wind roses (Fig. 9.6) and depict the proportion of observations at various compass directions. (ii) Progressive vector diagrams, which sum the current vectors over the recording period (Fig. 6.5). (iii) Stick diagrams which depict the instantaneous current vector as a line whose magnitude and direction mimic that of the observation. Each record is depicted by a line whose base is positioned along an axis that represents the time at which the reading was taken (Fig. 10.8). (iv) Time-series plots of the current components. Generally alongshore and onshore components are preferable for the horizontal components. Plots of speed and direction as two separate time series are very difficult to interpret and should be avoided.

Before plotting data they need to be processed, a procedure sometimes known as data massaging. Obvious errors in the data need to be corrected. In most cases the mere act of plotting the data will reveal these errors and they can then be eliminated and the corrected version replotted. The analyst will need to decide whether he wants to plot the data as collected, or whether he wants to sample it and plot daily midday values, say, or whether he wants to smooth it and plot daily mean values.

After one has a good idea of the nature of the collected data, the next step is to try and determine the interrelationships between data variables. Once again there are many different ways of doing this, but scatter plots are easy and informative. These plot one variable (e.g. temperature) against another (e.g. salinity) to determine if there is any relationship between the two (as in Fig. 5:3). If there is indeed a relationship, then one generally wishes to quantify it. This is done by statistical manipulation – usually based on linear regression. Most large computer installations carry program packages to do these statistical manipulations. GENSTAT (General Statistical Package) and SPSS (Statistical Package for the Social Sciences) are the most common. Despite its name, SPSS is also useful for those outside the social sciences, for it will manipulate large amounts of data, calculate the standard statistics of these data sets, and produce line printer plots of scatter diagrams.

Data management and processing is an important task in any large, interdisciplinary study which requires a separate person (or group) solely devoted to it. The reason is that most specialists are more interested in collecting than in processing data so that they will not bother to graph them until the completion of the study. In an interdisciplinary study the biologist will often need the meteorologist's wind data in order to understand his own results, and the hydrologist may be tearing out his hair waiting for the oceanographer to deliver the tide heights to him. In these cases, the best solution is for them all to deposit their results in a data archive, from which the data manager produces graphs of all the data. These graphs are then distributed to all the participants at agreed upon intervals. A duty statement for such a person can read as follows:

(i) prepare all raw data in computer compatible form;
(ii) acquire, read and store data from magnetic tapes;
(iii) verify and correct all data;
(iv) develop a data archival system compatible with the installed computer system that permits easy retrieval in various output forms and formats;
(v) retrieve information from the archival system, prepare and disseminate this information to the research coordinator and other team members both routinely and on request.

12.2 Data Analysis and Statistics

A data analyst should always try to understand – to "get a feel" for – his data, and there are many tools available to him from the field of statistics. The appropriate tool depends on the analyst's final objective, the nature of the data, and the amount of finance available. Numerous statistics books are available that are supposed to help the beginner. The majority of these are useless in environmental oceanography because they concentrate on the properties of the normal distribution. Though this distribution, also known as the Gaussian distribution, is a cornerstone of mathematical statistics and the theory of errors in observations, most environmental parameters are not normally distributed.

The depth of the tropical mixed layer is an exception, since it comprises one environmental parameter that is normally distributed. It is plotted in Fig. 12.1 on special graph paper that is designed to produce a straight line for the cumulative frequency distribution (i.e. the probability of occurrence of a particular depth and all lesser depths) of a normal distribution. The observed points — obtained over a 5-year interval in the Louisiade archipelago — lie very close to a straight line. The mean depth is found from the depth at which the probability of exceedance equals 50%.

Robust statistics (as opposed to normal, or Gaussian statistics) are those statistics that are applicable regardless of the nature of the statistical distribution of the data. The mean, $\bar{y}$, of a series of numbers is a robust measure of the central tendency. It is obtained by adding all the numbers together and dividing the sum by the number (n) of data points.

$$\bar{y} = (y_1 + y_2 + \ldots + y_n)/n = (\sum_{t=1}^{n} y_t)/n. \qquad (12.1)$$

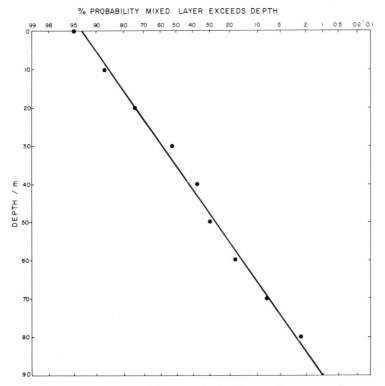

FIG. 12.1. *The depth of the tropical mixed layer varies as a normal distribution with a mean depth of 35 m. Mixed layer statistics are plotted on normal probability graph paper which produces a straight line for normal distributions.*

The variance, σ^2, is a robust measure of the variability of the data which is defined in terms of the mean square deviation from the mean

$$\sigma^2 = \sum_{t=1}^{n} (y_t - \bar{y})^2 / n. \qquad (12.2)$$

The square root of the variance is called the standard deviation.

For a normal distribution, such as that of Fig. 12.1, the standard deviation is the depth interval between 16% and 50% probabilities, and is the same as between 50% and 84% probabilities. The standard deviation of the data of Fig. 12.1 is 23.5 m.

Engineers who compute design criteria are particularly interested in the statistics of extreme and rare events. A typical problem would be as follows: Our company wishes to construct an underwater structure that is designed to last for 30 years. How heavy should it be to ensure that it does not topple? If one knows the general shape of the structure and is willing to make some assumptions about its fluid drag, the problem becomes one of estimating the maximum current speed to be expected in 30 years. Statistics enter into consideration because no-one has 30 years of underwater current data and it is necessary to extrapolate the short data record that one actually possesses in order to estimate the 30-year peak. Figure 12.2 illustrates an even more indirect way of arriving at an estimate. For the site in question there were no current meter data, but the wind statistics could be calculated on the basis of 17 years of record. Figure 12.2 plots this on special probability graph paper, under the assumption that these extreme winds obey a statistical distribution known as a Gumbel distribution, and if this is the case then the plotted points should lie on a straight line. The straight line can then be extended to estimate that over a 30-year period one can expect a 42 m s⁻¹ wind.

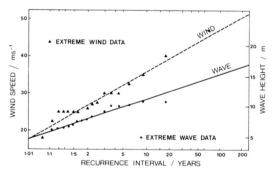

FIG. 12.2. *The recurrence interval of extreme winds is estimated by plotting the existing information (17 years in this case) on extreme value probability graph paper and extrapolating a straight line. The wind data is used to calculate expected wave heights.*

The next step is to convert the 30-year wind into a 30-year current. This particular site was 80 m deep and it was assumed that a wind of this strength would mix the whole body of water and move it in the direction of the wind at 0.03 of the wind speed — as explained in Chapter 9.5 — to produce a 30-year steady design current of 1.26 m s^{-1}. To this one must add the maximum expected tidal current speed (0.33 m s^{-1} in this case) and the maximum expected wave-induced currents generated, at the appropriate depth, by the 42 m s^{-1} wind (0.06 m s^{-1}). The structure must therefore be designed to withstand an overall current of 1.65 m s^{-1}.

12.3 Time-series Analysis

Geophysical data often arrives in the form of a time series of equally spaced observations obtained by a recording instrument that samples at predetermined intervals of time. Time-series analysis forms another branch of statistics with its own techniques and its own vocabulary. The easiest one to understand is smoothing. Spurious "noise" can appear in the time-series record (an electric connection, for example, may have been loose and sparking) and this noise can be reduced by smoothing.

TABLE 12.1

Time, t	=	1,	2,	3,	4,	5,	6,	7,	8,	9,	10
Time series, y_t	=	1,	2,	0,	1,	1,	0,	2,	2,	1,	0

A three-point running mean is an example of smoothing. For the data record of Table 12.1 a three-point running mean produces the values:

$$-, \quad 1, \quad 1, \quad 2/3, \quad 2/3, \quad 1, \quad 4/3, \quad 5/3, \quad 1, \quad -.$$

Each value is obtained by summing the value of y_t at time t and the values on either side of it, which are represented by y_{t-1} and y_{t+1} and then dividing the total by three. This produces a new time series which we shall denote by $\hat{y}_t$ where

$$\hat{y}_t = (y_{t-1} + y_t + y_{t+1})/3$$
$$= (1/3)\,y_{t-1} + (1/3)y_t + (1/3)y_{t+1}. \tag{12.3}$$

The running mean series, $\hat{y}_t$ is smoother than the original series y_t. The original series jumped between 0 and 2, whereas the running mean varies only between 2/3 and 5/3. There are two undefined values at either end of the time series which can be handled at the analyst's discretion.

There are technical reasons that make a weighted running mean superior to the ordinary running mean of equation (12.3). Weights of (0.25, 0.5, 0.25), known as Hanning weights, are frequently used to produce a series

$$\hat{y}_t = (0.25y_{t-1} + 0.5y_t + 0.25y_{t+1}). \tag{12.4}$$

Notice that the weights are normalised — that is to say that when they are all added together they sum to unity. Another popular choice is the exponentially weighted past running mean

$$\hat{y}_t = (1/2)y_t + (1/4)y_{t-1} + (1/8)y_{t-2} + (1/16)y_{t-3} + \dots \qquad (12.5a)$$

Its popularity rests on its ease of programming in recursive form:

$$\hat{y}_t = (1/2)y_t + (1/2)\hat{y}_{t-1}. \qquad (12.5b)$$

The advantage of a recursive form, such as equation (12.5b), is that it can be executed in real time, as each new data point is collected, and it requires only one storage register. As each new data point is collected it is added to the value in the data register, and the resulting sum is divided by two to produce the new value of $\hat{y}_t$.

What would happen if we used negative weights? Say $(1, -1, 0)$ to produce a series $\tilde{y}_t$ given by

$$\tilde{y}_t = y_t - y_{t-1}. \qquad (12.6)$$

The time series $\tilde{y}_t$ is a measure of the derivative of the time series y_t and it will tend to emphasise, and even amplify, any noise in the data. Negative weights such as these do not smooth the series and there is no necessity for them to be normalised to unity. Equation (12.6) is normally used for trend removal, as it will eliminate any long-term upward or downward trend in the time-series data.

All of the procedures defined by equations (12.3) to (12.6) are examples of filters. Equations (12.3) to (12.5) define different types of low pass filters; in which the low-frequency variations of the time series y_t are reproduced in the filtered series $\hat{y}_t$. Equation (12.6) defines a type of high pass filtering in which the high-frequency fluctuations of y_t are reproduced in $\tilde{y}_t$.

The Z-transform

The complicated process of filtering involves three sets of numbers: the raw data of the original time series, the filtered data of the final time series, and the filter itself. Figure 12.3a depicts a graphical representation of the process, with the symbol $\otimes$ representing the mathematical manipulations that are involved. The process of taking a running mean consists of a convolution between the filter, say $(1/3, 1/3, 1/3)$ and the data set represented by y_t. Differencing the data, as in equation (12.6), consists of a convolution between the filter $(1, -1)$ and the data set y_t. Hence the symbol $\otimes$ represents convolution.

An alternate notation is used in systems analysis. To understand this we must introduce an operator, Z, whose sole function in life is to shift a time series, or an element of the time series, forward one unit in time

$$y_{t+1} = Zy_t = Z^2 y_{t-1}. \qquad (12.7)$$

The operator Z, which is also called the forward shift operator, possesses an inverse Z^{-1} which is the backward shift operator, that behaves such that a)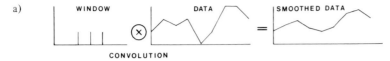

CONVOLUTION

b)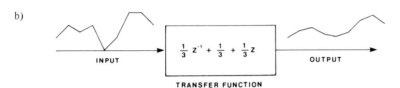

TRANSFER FUNCTION

FIG. 12.3. *Filtering can be treated as either (a) a convolution between the input data and the filter (also known as a window), or (b) as a transfer function process in which the filter defines the characteristics of the transfer function.*

$$y_{t-1} = Z^{-1} y_t = Z^{-2} y_{t+1}. \tag{12.8}$$

In this shift notation — known as the Z transform — the three-point running mean (12.3) is written

$$\hat{y}_t = (1/3)Z^{-1}y_t + (1/3)y_t + (1/3)Zy_t$$
$$= [(Z^{-1}/3) + (1/3) + (Z/3)]y_t \tag{12.9}$$

The Z transform notation converts the complicated mathematical process of convolution into an ordinary multiplication. The filtered series $\hat{y}_t$ is the product of the original time series y_t and the Z transform of the filter.

Figure 12.3b shows how the Z transform notation can be used to produce a systems diagram that depicts smoothing by a three-point running mean. This is also called a transfer function, or input–output, representation. The transfer function $Z^{-1}/3 + 1/3 + Z/3$ transforms the input y_t into the output $\hat{y}_t$.

Figure 10.6 has already depicted a complicated systems diagram for a particular environmental problem. The model, as given in Fig. 10.6, is a conceptual one because it has not been quantified. No mathematical forms have been given to the transfer functions. It is very difficult, if not impossible, to find the correct mathematical representation for each of the transfer functions. Conversely, a simple systems diagram such as that of Fig. 12.3b is unlikely to have much relevance to environmental systems. The task of a systems modeller, to be described in section 12.4, is to bridge the gap.

Autocorrelation and Cross-correlation

A correlation coefficient highlights the similarity between two data sets. A correlation coefficient near +1 means that both time series vary together, whereas a coefficient near -1 means that a rise in one data set corresponds to a fall in the other. A correlation coefficient of zero indicates that there is no relationship between the two sets of data as they stand, If there are cyclic changes in the two data sets that are not in phase, then it is possible that the two are indeed related even though the correlation coefficient was zero. This will be discovered by shifting one of the data sets by the appropriate time interval and again finding the correlation coefficient.

Often one wishes to examine the persistence of a data set. How long does the current stay the same? This is done by convoluting the data set with itself in order to produce an autocorrelation function. Multiply together each term of the two series (i.e. the data set and its replicate), sum the numbers and normalise the sum so as to lie between ± 1. The procedure is repeated by lagging (i.e. shifting) one of the data sets by one time interval, then by two time intervals, and so on. The autocorrelation function, which is defined at lag τ by

$$a_\tau = \frac{y_0 y_\tau + y_1 y_{\tau+1} + y_2 y_{\tau+2} + \ldots + y_t y_{\tau+t} + \ldots}{(y_0^2 + y_1^2 + y_2^2 + \ldots y_t^2 + \ldots)}$$

is then plotted as a function of τ. If there is little or no persistence in the data, the autocorrelation will drop quickly to zero.

Cross-correlations measure the relationship between two different data sets, x_t and y_t, by convoluting the two. The cross-correlation function at lag τ (and τ may be positive or negative) is similarly defined as

$$c_\tau = \frac{x_0 y_\tau + x_1 y_{\tau+1} + x_2 y_{\tau+2} + \ldots + x_t y_{\tau+t} + \ldots}{\sqrt{(x_0^2 + x_1^2 + \ldots + x_t^2 + \ldots)(y_0^2 + y_1^2 + \ldots + y_t^2 + \ldots)}}$$

The cross-correlation function is particularly useful if one wants to find the time that a particular event took to travel between two points. For example, the travel time of a tsunami can be found by cross-correlating time series of sea level between two stations. The cross-correlation function will have a maximum value at a particular lag which corresponds to the appropriate travel time.

Figure 12.4 depicts auto- and cross-correlations for 3-hourly coastal wind data in the South Australian gulfs. Two stations are depicted: Port Augusta, whose wind rose is shown in Fig. 9.6, and Port Pirie, situated 85 km due south. The wind data was separated into north–south (X) and east–west (Y) components and each component was examined separately. The analysis covers a summer month (16 February to 28 March 1976) so that the bumps in the curves at lags of 8, 16, 24 and 32 are caused by diurnal sea breezes. Because both locations experience sea breezes and they are sufficiently close to experience the same synoptic weather, their instantaneous cross-correlation coefficient is high (0.75). The fact that the cross-correlations and auto-correlations are so similar indicates that the records are virtually interchangeable, as far as the synoptic weather is concerned, so that one anemometer would provide wind information relevant to

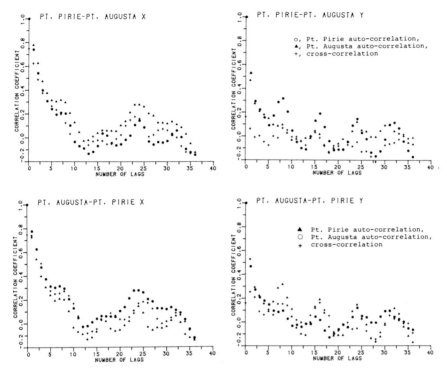

FIG. 12.4. *The auto-correlation of Port Augusta (triangles in top graphs, circles in bottom graphs) and Port Pirie (circles at top; triangles at bottom) wind data as well as their cross-correlation (crosses). Three-hourly wind data for the X(N–S) and Y(E–W) components were used. Daily sea breeze effects are apparent at lags 8, 16, 24, and 32 (namely 1, 2, 3 and 4 days), whereas the overall rise between lags 12 and 24 reflects the mean time between the passage of fronts.*

the dynamics of the gulf. The overall rise in the X component record at long lags reflects the predominance of 3-day wavelike cycles in South Australia's summer weather.

Harmonic Analysis

Much data collected in oceanography are a result of periodic disturbances such as waves or tides. Harmonic analysis, or Fourier analysis, is a means whereby a time series is decomposed into a set of sinusoidal waves of fixed frequencies. This process has already been illustrated in Figs 4.2 and 4.3 and in many cases the final result is depicted as a power spectrum as in Fig. 3.11.

If one has a time series of 100 data points then a harmonic decomposition will yield a total of 100 sine and cosine waves. These 100 waves will not all be at different frequencies because both a sine wave and a cosine wave are needed to specify the amplitude and phase at each frequency. If the time series consists of N data points in the time domain, then a Fourier transform will represent the data set by $(N/2 + 1)$ independent frequencies, in the frequency domain. These frequencies range from a wave of zero frequency (the mean value of the data set) to a wave of frequency $1/(2\Delta t)$, where Δt is the time interval between samples of the time series. If daily data is collected, then $\Delta t = 1$ day and one obtains frequency components that range from zero cycles per day (the mean) to 0.5 cycles per day (see Fig. 3.11).

The usual way to transform the data from the time domain to the frequency domain is to perform a Fourier transform upon it. In recent years an algorithm known as the Fast Fourier Transform (FFT) has been developed and incorporated into many packages of computer subroutines. The IMSL (International Mathematical and Statistical Library) packages, which are found on most large computer systems, incorporate a number of FFT subroutines as does the more specialised ARAND package developed by Oregon University specifically to analyse oceanographic data. One requirement for FFT processing is that the length of time-series data must be a power of 2. There must be either 2, 4, 8, 16, ... data points. Though this may appear restrictive, it can usually be achieved by subtracting the mean from the time series to produce a new time series of zero mean and then adding sufficient zeros at the end to bring its length up to a power of two. Programs also exist to calculate the Fourier transform of any number of data points. They are neither fast nor economical of data storage space.

Another use for the FFT is that of filling gaps in a collected data record due, for instance, to a temporary instrument malfunction. If the gap is small, and in the midst of sufficient data points on either side, then an iterative use of an FFT algorithm will reconstruct a complete record with the same spectral composition as the observed record. The method is iterative in that the gap is first of all replaced by a straight line. An FFT is applied and the points in the gap replaced by the first Fourier frequency. The FFT is reapplied and the gap filled in from the sum of the first two Fourier frequencies, and one continues to work up to all Fourier frequencies that characterise that number of data points.

A completely different method of producing power spectra utilises a technique called stochastic estimation. It relies on the fact that there is a mathematical link between a Z transform and a Fourier transform and uses statistical estimation techniques to find the Z transform. There are computer packages available that will estimate a transfer function in Z transform form. The principal package for this is the CAPTAIN (Computer Aided Programs for Time-Series Analysis Including Noise) package marketed through the UK Institute of Hydrology. The trick in using the transfer function method for power spectral computations is that the input is taken as a series of normally distributed random numbers whereas the output is the time series itself. Algorithms within the program (which are generally based on either the maximum entropy or maximum likelihood method) then calculate the transfer function, which can then be converted to a power spectrum.

12.4 Modelling

In the management and planning of environmental systems one of the major needs is for adequate forecasting of possible future conditions. However, it is rarely, if ever, possible or even desirable to explain all the phenomena associated with air and water systems by precise laws or relationships. The complex interactions between physicochemical variables, biological components and socio-economic aspects ensure that forecasting is a difficult procedure.

Models are built in order to assist in forecasting and prediction. There are many different types of models. They range from physical models that are scaled down representations of the system under consideration to mathematical models that consist only of a computer program. The choice of model is determined by the objectives of the study. A physical model would be appropriate if one needed to estimate tide heights in a complicated waterway, but it would be inappropriate for detailed estimates of pollutant dispersion.

Environmental and socio-economic systems have been characterised as poorly defined systems. This means that the investigator rarely has good *a priori* information on the nature of the various mechanisms which characterise the system and result in the observed behaviour. A laboratory researcher can carefully plan experiments to discover more about his system and so remove any ambiguities present in his observations. An environmental analyst can rarely resort to the luxury of planned experimentation if he wishes to investigate the system. (There are exceptions. One Californian team persuaded the Navy to speed a destroyer up the coast in an unsuccessful attempt to generate edge waves.) Usually one must make do with passive monitoring exercises aimed at observing the system behaviour during its normal operations.

Figure 12.5 depicts the major stages in model building. There are four major stages: first, the formulation and identification of plausible models; second, the choice or identification of suitable model parameters and linking them together into the structure of the model; thirdly, estimation of those parameters which characterise the chosen model structure; and finally, validation of the model.

Initial Model Formulation

In the case of badly defined systems, such as those encountered in most large-scale environmental investigations, models to simulate the system are often patchworks of sub-models each of which was written by a mono-disciplinary expert on one component process of the system. This tends to make simulation models very complex and with judicious "fiddling" they can be made to repro-

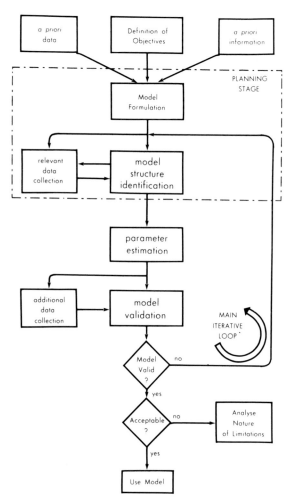

FIG. 12.5. *The model building process contains a number of feedback loops, the most important of which requires a restructuring of the initial model if subsequent data indicate that the model is invalid.*

duce almost any behaviour. There has been a regrettable tendency for modellers to believe that a complicated model is a better model. This is false. In modelling, one should always apply Occam's razor to prune unnecessary fat, for the best model is the simplest model consistent with the study objectives.

Models suitable for coastal investigations may generally be divided into four types:

(i) Stochastic models

These are any form of model in which statistical techniques are used. For example, statistical functions may be used to simulate the movement of pollutants in an estuary. Stochastic models can be used as preliminary speculative models designed to find the dominant behaviour of the system. Used like this, one builds a large patchwork model and allows the model parameters to vary randomly within specified bounds (this is called Monte Carlo simulation). The results of each model run are stored and it will generally be found that the system behaviour is controlled by relatively few variables — the rest can be eliminated. In the *Cladophora* problem described in Chapter 10, Monte Carlo simulation modelling indicated that phosphorus, nitrogen and light would be important, whereas carbon, ammonia and dissolved oxygen would not.

Alternatively, stochastic models can be used to model collected data. Rainfall-runoff models that use transfer function techniques have been particularly successful in simulating river flow. In this case the time series of rainfall is initially filtered to allow for soil moisture effects; the resulting effective rainfall is treated as the input, the observed flow is taken as the output and the Z transform transfer function linking the two is calculated.

(ii) Simulation models

This covers: models based upon the analogy between fluid and electric current flows which model a stretch of water by a bank of resistances and capacitors; models using electrical circuits in a general purpose analogue computer to perform mathematical functions such as integration; and physical models in which water is used as the flow medium.

Physical models are expensive to build, but for certain problems offer excellent results. Because they are built to scale they cannot answer all questions about the system. The laws of scaling require that the non-dimensional number characterising the phenomenon of interest be the same in the model and in the prototype. If turbulent effects are to be modelled, then the Reynolds number ($\rho r u/\mu$, see Chapter 8.1) must stay the same. For density stratification the Richardson numbers $[-(g/\rho)(d\rho/dz)/(dU/dz)^2$, Chapter 8.1] must be identical. Gravitational effects are controlled by a Froude number ($u/\sqrt{gr}$), whereas diffusive effects are related to the Peclet number (Λ/ur). The list goes on and on, and it is impossible for any scale model to match all of them. Hence their restricted use.

(iii) *Analytical models*

If the phenomenon of interest can be described by well-validated equations with simple solutions, then the direct use of these solutions constitutes an analytical model. Tidal inflow into deep, regular-shaped estuaries constitutes the most frequent example of the use of analytical models.

(iv) *Numerical models*

When the phenomenon of interest can be described by well-validated equations but these equations do not have simple solutions, one must resort to numerical modelling. Most such equations are differential equations and numerical techniques revolve around methods of solving them. The three main approaches consist of the method of characteristics, finite difference methods or the finite element method.

One particular danger with numerical models is that the solution technique may introduce a spurious solution. The process of solving an advection equation using a finite difference technique will introduce spurious diffusion (known as numerical dispersion) into the model even when there is no dispersion present. A poor choice of time increment can produce numerical instabilities, and so on.

Model Structure Identification and Estimation

We have seen how a stochastic simulation model reveals the important parameters in a preliminary speculative model. A coordinated systems analysis strategy of modelling and data collection plans and initiates relevant data collection at the same time as the initial modelling. This data set will be used in the next step in model building; namely, identifying a suitable model of the system, and discovering the parameter values that characterise the model.

In an oil spill trajectory model the choice of an oil slick velocity vector U_0 (Chapter 9.5) as

$$U_0 = U_c + \zeta W$$

identifies the model. Field data from simulated small (200 ml) oil spills can be used to test the model and to parameterise (i.e. find the best value) for the wind factor ζ. Experiments near the coast of a shallow gulf indicated that the "standard" model in which ζ is a scalar with a value of 0.035 is not the best model. In that case ζ had to be treated as a matrix with unequal diagonal elements and, in addition, the cross-shore (onshore-offshore) component of the current was found to be so weak and variable that it played no role in the oil transport. For an oil spill spreading model one would need to estimate the parameters con-trolling the spread. This depends on the size of the spill, but as it is environ-mentally unacceptable to spill hundreds of tonnes of oil for an experiment, one parameterises an oil spill spread model with data from spills of opportunity (i.e. rush out and take readings when a large spill accidentally occurs) or from scaled laboratory experiments.

Model Validation

The final and continuing stage in model building is validation. Here the model's forecasting ability is evaluated on data other than that used in the identification and estimation studies. If the model continues to forecast well over this test data interval, it is assumed that it is conditionally acceptable in the sense that, as far as it is possible to test, the model seems satisfactory.

Validation is a continuing procedure since the model will need to be reassessed in the light of future developments and additional data. If major changes in the system take place, for instance, it is likely that the model will need to be modi-fied in some manner because it will not necessarily mirror the changed behaviour in the new situation. Of course, the only real validation of a model is that it satisfies the purposes for which it was intended; in other words that it "works" in practice.

Despite the practical common sense in model validation it is one of the most frequently omitted steps in model building. Many modellers are so confident of their knowledge of the system that they believe that their cherished model is the system. In particularly simple situations this may be justified, and subsequent experiments will validate the model. In complicated models such confidence is rarely justified. It is shabby model building to present or publish the results of a model — even if every step of the model follows accepted scientific norms — if there is no validation data against which the results of the model can be com-pared. Such shabby model building is far too prevalent.

12.5 Ecosystems Analysis

The theoretical basis for analysing, modelling and forecasting biological systems is more meagre than that of physical systems. The field of theoretical ecology has made rapid strides recently and there exist quantitative methods by which biological data can be analysed for environmental assessment. The basic data that are needed consist of more than just species lists. One needs an estimate of the number of individuals, or the biomass, within each species.

Species diversity is one measure that has been used to compare different ecosystems, or the same ecosystem at different times (as, for example, before and after pollution). Considerable argument exists over the definition of a diversity index and even of its utility. One index that has been proposed to categorise the diversity of an ecosystem is the slope of a curve that plots cumulative number of species against the logarithm of the individuals counted. This has been advocated on heuristic grounds because the resulting curve is often a straight line.

Another choice for the diversity index is based on information theory, and defines an index D_i as

$$D_i = - \Sigma\, n \log n, \qquad\qquad (12.10)$$

where n is the number of individuals in that species divided by the total number of individuals in the ecosystem, and the sum Σ extends over the total number of species present.

One attraction of equation (12.10) is that it links biology with information theory, which can in turn be linked to the thermodynamic concept of entropy. Entropy can in turn be related to the physical idea of energy flow. Considerable space was devoted in Chapter 3 to the energy flow of wave motion. In that situation the energy can be well defined and expressed quantitatively for any given wave. Energy flows in an ecosystem are more difficult to determine, though ecologists have managed to study a limited number of systems in detail. Primary producers, which constitute the lowest link in the food chain, capture only about 1% of the total incident solar radiation, as outlined in Chapter 5.6. When compared to the incident PAR (photosynthetically active radiation, as defined in Chapter 11) the ecological efficiency of energy capture rises to about 10%.

As energy passes along the food chain, entropy is produced and the diversity index (12.10) increases. About 10% of the energy passes from one level to the one above, with 90% being dissipated as heat during the work processes involved.

Environmental studies of biological systems are then often designed to yield information on energy flows. In practice this is achieved by determining annual nutrient budgets for the ecosystem under study. This forms a methodology of static ecosystems analysis. Dynamic ecosystems analysis attempts to model the biological system by a set of differential equations, in a manner analogous to the differential equations of fluid motion. The dynamic approach has proved very formidable, because there is no firm theoretical base for the differential equations that are used, and equations suitable for one species may give unreliable results when applied to another species. There are indications, however, that data based modelling techniques may overcome some of the past problems, particularly when they are used in conjunction with Monte Carlo simulations.

Further Reading

Time Series Analysis and Statistics

J. W. TUKEY: *Exploratory Data Analysis*, Addison-Wesley, Reading, Mass., 1977.
E. R. KANESEWICH: *Time Sequence Analysis in Geophysics* (2nd edition), University of Alberta Press, Edmonton, 1975.
G. M. JENKINS and D. G. WATTS: *Spectral Analysis and Its Applications*, Holden Day, San Francisco, 1968.

Modelling

There is an extensive literature on modelling, but little is of direct relevance to coastal waters.

D. M. McDOWELL and B. A. O'CONNOR: *Hydraulic Behaviour of Estuaries*, Macmillan, London, 1977,

has three excellent chapters on modelling estuarine systems.
Wider aspects of marine modelling (including ecosystems analyses), are covered by

J. C. J. NIHOUL (ed.): *Modelling of Marine Systems*, Elsevier, Amsterdam, 1975.
E. D. GOLDBERG, I. N. McCAVE, J. J. O'BRIEN & J. H. STEELE (eds.): *The Sea*, vol. 6 (Marine Modelling), John Wiley, New York, 1977,

and

E. B. KRAUS (ed.): *Modelling and Prediction of the Upper Layers of the Ocean*, Pergamon, Oxford, 1977,

whereas references on the wider aspects of modelling in general include

V. VEMURI: *Modelling of Complex Systems,* Academic, N.Y., 1978.
R. G. BENNETT and R. J. CHORLEY: *Environmental Systems*, Methuen & Co. Ltd, London, 1978.
G. C. VANSTEENKISTE (ed.): *Modelling, Identification and Control in Environmental Systems*, North Holland Publishing Co., Amsterdam, 1978.

CHAPTER 13

Coastal Assessment

13.1 Introduction

Until now I have tried to describe the dominant physical processes in the coastal environment in order to demystify the subject for environmental managers. Let us now consider the institutional, legal and mental framework in which an environmental manager operates.

Environmental assessment is a prelude to environmental management. The piece of coast to be managed may be under actual pressure such as eutrophication, pollution or overcrowding, or it may be under threat of pressure from some proposed development. To ensure that this latter possibility is properly considered, many states have enacted environmental impact legislation. This type of law places a legal requirement on a developer to assess the environment in order to create and maintain conditions under which man and nature can exist in productive harmony.

Except for rare and specific cases, the law does not specify exactly how this desirable harmony will be achieved, though its attainment should involve (a) an interdisciplinary approach, (b) an integration of natural and social sciences and environmental design arts and (c) unquantifiable environmental amenities and values should be given appropriate consideration along with economic and technical considerations.

These are high expectations, and it is important to realise that the *means* by which they are achieved are themselves of crucial importance. Only a team, led by a wise and forceful environmental manager, can provide the requisite multidisciplinary skills. Its teamwork must be facilitated by effective trust and communication which, during the course of the study, must be extended to the community at large. Public involvement in environmental impact assessment through open meetings, and through public comments on draft environmental impact statements, should be integral to the assessment process. Technical workshops with scientific specialists and meetings with the government officials charged with regulatory powers are equally important.

Sadly, there are many environmental investigations that were shabbily planned and poorly executed. Some of the problems that I have witnessed include the four great lacks:

(i) *Lack of well-defined objectives*

Government departments initiating a study under strong political pressure are particularly prone to this fault. A promise to maintain the environmental integrity of the coastal zone may win votes, but will induce migraines in the government official who has to implement the policy. He must zoom in on the salient problems and redefine his objectives in those terms.

(ii) *Lack of analysis*

These studies appear to have measured the adequacy of assessment in terms of the volume of data collected. It was stated in Chapter 12 that information arises only from analysis and interpretation of collected data. Lists of tidal constituents do not constitute an adequate physical oceanographic investigation. The tides have to be interpreted and the amplitudes and circulations explained in terms of the aims of the study. Species lists alone do not comprise a biological investigation. The observed species must be explained within an ecological context.

(iii) *Lack of coordination*

A gaggle of academics often appears to suffer a lack of coordination. Each specialist is so concerned with the fascinating ramification of his own arcane work and explores it to such great depths that no-one else can understand it. These studies are particularly harmful because the participants will all finally depart believing the study to have been a great success and proceed to plan yet another uncoordinated study of some real or imagined problem. No harm is done if these studies are presented as contributions to pure science, but they should not be advertised as contributions to environmental assessment.

(iv) *Lack of leadership*

Environmental protection and management are of little import in certain decision-makers' eyes and these people will appoint, or delegate, responsibilities to juniors far too inexperienced to fulfill the role of an environmental manager.

Let us assume that all hurdles have been surmounted and the physical oceanographer is part of a functional assessment team. There are two further factors that should govern his operations. These are the realisation that (i) the results of his work will be judged within an economic framework based on cost-benefit analysis and that generally (ii) coastal waters management uses oceanographic data in order to maintain the aquatic ecosystem.

13.2 Cost-Benefit Analysis

The basic idea behind cost-benefit analysis is that one can assign a dollar value to everything of importance, sum the costs, total the benefits and proceed if the benefits are greater than the costs. Dollars are used because they are the most convenient measuring rod, though they are not necessarily particularly easy to use when one has to value a "priceless" commodity such as a scenic view.

Cost-benefit analysis forms an active branch of economics which has its own special approaches and its own set of technical terms. This brief outline is mainly intended to familiarise you with some of these terms and enable you to appreciate some of the unique problems that environmental cost-benefit analysts face.

In theory, a cost-benefit analysis should be an exercise in which various project alternatives (including the no-action or no-build alternative) are evaluated for the potential to produce maximum benefits and minimum costs. Since everyone has at least an intuitive appreciation for just what constitutes a benefit and what constitutes a cost, a cost-benefit approach to impact assessment appears quite rational. The problem in a world composed more often of greys than of simple black and white, is the difficulty in assigning those dollar values to intangibles. Private costs and private benefits are generally easier to calculate than social costs and social benefits. The private costs and benefits are those that accrue to a single individual or corporation upon completion of a particular project. They differ from social costs and benefits because they neglect external effects that are not reflected in market prices.

These effects are known as externalities, and an example in which they arise would be that of a producer releasing untreated gaseous or liquid waste. The social cost is difficult to assess because it depends on the assimilative capability of the medium. If this capability is not overburdened then the costs may be low or even zero. However, if the waterway into which the wastes are dumped is required for downstream drinking purposes and this added effluent requires additional expenditure to return the water to an acceptable quality for human consumption, then the cost of this aspect of the externality can be assessed.

Costs are then defined as the monetary expenditure required to satisfactorily complete a project or alternatively as the monetary value of foregone opportunities. In other words, the benefit that we would have gained had we gone ahead with the project becomes the cost of not proceeding with the project. Benefits are usually defined by how much people would be willing to pay for the favourable effects resulting from that project.

That there is a certain arbitrariness to all this can be illustrated by the Peel Inlet *Cladophora* problem outlined in Chapter 10. The monetary value of the benefit (i.e. elimination of the weed nuisance) was determined by a questionnaire in which the residents of Mandurah were asked the level of extra taxes they would be willing to pay in order to alleviate the problem.

There are two immediate problems. The first is the "free rider" problem in which people will not be willing to pay if they believe that they can get the benefit without having to pay for it. Conversely, there will be people who will grossly overstate what they would be willing to pay when questioned but would renege if actually required to pay the amount they claimed.

Finally, it is worth pointing out that coastal waters tend to be thought of as an undepletable amenity resource. It cannot be bought or sold, but it can be exploited. Such resources are prone to the "tragedy of the commons". This refers to the overexploitation of the free grazing areas, known as the commons, that existed in rural England. Each landowner, and each peasant, felt that they could obtain the best short term benefit from the commons by grazing as many of their cows on it as they possibly could — even though this unco-operative attitude was ruinous in the long term. To avoid this tragedy of overexploitation, affluent, highly industrialised countries place great emphasis on amenity resources and their preservation. This is because these same affluent countries make high demands upon the world's product resources of minerals, forests, fish, oil and any other commodity that can be bought, sold and transported. The high level of pollution and energy consumption associated with their economic activity then places a great burden on their amenity resources.

13.3 Aquatic Ecosystems

Present-day approaches to the management of the coastal environment depend heavily upon what is known as the ecosystem management concept. Beneficial management involves manipulation to maximise the returns to man, whilst exploitation is management that results in the reduction of the productivity of the ecosystem to mankind over a period of time.

One method of delineating an ecosystem is through its trophic structure: who eats whom? The feeding relations of the species in the community will determine the flow of energy and nutrient materials from the physical environment to plants, which, as the first trophic level, act as food producers and from them to the higher trophic levels of the consumers (Fig. 13.1).

Theoretical approaches to potential fisheries production require an estimate of the region's primary productivity, and the ecological efficiency of the chain of trophic levels required to convert the producers (plankton and other plants) into fish. Table 13.1 indicates how this can be done for the world as a whole and shows why coastal and upwelling areas sustain larger fish yields than the open ocean. Basically, there are less trophic levels so that the conversion of nutrients into edible fish proceeds more efficiently.

The rate of primary productivity depends on the supply of light and nutrients. In addition, productivity depends on the amount of material present, for it is this existing material that reworks the nutrients into new protoplasm. When sufficient nutrients are present, then the rate of phytoplankton photosynthesis

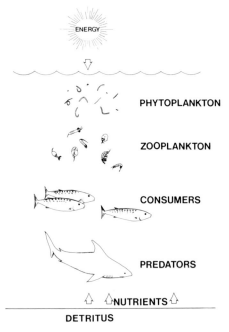

FIG. 13.1. *The trophic web. The diagram emphasises that the light energy for primary production decreases with depth and is thus limited to surface waters; whereas the nutrients are reworked from detritus and are most accessible near the bottom. The two regions overlap in high productivity areas.*

TABLE 13.1. *Estimate of Potential Annual Fish Production*

Province	Area (km²)	Productivity (g carbon m⁻² a⁻¹)	Carbon (G tonnes)	Trophic levels	Efficiency of each trophic level (%)	Fish production (tonnes)
Oceanic	326×10^6	50	16.3	5	10	16×10^5
Coastal	36×10^6	100	3.6	3	15	12×10^7
Upwelling	3.6×10^5	300	0.1	1.5	20	12×10^7

is proportional to (i) the relative photosynthesis rate – obtained from a curve like that of Fig. 11.9 – (ii) the concentration of phytoplankton present, which is generally expressed in terms of chlorophyll per cubic metre of water in the water column, and the rate of photosynthesis is inversely proportional to (iii) the extinction coefficient, κ, of the light.

In upwelling areas there is an abundance of nutrients for the phytoplankton, so that primary production is limited by the availability of light. However, in most coastal waters outside of upwelling zones, phytoplankton growth is controlled by the availability of nitrogen. Figure 10.5 illustrated this. We can see that phytoplankton growth (as measured by chlorophyll) did not begin until after the addition of abundant amounts of nitrogen. Other primary producers with slower growth dynamics are sometimes able to amass sufficient nitrogen that their growth is controlled by the input of phosphorus.

Turn again to Fig. 10.5 and notice the strong sharp peaks in chlorophyll concentration. These are called algal blooms and show up in the Peel Inlet as large areas of floating green scum. In that particular estuary they caused no noticeable harm, but elsewhere algal blooms have caused fish kills either by lowering the dissolved oxygen concentration or by forming toxic materials; or occasionally both. The Florida red tide is a plankton bloom, caused by a type of phytoplankton known as a dinoflagellate, which kills great numbers of fish and shellfish in the south-eastern waters of the United States.

The idea that the growth rate of an organism is limited by the availability of the growth factor that is in shortest supply is known as Liebig's law of the minimum. It is schematically illustrated in Fig. 13.2 which shows a hypo-

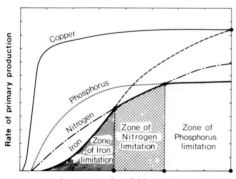

FIG. 13.2. *Hypothetical illustration of a sequence of nutrient factors limiting primary productivity, whose rate will follow the heavy line and be limited first by iron, then (as iron becomes available) by nitrogen and finally by phosphorus. Some nutrients, such as copper, may always be present in superabundance.*

thetical sequence of nutrient factors limiting primary productivity. In this particular example trace elements such as copper are in abundant supply, but the rate of primary production will follow the heavy line and be limited first by iron, then (as more iron becomes available) by nitrogen and finally by phosphorus.

Ecosystems management requires a knowledge of the complete trophic web and the pressures liable to be placed upon it. Fisheries management, which operates almost exclusively at the highest trophic level, indicates some of the problems. Prior to the twentieth century, the prevalent fisheries philosophy was that the fish populations in the ocean were virtually inexhaustible. By the turn of the century, however, it was noticeable that the catches of certain heavily fished populations were not increasing in response to increasing fishing pressure, and it became apparent that all fisheries have an upper limit of exploitation and can be overfished.

The management basis for many fisheries nowadays is the maximum sustainable yield (MSY). This theoretical concept — which has many opponents — assumes that there exists an optimum catch that balances the underexploitation of low fishing effort and the dangers of overfishing. However, when the world's conventional fisheries are examined with respect to MSY, we find that most are nearing MSY, have reached MSY or are overexploited. Overexploitation has occurred because wild fish stocks are common property resources and can be exploited by anyone. In dealing with common property resources, the individual rarely behaves in terms of the group optimum but concentrates instead on short-term gains. One hopes that the proclamation of exclusive fishing zones will lead to better management of this particular resource.

13.4 Pollution

Various pollution aspects have been considered in previous chapters. They can be conveniently grouped under seven headings, namely: sediment; organic matter; chemicals; herbicides and insecticides; oils; radionuclides; heat and general rubbish. In the past, pollution control consisted of regular monitoring to ensure that water quality standards were not breached and heavy fines, or a complete closure of operations, were imposed upon offenders. The problem with this system is that it virtually ensures that receiving waters will be polluted to just below their legal limits. The present-day viewpoint is that any potential offenders should be required to institute "best management practices" or "best available technology" to minimise the pollution load of their own effluent. At the same time a contingency fund is established — and a tax imposed on the appropriate industry — to finance the requisite action in case of catastrophic disaster, such as an oil tanker spill, or a major release of a dangerous chemical.

Sediments

Natural sediment loads from a river can often be high, but in general they are restricted to periods following large storms. Harbour works, dredging, and other such maritime construction can disturb silt and produce detrimental effects. Light penetration and photosynthetic activity is reduced. Bottom dwelling animals and plants are smothered, fish spawning is impaired. The waste assimilation capacity of the water is reduced. And shellfish, particularly oysters, clog up and may die.

Organic Matter

This is perhaps the most common type of pollution and its effect is largely indirect. Low dissolved oxygen levels, and eutrophication in estuaries are two different manifestations of this problem. They were discussed in Chapters 5 and 10 respectively.

Organic enrichment arising from city sewage disposal can cause problems. There are now well-established methods of treating such putrescible material. In modern sewage works, the solids in the sewage are allowed to settle out to undergo anaerobic fermentation. A large part of the carbon is set free, bound to hydrogen in methane gas. This gas may be collected and used as fuel, whilst the spent sludge makes good fertiliser. After settling out the solids, the clarified liquor may be sprayed down a trickle filter, where the remaining inorganic matter is oxidised by a bed of clinker, well infected with bacteria, protozoa, fungi and algae, together with fly larvae and worms. The film of bacteria and fungi break down the organic matter into simpler harmless forms, and the insects and other animals clear away excessive growths of the bacterial film. The liquor now contains very little putrescible matter and can safely be discharged to natural waters.

Chemicals

Chemical pollution causes direct damage because poisons are involved. The substances vary as much as the industry itself varies: phenols, cyanides, arsenic (especially from sheep and cattle dips), chlorine, slaked lime and compounds of many heavy metals. Poisonous chemicals can directly cause fish kills. Paint remover tipped into a salmon or trout stream can kill all the fish there. The only way to treat such poisonous residues is dilution to the point where they become harmless.

Heavy metals are particularly harmful. Oysters and cockles can accumulate heavy metals, such as mercury or cadmium, and concentrate them in their bodies until they become dangerous as food. Certain fish also accumulate heavy metals and can cause Minimata disease in humans who eat them, as explained in Chapter 5.

Chemical pollution can also be indirect. A number of Sydney's famed beaches were noted for their beautiful Norfolk Pine trees. These mysteriously died in the mid-1960s and intensive environmental investigation revealed that the cause was washing detergent discharged from sullage outlets near the beaches. Washing detergent lowers the surface tension of water, and when detergent contaminated sea spray washed over the pine needles, the lowered surface tension allowed salt to penetrate the leaf material and destroy it.

Insecticides and Herbicides

Seabirds can accumulate high concentrations of persistent insecticides such as DDT. The insecticide residue becomes ever more concentrated as it progresses up the food chain. The sea birds then lay easily broken, thin-shelled, eggs and so fail to reproduce. In addition DDT and other chlorinated hydrocarbons, such as endrin, aldrin and dieldrin, are extremely toxic to fish. Heavy fish kills can follow crop spraying if some of the spray is blown into the water.

Oils

The behaviour of a natural slick was discussed in Chapter 9. Present methods of prevention and clean-up rely on booms, which are floating sausage-like bags, for containment followed by pumping skimmers for clean-up. The use of detergents is in disfavour, because the excessive quantities used to clean the beaches after the *Torrey Canyon* spill did far more ecological damage than the oil itself would have done.

Environmental planning with respect to oil spills — or any other hazardous discharge — often consists of the delineation of exclusion zones, zones in which that particular activity is precluded. For example: if one wishes to ensure that a particular marine park will not be subject to oil pollution from exploration, in what areas should there be a total ban on drilling? A simple method of doing this is shown in Fig. 13.3. It consists of plotting the assumed trajectories if oil were to be spilled from the location to be protected, and plotting sufficient of these trajectories to be able to assign statistical confidence limits to them. The exclusion zone is then determined by tracing onto a transparency the extreme trajectories within which 95% of the other trajectories lie, and rotating the transparency through 180°. The resulting lines mark the boundaries of the exclusion zone, whose far boundary needs to be set according to an assumed speed and decay time for the oil.

Notice in Fig. 13.3 that the initial calculation needs to use wind and current information from locations rotated by 180°, and the resulting modelled oil spills all occur over land!

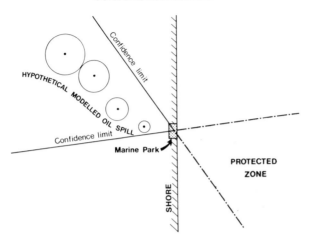

FIG. 13.3. *Protection zones in which, for example, oil exploration is completely banned may be set by determining confidence limits within which 95% of any spilled oil will lie. The protected zones are based on simulated spill trajectories rotated through 180°.*

Radionuclides

Britain's nuclear power stations are situated on the coasts and will regularly discharge their effluents into estuaries and coastal waters to form one of the largest concentrations of marine radioactive disposal areas in the world. Careful control, and siting where natural currents will disperse the effluents, reduce their pollution potential. An exception is Windscale, in Cumberland, situated on the Irish Sea. At this plant, spent nuclear fuels are processed and some of the fission products discharged into the Irish Sea. Some of the ruthenium-106 becomes concentrated in the alga *Porphyra*, from which the Welsh seafood "laverbread" is made. But upon testing, the exposure to radionuclides of the consumers was found to be well within safety limits.

The general conclusion from this, and other studies, is that the present situation with regard to radioactive pollution is reassuring. The nuclear industry prides itself on the protection standards which were adopted before the technology became widespread. However, public concern is still lively and any possible radioactivity needs to be scrupulously investigated and meticulously documented in any environmental assessment.

Thermal Pollution

Hot water is a pollutant because it contains far less dissolved oxygen than water at lower temperatures; and also because, at temperatures above about 37°C, the number of plants and animals able to tolerate the heat rapidly diminish. Above 42°C very few can live.

In temperate climates it seems that the effect of heated water, released by the cooling towers of electricity generators, has been beneficial to estuarine eco-systems. It has the impact of an earlier and longer-lasting summer growth period. But the situation is different in hotter climates. On the south-eastern coasts of the United States and in the Gulf of Mexico, summer temperatures are already near the upper limit of tolerance for much marine life.

In addition, large numbers of small invertebrates are sucked into the cooling systems and power stations. They are then subjected to severe buffeting, heat, and to the weak chlorine concentration added to the water to inhibit sedentary organisms settling in the pipes. Phytoplankton appear to pass through all this unharmed, but there is no certainty that the young of fish species that spawn in estuaries will also be as tolerant.

General Rubbish

The wholesale dumping of rubbish in water bodies is one of the uglier features of the modern environment. It is made worse by the greater mobility of societies today, which allows people to visit even remote beauty spots in large numbers. Where public spirit is wanting, they will leave their rubbish behind them.

Further Reading

An excellent guide to environmental assessment is:

P. A. ERICKSON: *Environmental Impact Assessment (Principles and Applications)*, Academic Press, New York, 1979 (395 pp.),

whereas management is dealt with by:

J. R. CLARK: *Coastal Ecosystems Management (A Technical Manual for the Conservation of Coastal Zone Resources)*, John Wiley & Sons, New York, 1977 (928 pp.).
G. A. ROUNSEFELL: *Ecology, Utilization, and Management of Marine Fisheries*, C. V. Mosby Co., St. Louis, 1975 (516 pp.).

There are numerous texts on ecology. Three which deal specifically with aquatic systems are, in order of increasing sophistication:

C. F. HICKLING: *Water as a Productive Environment*, Croom Helm, London, 1975.
G. K. REID & R. D. WOOD: *Ecology of Inland Waters and Estuaries* (2nd edition), D. Van Nostrand Co., New York, 1976.
R. S. K. BARNES & K. H. MANN (eds.): *Fundamentals of Aquatic Ecosystems*, Blackwell Scientific, Oxford, 1980 (229 pp.).

Finally, I would highly recommend:

W. CUFF & M. TOMCZAK jr. (eds.): *Synthesis and Modelling of Intermittent Estuaries*,
Springer Verlag, New York, 1981,

because this is the only book to thoroughly examine a multidisciplinary environmental
study that failed to achieve its goal and discusses the reasons for this failure.

Some Physical Quantities in SI units

Quantity	Name	Symbol	Expression in terms of other units	Dimensions
area	square metre	m^2	–	$[L^2]$
volume	cubic metre	m^3	–	$[L^3]$
speed, velocity	metre per second	m/s	–	$[LT^{-1}]$
acceleration	metre per second squared	m/s^2	–	$[LT^{-2}]$
wave number	per metre	m^{-1}	–	$[L^{-1}]$
frequency	hertz	Hz	c/s	$[T^{-1}]$
force	newton	N	$kg \cdot m/s^2$	$[ML\,T^{-2}]$
pressure, stress	pascal	Pa	N/m^2	$[ML^{-1}\,T^{-2}]$
energy, work, quantity of heat	joule	J	N.m	$[ML^2\,T^{-2}]$
power	watt	W	J/s	$[ML^2\,T^{-3}]$
electric charge	coulomb	C	A.s	$[T\,A]$
electric potential	volt	V	W/A	$[ML^2\,T^{-3}\,A^{-1}]$
electric resistance	ohm	Ω	V/A	$[ML^2\,T^{-3}\,A^{-2}]$
conductance	siemens	S	A/V	$[M^{-1}\,L^{-2}\,T^3\,A^2]$
density	kilogram per cubic metre	kg/m^3	–	$[M\,L^{-3}]$
specific volume	cubic metre per kilogram	m^3/kg	–	$[M^{-1}\,L^3]$
dynamic viscosity	pascal second	Pa . s	$N \cdot s/m^2$	$[ML^{-1}\,T^{-1}]$
kinematic viscosity	metre squared per second	m^2/s	–	$[L^2\,T^{-1}]$
moment of force	newton metre	N.m	$kg\,m^2/s^2$	$[ML^2\,T^{-2}]$
surface tension	newton per metre	N/m	kg/s^2	$[MT^{-2}]$
heat flux, irradiance	watt per square metre	W/m^2	$J/(m^2\,s)$	$[MT^{-3}]$
specific heat	joule per kilogram kelvin	J/(kg K)	$m^2/(K.s^2)$	$[L^2\,T^{-2}\,K^{-1}]$

Sample Equipment List

The following is an example of a check-list of oceanographic field equipment for a coastal environmental investigation. The particular investigation concerned the behaviour of a hypothetical oil spill in the Spencer Gulf of South Australia. An oil spill trajectory model for this region was developed and the results of the model incorporated in the Environmental Impact Statement. However, as discussed in Chapter 12, field experiments are needed to validate the model and in this case small (200 ml) oil patches were followed by boat and tracked by shore based surveyors whilst an anemometer and a current meter (deployed from the boat) automatically took records. In addition the behaviour of computer cards — which were used in lieu of drift cards — was monitored.

THIS LIST IS ONLY AN EXAMPLE

Each study will need to prepare its own list of equipment. The main object in reproducing it is to emphasise how detailed it must be, down to pencils and pencil sharpeners.

Equipment Checklist

Current Meter

1. 2 × current meters (Alekseev)
2. 2 × spare recording mechanisms
3. 2 × carabina clip attachments
4. 2 × taut wire mooring frames
5. 2 × sets of subsurface floats
6. 1 × coil 25-mm rope
7. 2 sets of 25-mm thimbles, shackles and swivels
8. 20 m × 12 mm chain
9. 2 × anchor weights
10. 8 × 20 mm polystyrene floats
11. 1 × coil 8-mm rope
12. 1 set thimbles, shackles
13. 1 × profiling current meter

Tracking Exercises

3 × two-way radios
40 litres of diesel fuel in steel jerrycans
Condensate and crude oil, as available (to be collected in Adelaide)
50 × 5 litre, 50 × 1 litre plastic screw-top juice bottles
30,000 computer cards (10,000 each of red, orange & yellow)
6 drogues — 6 × met. balloons
    6 × 4" styrene buoys
    6 × fencing wire masts and orange flags.

10 × orange sheet marker floats and anchors, consisting of:
    12 broomsticks
    24 × 8″ styrene buoys
    30 × 2 m × 1 m Dayglo orange high-density polystyrene sheets, with black coded
      symbols for I.D.
    12 × 30-m anchor ropes, eyes both ends
    12 × sets of scrap steel anchors, & chains & shackles
Small box, containing:
    Life jackets
    Flares
    Water,
    Waterproof clothing
    Small plane
    First aid kit

General

300-m roll 12-mm O.D. polypropylene rope
150-m roll sashcord
1 roll 10-gauge galvanised fencing wire
1 roll tie-wire (galvanised)
Chain
Field notebooks (aluminium)
3 ring binder for note filing
3 ring binder pages for above
Pencils, drawing equipment, pencil sharpeners
Waterproof marker pens
Camera, with polarising filter
20 rolls Kodachrome 36 exp. 64 ASA film
Whyalla town map
S.A. road maps
Alarm clock
Full admiralty chart coverage of both S.A. gulfs
2 Eskies (a type of ice box)
2 water cooler bottles

Toolkit

Hand-drill, selection of drills
Multigrips
Pliers
Wire cutters
Insulation tape (4 rolls)
Tie wire (corrosion resistant)
WD 40 (a spray to loosen rusted or corroded screws)
Torch
Screwdrivers (selection)
Spanners
Scissors (large size, 2 pairs)
Stanley trimmer & spare blades
Heavy duty stapler
Plastic adhesive (polythene, marine resistant)
Super glue, araldite
Polyethylene binding tape
1 roll masking tape

Permanent, waterproof marking pens
Hacksaw and blades
Pocket knife
Splicing knife
Matches
Heavy polythene bags (12 × 15 in)
Rubber bands
Seasickness pills

Wave Glossary

Acoustic wave: A wave due to the compressibility of water.

Airy wave: Surface gravity waves predicted by a simple linearised theory that treats them as sinusoids.

Baroclinic wave: Waves in which the isopycnals and isobars are not parallel. This generally means that they have a vertical phase structure. Internal waves in a stratified fluid are baroclinic waves.

Barotropic wave: Waves in which the isopycnals and isobars are parallel. Surface waves are barotropic waves.

Boussinesq wave: Waves which would be found in a theoretical medium that is stratified but incompressible. Their frequency lies between the buoyancy frequency and the inertial frequency of rotation.

Buoyancy wave: A wave whose frequency equals the buoyancy (or Vaisala-Brunt) frequency. This is the frequency of oscillation of a water particle in a stratified fluid when displaced from its equilibrium position.

Capillary wave: A wave in which surface tension forces dominate.

Cnoidal wave: A Crapper wave (see below).

Continental shelf wave: A low-frequency wave trapped along the continental shelf that can only propagate with the coast on its left in the Southern Hemisphere and the coast on its right in the Northern Hemisphere. Their period must exceed the inertial period.

Crapper wave: A type of surface gravity wave predicted by a non-linear theory that accounts for their finite amplitude. The solutions are in terms of elliptic function, cn, and so they are sometimes called cnoidal waves.

Deep water wave: Surface waves in deep water ($H/\lambda > 0.25$) which disperse and satisfy a dispersion relation $\omega^2 = gk$.

Edge wave: Gravity waves with period less than the inertial period that are trapped along a beach or along a coastline and can only propagate parallel to it.

Equatorial wave: Any of a large variety of wave modes that are trapped by the equator and constrained to propagate parallel to it.

Equatorial Kelvin wave: An equatorial wave mode that has a phase speed equal to that of a Kelvin wave, and has an exponential decrease in amplitude on either side of the equator.

Evanescent wave: A wave with no vertical phase structure. Suface waves are evanescent.

Gerstner wave: A type of surface gravity wave predicted by non-linear theory which accounts for their finite amplitude. The wave shapes are trochoidal, that is a curve traced out by a point rolling along the rim of a wheel.

Gravity wave: Any wave in which gravity (as opposed to say, surface tension) is a dominant restoring force.

Inertial wave: Any wave whose period equals the inertial period of $(12/\sin\phi)$ hours at latitude ϕ.

Internal wave: A wave due to density gradients and stratification in the interior of a fluid.

Kelvin wave: A wave trapped along a coast or in a channel that propagates at the shallow water wave speed parallel to the boundary and in the same direction as a continental shelf wave. It has an amplitude that decays exponentially from the boundary.

Planetary wave: A long period long wavelength wave whose dominant restoring force is the latitudinal variation in the Coriolis force.

Poincaré wave: A special class of edge waves.

Rossby wave: A planetary wave on a plane (usually called the beta plane) rather than on a sphere.

Seismic sea wave: A tsunami.

Shallow water wave: Surface waves in shallow water ($H/\lambda < 0.05$) which are non-dispersive with phase and group speeds of $(gH)^{1/2}$.

Sinusoidal wave: Any wave whose form is that of a sinusoid. Most linear waves are assumed to be sinusoidal.

Solitary wave (or soliton): A non-linear wave characterised by a single crest. Solitons satisfy the Korteweg de Vries equation.

Stokes wave: A type of non-linear surface gravity wave that is obtained by a higher order approximation to the Airy wave. The wave height appears in the dispersion relation for these waves.

Surface wave: A wave on the surface of the water.

Surface tension wave: A capillary wave.

Swell waves: Surface gravity waves with period of about 10 s generated by distant storms.

Tidal wave: An obsolete term for a tsunami.

Trochoidal wave: A Gerstner wave.

Tsunami: A long wavelength surface gravity wave generated by earthquakes. The breaking of a tsunami upon a coast generally causes great damage.

Wind waves: Any wave generated by the wind. The term is generally used for short period (about 1 s) surface gravity waves directly generated by wind.

Yanai wave: A type of equatorial wave mode.

Oceanographic Glossary

Alga: A type of phytoplankton (see below).

Amphidromic: A representation of tides within an ocean basin.

Atoll: A ring-shaped coral reef, often carrying low sand islands, enclosing a lagoon.

Baroclinic: When surfaces of constant pressure intersect surfaces of constant density. See Wave Glossary.

Barotropic: When surfaces of constant pressure are parallel to surfaces of constant density. See Wave Glossary.

Bathymetry: The depth of water and information related to it.

Bayou: A swamplike estuarine creek, also called a slough.

Benthic: Related to the bottom of a body of water.

Bore: A rapid rise in water height that propagates into estuaries.

Boundary currents: A current whose properties are influenced by the presence of a solid boundary.

Cabbeling: Sinking due to mixing of waters of equal density but differing temperatures and salinities.

Cay: A low island of sand or coral. The same as a **Key**.

Celerity: Wave speed.

Chop: Short-crested waves that spring up quickly in a moderate breeze.

Clapotis: A standing wave formed by reflection from a seawall.

Coastline: The line that forms the boundary between the coast and the shore.

Copepods: A type of zooplankton (see below).

Cumec: One cubic metre per second.

Cusp: Low mounds of beach material separated by crescent-shaped troughs.

Dinoflagellates: A type of phytoplankton (see below), responsible for "red tides".

Diurnal: Once every 24 hr.

Ebb: Associated with a falling tide.

Ecosystem: A community functioning as a dynamic system within its environment.

Eddy: A circular movement of water.

Euphotic zone: The upper layers of a water body into which sufficient light penetrates to permit plant growth.

Eutrophication: An oversupply of nutrients to a water body.

Fathom: An imperial unit of measure equal to 1.83 m.

Fjord: A narrow, deep, steep-walled inlet of the sea usually associated with a deep glacial trough.

Flocculation: Small, loosely aggregated bits of material (floccules), usually clay, forming through electrochemical reactions in saltwater.

Flood (current or tide): Associated with a rising tide.

Flushing: The movement of water out of a waterway, characterised by a flushing time.

Flux: The rate of change of a quantity per unit area per unit time (for three-dimensional quantities) or per unit distance per unit time (for two-dimensional quantities).

Fronts: Regions of separation between fluid masses of different physical properties.

Fumigation: An air pollution event characterised by a plume spreading only downwards.

Gelbstoff: A general name for soluble humus-like products that give coastal waters a characteristic shift towards the yellow part of the spectrum.

Geomorphology: The study of the shape of the land.
Gilvin: Gelbstoff (see above).
Groin (groyne): A shore protection structure built to trap littoral sand drift.
Gyre: A circular or spiral motion. Oceanographers use gyre for large-scale (hundreds to thousands of kilometres) motion, and eddy for small-scale motions.
Halocline: A region within which salinity changes markedly in the vertical.
Hydrography: The description and study of seas, lakes, rivers and other waters and especially the configuration of underwater surfaces.
Iso-: A prefix for a line or surface joining points with an equal physical property. The general term is isopleth. Specific terms include: Isobar − isopleths of constant pressure; Isohaline − isopleths of constant salinity; Isohyet − isopleths of constant rainfall; Isotherm − isopleths of constant temperature; Isopycnic or isopycnal − isopleths of density.
Jet: A narrow strong current.
Key: A low island of sand or coral. The same as **Cay**.
Lagoon: A shallow body of water usually connected to the sea.
Lee: The region toward which the wind blows. The lee of an object is sheltered.
Levee: A dike, or embankment, to protect land from inundation.
Liman: An estuarine lagoon.
Littoral zone: A zone affected by the action of both tides and breaking waves.
Mangrove: A tree found in brackish waters that has large prop root systems that are important in coastal land building.
Nephelometry: The study of particles suspended in a fluid.
Neritic: Related to coastal waters.
Normal: A mathematical term synonymous with perpendicular.
Normal curve (normal distribution): A bell-shaped symmetric curve describing the distribution of measurement errors. It is also called the Gaussian curve, or the error function.
Orthogonal: A line drawn perpendicular to water wave crests. It corresponds to a ray.
Outfall: A structure extending into a body of water for the purpose of discharging wastewater or sewage.
PAR − photosynthetically active radiation: Electromagnetic radiation between 350 nm and 700 nm within which band plant photosynthesis occurs.
Pelagic: Relating to oceanic and coastal waters.
Phytoplankton: Floating plant life of natural waters.
Pocket beach: A small beach between two barriers.
Prism: See **Tidal prism**.
Pycnocline: A region within which density changes markedly in the vertical. A pycnocline must also be a thermocline, a halocline or both.
Ray: The path along which wave energy travels. For water waves it is the same as an orthogonal (see above).
Reef: An offshore navigation hazard of rock, coral or sand whose depth is less than 10 m. A sand reef is called a bar.
Ria: A long narrow inlet, with depth gradually diminishing inward.
Ring: An eddy formed by a strong current but detached from it.
Rip: A narrow strong current flowing outward from the shore, caused by waves.
Scattering: The effect that causes light to deviate from a straight line. Various types include Rayleigh, Mie, Raman, Brillouin scattering depending on the wavelength of light and the size of the scatterers.
Set-up: Super-elevation of the water surface due to either wind stress (wind set-up), wave action (wave set-up) or both.
Shear: Relative motion between bodies in contact, moving parallel at different speeds.
Shingle: Coarse beach material composed of smooth, rounded pebbles.
Shoreline: The line where water meets the shore.
Siome: A visible line of demarcation between two water masses.
Stochastic: Involving statistical probability or randomness.
Stress: A force per unit area.
Sullage: Wastewater from storms, baths, etc., that does not require sewage treatment.
Swash: The rush of water onto the beach following the breaking of a wave.

Thermocline: A region within which temperature changes markedly in the vertical.

Thermohaline: Effects arising from combined temperature and salinity differences in bodies of water.

Tidal prism: The total volume of water that flows into a harbour or estuary with the movement of the tide (excluding any freshwater flow).

Tombolo: A bar or spit that connects an island to the mainland or to another island.

Vigia: A presumed reef whose existence and location is uncertain.

Vorticity: Rotational motion formed either by fluid spin or shear.

Windrows: Rows of visible matter on the surface of choppy water aligned parallel to the wind.

Yellow substance: See Gelbstoff.

Zooplankton: Minute animal life found passively floating or weakly swimming inside natural waters.

Index

WG denotes the wave glossary of Appendix 3
G denotes the glossary of Appendix 4

Absorption   205–209
Accretion   27
Acoustics   7, 12, 144, 196–202, WG
Aerosols   160
Agulhas Current   52, 101
Air pollution   160–161
Albedo   151
Alga   95, 183, 186, 241, G
Alternative technology   13–14
Analysis   237
  cost-benefit   238–239
  data   219–235
  water quality   97–98
AOU   91
Assessment   236–247
Atoll   185, G
Attenuation   197–199, 205–211
Amphidromic system   68, G
Austausch   *see* Eddy
Autocorrelation   225–226
Autotrophic   182

Bacteria   92, 182
Baltic Sea   170, 208
Baroclinic   60, 104, 167, 252, G, WG
Barotropic   60, 252, G, WG
Bathymetry   G
  beach   20
  continental shelf   7
  satellite mapping   215
Bayou   170, G
Beach
  pocket   28
  processes   26–31
Beaufort Scale   154
Beats   71–73
Beneficial uses   97
Benefit-cost analysis   238–239
Benguela Current   101, 122

Benthic Boundary Layer   125–126, G
Bicarbonate   93, 95
Bioenhancement   96
BOD   92
Bore   73, G
Boundary
  currents   105, 143, G
  layers   117–129
Bowen ratio   152
Breakers   23–25,
  forces of   45–48
Breakwater   31–32
Buoyancy   132–134
  frequency   252, WG

Cabbeling   90, G
California Current   101, 144
Canyons   23, 80
Carbonate   93, 186
Carbon dioxide   93
Cay   G
Celerity   G
  see also Velocity, phase
Chemicals   96–99, 243
Chlorophyll   183, 241
Chop   37, G
Circulation   100–116, 176, 178
Cladophora   183–184
Clapotis   33, G
Coastal
  engineering   31–33, 139, 189
  front   140–141
  jet   127, 140–141
  low   165–167
  management   31–33, 139, 189
  oceanography   1–19
  plain   7, 170
  waters   2–6
  zone   3, 33–36

257

Coastline   G
Cockerell raft   44
Colloids   28, 93
Commons   239
Computer   191–192
Conductivity
  electrical   87
  thermal   131
Continental
  margin   4
  shelf   3
  slope   4
Convection   132–134
Convergence   23
Convolution   224–225
Co-ordination   237
Copepods   200, G
Coral   186
Coriolis   106
  deflection   153
  force   106–109
  parameter   109, 119
Correlation   225–227
Cost-benefit analysis   238–239
Cross-correlation   225–226
Cross-flow   127–128
Cumec   101, G
Currents
  representation of   219; *see also dia-grams*
  cross-shore   127
  longshore   29, 126–128
  nearshore   29–31
  oceanic   101
  riverine   174
  separation   105
  shear   132, 137
  western   105, 143
  Agulhas   52, 101
  Benguela   101, 122
  California   101, 144
  East Australian   101, 105
  Florida   105
  Gulf Stream   101, 105, 143
  Kuroshio   101, 105, 143
  Leeuwin   145
  West Australia   101, 144
Cusp   54, G

Data
  analysis   219–235
  collection   191–192
  presentation   219–220
Decomposers   182
Degradation   26
Density   84–85

Detritus   94
Diagrams   219
  progressive vector   107, 195
  roses   156
  stick   111, 188
Diffusion   111–112, 131, 231
  double diffusion   133
Dimensions   15, 231
  dimensional analysis   16, 39, 107, 120, 130
Dinoflagellates   241, G
Dispersion   43, 58, 136–139 252
Dissolved
  carbonates   93
  gases   90–94
  nitrogen   94
  nutrients   94, 184
  oxygen   91
  salts   86, 95
Divergence   23
Diversity   233–234
DO (Dissolved Oxygen)   91
Double diffusion   133
Drift cards   249
Drogue   127, 195

East Australian Current   101, 105
Ebb   176, G
Ecosystem   G
  analysis   233–234
  cycles   186
  delineation   239
  management   242
  models   10, 233
Echo sounder   194, 198
Eddy   G
  diffusion   112
  large scale   144
  length   130
  viscosity   115, 118
EEZ   5
Effluent   139
Ekman, V. W.   119
  Ekman spiral   119–123
Electromagnetic radiation   202–204
Emissivity   204
Energy
  alternative   13–15
  budget   149–152
  flow   234, 239
  flux   44–45, 205
  OTEC   14
  in photosynthesis   94
  solar   205
  spectra   48–51, 57, 227–229
  tide   73–75

units and dimensions 248
  wave 41–45
Entrainment 113, 134–136
Entropy 229, 234
Equivalent depth 60, 104, 167
Erosion 26
Estimation 232
Estuarine 169–185
  classification 170–172
  hydrology 172–178
  pollution 178–185
Eulerian 40–41, 111, 195
Euphotic zone 8, 94, 211, G
Eutrophication 182–183, G
Evaporation 148–151
  oil 164
Exclusive economic zone 5
Exclusion zone 244–245
Exploitation 239
Externalities 238

Fathom G
Fetch 50, 172
Filter 224
Fish kills 241, 244
Fishing 6–10, 80–81, 178, 239
Fjord 170, G
Flinders Current 101
Flocculation 93, 181, G
Flood (current or tide) 176, G
Florida Current 105
  red tide 241
Flow see Currents
Flourescence 207, 209
  tracing 138–139
Flushing 175, 179, G
Flux 44, 112, 130, G
Fog 150–151, 155
Fourier, J. B. 50
  see also Spectra, harmonic analysis
Fractal 6
Freezing point 85
Friction see Viscosity
Fronts 139–141, G
Froude number 125, 231
Fully developed sea 50
Fumigation 161, G

Gasses
  atmospheric 160–161
  dissolved 90–94
Gaussian 137, 221
Gelbstoff 206–208, G
Geoid 110
Geomorphology 26–28, 170–172, G

Geopotential 110–111
Geostrophic motions 109–111
Giant waves 51–52
Gilvin 206–208, G
Gosstcomp 9
Gravity
  acceleration due to 15, 102
  modified 60, 104
  reduced 60, 104
Groin (groyne) 33, G
Grunion 81
Gulf Stream 101, 105, 143
Gyre 141–142, G

Halocline 88, 177–178, G
Harbour
  design 22
  resonance 55
Harmonic analysis 66, 69–73, 227–229
Heat
  pollution 245
  see also Energy budget
Heavy metals 98–99, 243
Henry's Law 92
Heterotrophic 182
Hjulstrom curve 28–29
Hurricane see Tropical cyclone
Hydrography 176, G
Hydrology
  cycle 146–153
  estuarine 172–178
Hydrodynamics 100–116
Hydrostatic equation 16, 83, 157

Identification 232
Inertial
  oscillations 107–109
  period 56
Infra-red 215–217
Insecticides 244
Instruments 191–195
Internal waves 59–60, 198
Inverse barometer 157
Ions
  rivers 95
  sea 86–87
Isobars 110
Isohalines 177
Isohyets 147
Isopycnals 89
Isotherms 86

Jet 113, 127, 140–141, G
Jetty 31–32

Kelvin wave   58, 167, WG
Key   G
Kirchhoff's Law   204
Knudsen parameter   84
Kuroshio   101, 105, 143

Lagoon   G
   estuarine   170–172
   reef   55, 185, 187
Landsat   215
Langmuir, I   124
   Langmuir cells   123–125
Lagrangian   40–41, 111, 195
Laplace, P. S.   68
Latent heat   152
Law of the Sea   4
Layered
   convection   133
   system   60, 79, 104
Leadership   237
Leeuwin Current   145
Lee   185, G
Leeway   163
Levee   G
Liebig's Law   241
Liman   170, G
Littoral Zone   80–81

Macrotides   74
Management
   coastal zone   33–36, 236
   ecosystem   239–242
   estuarine   183–185
   fisheries   242
   water quality   96–99
Mangrove   169, 172, G
Marine
   ecosystems   239–242
   optics   204–205
   parks   35–36
   resources   5, 6, 10
Marsh   183
Masuda buoy   14, 44
Maximum sustainable yield   242
Mean   66, 223–224, 228
Merians formula   54
Meteorology   2, 115, 146–168
Microwaves   212, 217
Minimata disease   99, 243
Mining   99
Mixed layer   86, 118, 121, 134
Mixing length   130
Modelling   175–176, 229–233
Momentum
   of waves   44–45, 46
   transfers   114, 117, 130

Monte Carlo   231
MSY   242

Navigation   192–193
Nearshore currents   29–31
Nephelometry   194, 210, G
Neritic   G
   see also Coastal
Nitrogen   92
Newton, Sir I.   64
   Law of Motion   102
Normal   G
   wave normal   22
Normal curve   see Gaussian
Nuclear waste   245
Nutrients   94–96, 182–183, 241
Nyquist frequency   228

Objectives   230, 237
Oil spills   161–165, 244, 249
Optics   204–205
Orthogonal   G
   see also Ray
Oscillation   see Wave
OTEC   14
Outfall   139, G
Oxygen   91, 94, 186

PAR (photosynthetically active radiation)
   211–212, G
Peclet number   231
Peel Inlet study   171, 173, 183–185,
   238
Pelagic   G
Penman equation   152–153
pH   92–93
Phi units   28
Photosynthesis   94, 186, 211–212
Phytoplankton
   blooms   241
   models   10–11
   role in spawning   80–81, G
Pixel   213
Pocket beach   28, G
Pollution
   air   160–161
   estuarine   178–185
   water   161–165, 242–246
Power   see Energy
Precipitation   147–148, 172–175, 212,
   217
Pressure
   forces   102–105
   gradient   104

partial 92, 150
sound 197
units 16, 248
vapour 175, G
Prism, tidal 175, G
Productivity 211, 239–240
Progradation 27
Progressive vector diagrams 107, 195, 219
Psychrometric constant 152
Pumping 176
Pycnocline 88, 104, 134, 197, G

Radar 212
Radiation 151, 196, 203, 211
Radionuclides 245
Rainfall 147–148, 172–175, 212, 217
Ray 22, 53–54, G
Recursion 224
Reef 35, 55, 185–189, G
Refraction 21–23
Reflection 54, 199–201
Remote sensing 195–218
Resources
exploitation 5
management 33, 242
non-renewable 10
renewable 6
Reynolds, O. 130
Reynolds number 130, 231
Reynolds stress 117
Rhodamine 139
Ria 170, G
Richardson L. F. 131
Richardson number 132, 231
Rigid lid 104
Ring 143–144, G
Rip 29, G
Rivers 94–96
Runoff 172

Sail 159
Salinity 84–85, 86–90
Salter cam 44–45
Satellites 9, 193, 213–217
Saturation coefficient 92
Scaling 231
Scattering
acoustic 197, 199
electromagnetic 209–211
Sea breeze 153–155
Seawall 33
Seasickness 61
Sea surface temperature 6–9
Sea surface slope 104, 110

Sea level
long term variations 77–78
see also Waves, Tides
Secchi disc 194, 210
Sediment transport 28–30, 172, 174, 179–182, 243
Segmentation 171–172
Seiching 54
Sensing 191–218
Set-up 45–48, 159, G
Sewage 139, 147, 182, 197, 243
Shear 132, 137, G
Shield's curve 28
Shingle 28, G
Shoreline 5, 20–36, G
SI (Systeme Internationale) 15, 248
Sigma 84
Sill 170
Siltation 181
Similarity approach 112, 130
Simulation 231
Siome 140, G
Snell's Law 22
Solar constant 205
Sound waves 7, 12, 144, 196–202
Spectra 48–51, 57, 202, 227–229
Speed see Velocity
Standards
oceanographic 15–16
water quality 96–99
State, equation of 86
Statistics 220–229, 231
Steric anomaly 84
Stick diagrams 111, 188, 219
Stochastic G
see also statistics
Stokes, G.G. 47
Stokes drift 47
Storm surge 155–159
Stratified
parameter 140
system 60, 79, 104
turbulence 131–132
Stress 114, 117, G
Sullage 244, G
Surf see Breakers
Surface tension 38, 217, 244
Sverdrup 16, 101
Swash G
Systems analysis 185, 225, 232, 233–234

Tailings 99
Taylor, G. I. 136
Temperature
sea surface 6
TS diagrams 88–90

units and dimensions   15
vertical distribution   85–86
Territorial waters   4
Thermal
    energy conversion   14
    pollution   245–246
Thermocline   86, 134, G
Thermohaline   G
    convection   132–133
    diagrams   89
Tidal energy   73–77
Tidal prediction   69–73
Tidal prism   175, G
Tides   63–82, 175
    astronomical theory   64–67
    dynamic theory   67–69
    internal tides   78–80
    long period tides   77–78
    red tides   241
Time series   223–229
Tombolo   G
Tragedy of the Commons   239
Training walls   31–32
Transfer function   225
Tripton   206
Trophic   182, 239–240
Tropical cyclone
    rainfall   148
    upwelling   122
Tsunami   56
Turbulence   112, 130–132
    atmospheric   150
    turbulent entrainment   134–136
Typhoon   see Tropical cyclone

Units   15
Upwelling   10, 86, 121–122, 148
    front   121–122, 140–141
    productivity   241

Validation   233
Variance   137, 222
Velocity
    entrainment   134

friction   125
group   42
phase   38, 42
shear   125
Vigia   27, G
Viscosity   114–115, 199
    negative   115, 131
Vorticity   142, 176, G

Water
    circulation   100–116
    composition   83–99
    quality   96–99, 210
Waves
    glossary   252
    in shore processes   20–36
    properties   37–62
Waves   WG
    acoustic   7, 12, 144, 196–202
    airy   46
    edge   53
    electromagnetic   196, 202–204
    giant   51–52
    internal   59–60, 198
    Kelvin   58
    long wavelength   55
    shelf   58
    Stokes   47
    trapped   53–55, 57–59
West Australian Current   101, 144
Wind   153–160
    factor   163–164, 223, 232
    roses   156
    stress   117, 119
Windrows   123–125, G

Yellow substance   206–208, G

Zoom   192, 237
Zooplankton   200, 240, G
Z transform   224–225